Europe, 1900-1980
A Brief History

EUROPE
1900-1980
A
BRIEF
HISTORY
BY
MICHAEL D.
RICHARDS

The Forum Press, Inc.
Arlington Heights, Illinois 60004

To my mother, Jane Smith Richards
and my mother-in-law, Ethel Hale Getgood,
both of whom have encouraged my interest
in the study and writing of history

85 86 87 88 McN 10 9 8 7 6 5 4 3 2

Printed in the United States of America

Library of Congress Catalog Card Number: 81-69869

ISBN: 0-88273-282-X

Cover Design by Tom Heggie

Maps by Dan Irwin

Contents

Preface

Europe, 1900-1980: A Brief History is intended to provide a comprehensive yet concise discussion of European experiences in the twentieth century. It is shorter by far than other treatments of this period, but I have endeavored to cover all the important aspects of European civilization in a century in which it has shown both its best and its worst sides. While not neglecting politics and economics, I have sought to emphasize social and cultural matters. Wherever possible, I have attempted to give some idea of how life was lived by the average man or woman.

A brief introduction at the start of the book summarizes the European experience in this century and indicates some of the most important features of that experience. The first section of the book is formed by Chapters 1-3 which deal with Europe before the war, with the destruction of much of that old Europe in war and revolution, and with attempts at the Paris Peace Conference and elsewhere to revive the old Europe. The next section, introduced by an "Overview, 1919-1939," is formed by Chapters 4-8. This section treats the efforts made to reconstruct postwar Europe in the image of prewar Europe, and the growing realization in the years of economic depression and diplomatic crisis that such was not possible. The last chapter in this section covers the descent into the barbarism of World War II and the first painful efforts at recovery afterwards. The last section, introduced by an "Overview, 1949-1979," reviews the startlingly swift recovery of Europe in the fifties, the new affluence and the new doubts of the sixties, and the concerns of the last decade.

Each chapter is followed by a list of "Suggested Readings." There are as well a number of maps and photographs designed to illustrate various points in the text. Finally, a list of abbreviations used in the book and an index will help in making use of the material in the book.

Anyone in academic life quickly accumulates a large number of debts to friends and former teachers. It gives me a great deal of pleasure to be able to acknowledge some of mine here. I owe much to those who taught me European history, particularly Professors Marvin Lowe of the University of Tulsa and Joel Colton of Duke University. My students at Sweet Briar College have probably taught me as much as I have taught them. My colleagues have been generous in their support and I want to thank them, especially my mentors in things European, Professor Lysbeth W. Muncy and the late Professor Gerhard Masur. This project would never have been started if it had not been for the initiative of Erby M. Young, the former managing director of Forum Press. It certainly never would have been finished except for the extraordinary patience and consistently good advice of Professor Peter N. Stearns, who served as editor for the book. I want to thank also W. A. Welsh, president of Forum Press, Alice Stifel, copy editor, and Pauline Spencer, who saw the book through production. Sarah Alcock contributed greatly through a careful typing of the entire manuscript. Various friends, colleagues, and family have offered encouragement and support, which I have greatly appreciated. I cannot name all the names here, but I would like to mention my friend and colleague, Gerald M. Berg, who was always ready to lend an editorial eye. Most of all, I would like to thank the members of my family: my wife, Anne, and my three sons, John, David, and Arie. They have helped me to learn what I know of life. To whatever extent this book reflects that knowledge, it is a good and true book.

Michael D. Richards

Europe, 1900-1980:
An Introduction

In less than two decades the twentieth century will end and a small army of scholars and journalists will set about summarizing the events of the century and assessing their significance. Certain names, each with its own terrible associations, will appear and reappear in the various post-mortems: Verdun, the Somme, Ypres, Kolyma, Auschwitz, Treblinka, Dresden, Hiroshima, Nagasaki, Biafra, My Lai, Kampuchea. These names refer to unprecedented extermination of human beings by other human beings, in wars and in related aggression. The view taken of this century at its end is likely to be based in large part on the images conjured up by those names and by such twentieth-century "inventions" as total war and concentration camps.

The prospects held by most observers at the beginning of the century were quite different. While a few professed to be weary of life and some felt a certain edginess about the new century, most looked forward to a continuation of progress in science and industry, to the spread of constitutional forms of government, and to the increased well-being of humanity. And certainly in the years between the turn of the century and World War I this view seemed confirmed by events. There were minor wars, frequent diplomatic alarms, and even the Revolution of 1905 in Russia, but these appeared to be unimportant compared to the growth of international cooperation and goodwill, the appearance of marvelous inventions such as the airplane and the development of others such as the automobile, and the extension of universal male suffrage and parliamentary government to countries which had only recently been governed by authoritarian monarchies. For the aristocracy and the middle classes, it was a good time in which to live, and for those from the working classes or the peasantry, it was not such a bad time, either.

The "guns of August" brought an end to what had been a kind of Indian summer in European history. In the first World War, the nineteenth century ended and the twentieth began. The years of fighting between 1914 and 1918 destroyed many expectations and illusions that Europeans had brought with them into the new century. War, cruelly experienced in the "hell of Verdun," in the futility of the Somme, and in the mud of Ypres, left some Europeans questioning whether their destiny was to advance continually toward a better life. For a few, a new Dark Ages seemed to be at hand.

The incredible resilience of human beings allowed most Europeans to set aside whatever lessons World War I might have taught them and to ignore the stirrings of revolution in Eastern Europe, the major result of which was a communist state in Russia. In similar fashion, Europeans tended to neglect the changing complexion of the world, including the rise of nationalism in the colonial empires and in states such as Turkey and China, which had long been at the mercy of Europe. Europeans could not help but be aware of the growing strength of the United States, but the implications of this were largely lost.

The twenties were a period of economic prosperity and cultural brilliance. Diplomatic issues seemed settled once again. Political stability was once again the keynote, at least by the mid-twenties when the Italian Fascist movement had taken power in Italy, ending instability in that country, and the Weimar Republic in Germany had gained a precarious political equilibrium. The innocence that had characterized the prewar period could not be regained and, in fact, some Europeans proclaimed rather self-consciously by their cynicism or hedonism that they were no longer innocent. Nevertheless, Europe could believe that it had recovered from the effects of war and revolution.

The decade that followed replaced cynicism with passionate commitment and hedonism with self-sacrifice. For many, of course, the Depression—the central fact of the thirties—brought only a numbing despair. For others, the old liberal political and economic practices no longer appeared effective. On both the left and the right, people in the thirties participated in a series of crusades—for communism; for democracy, both political and social; for fascism and the national state. Spain, with its civil war, was the arena in which the left and right lined up against one another. Nazi Germany, under the leadership of Adolf Hitler, was the instigator of crisis after crisis which destroyed any illusions that the reconstruction of Europe that had been brought about in the twenties could continue. When the Soviet Union, which had escaped the Depression but had suffered far more from efforts to industrialize the country and to consolidate the political power of the communist party, agreed to a Non-Aggression Pact with Germany in August 1939, World War II began.

World War II was even more wasteful of human lives and destructive of material goods than World War I had been. Barbarism on a level and scale unmatched in centuries was practiced in Nazi death camps, of which Auschwitz and Treblinka were simply the most notorious. The staggering power of atomic weaponry was revealed at Hiroshima and at Nagasaki and the still formidable destructiveness of conventional weaponry in the fire-bombing of Dresden.

Europe lay in ruins after World War II. Millions had died; millions more were homeless. The economy was in tatters. Quickly the allied powers divided into two camps and over the east-west confrontation hung the specter of atomic warfare. It was a bleak and fearful time for many. The human capacity for evil had been shown to be greater than anyone would have thought before the war. Europe was divided into hostile camps, its colonies rebelling against it; its once predominant position had been lost.

The recovery of Europe after World War II was nothing short of miraculous. Within a decade Western Europe was beginning to surpass prewar levels of production. Various explanations could be suggested for this. In part, despite the horrors of World War II, many emerged from the war determined to build a new society on the basis of programs outlined during the war. The extraordinary economic power that the United States had put together in the course of the war was utilized to aid the European recovery also. In Eastern Europe, it was only after Stalin's death and the events of 1956, particularly the Hungarian Revolution, that conditions began to improve.

From the late fifties through the sixties Europeans enjoyed an increasingly better life, at least in terms of material goods. Versions of the welfare state removed many anxieties of life and the abundance of consumer goods began to change the nature of society. Not only material conditions but also popular outlooks in Europe, both east and west, were strikingly different by the late sixties from what they had been in the thirties or even the early fifties.

Student-led protests in the late sixties against the organization of political and economic life did not achieve the goals of an egalitarian society and a radically different culture that the protesters had sought, but the protests did force many to question the emphasis in the past on reconstruction and the creation of material wealth. Even more unsettling was the rapid increase in the price of petroleum products in 1973 and the ensuing recession. Europe had enjoyed an unprecedented span of nearly twenty years of economic growth and prosperity. It could not, of course, go on forever as it had. Some Europeans felt that Europe no longer had a sense of mission. Economic recovery had largely been achieved, even if some problems remained. The Cold War was over and Europeans especially had no interest in reviving it. Some of the more idealistic projects, such as the political unification of Europe, now seemed unlikely. Europeans in the seventies could not help but question their role in world affairs.

Viewed from the perspective of 1900, when Europe reigned supreme in the world and many expected progress to be Europe's destiny in the twentieth century, the past eight decades form a tragedy in every sense of the word. From the perspective of 1945, the nadir of European civilization in the modern period, the European experience in this century takes on a more positive outlook. Shorn of many of its illusions and tempered to some extent by adversity, Europe remains a center of important developments in the arts, in social policy, in regional and international cooperation, and in economic affairs. Whether the period in which we live now will be only a temporary setback to the movement of European civilization since World War II, or whether it will be the prelude to yet another catastrophe on the scale of the two World Wars is something that we can hardly predict now. One thing can be said with some certainty: how that small army of scholars and journalists judge the twentieth century will depend to a substantial degree on whether Europeans regain a sense of purpose and are able not only to continue but also to expand the largely positive contribution of the past few decades.

1

Europe Before World War I, 1900-1914

In 1900 Europeans could have said, somewhat paradoxically, that
Europe was the world and the world was Europe's. At the beginning
of this century, art, science, manufacture, and commerce, all the
elements of civilization, were European. The overwhelming predominance of Europe in human affairs might be symbolized by the
quelling of the Boxer Rebellion in China in 1900 by a coalition of
European forces. The oldest continuous civilization in the world had
been defeated by a group of nations of which some had been in
existence only two generations.

Underlying Europe's dominance were a number of tensions that
gnawed at the heart of its civilization. These tensions, portrayed by
authors such as Joseph Conrad and Henrik Ibsen and painters such as
Vincent van Gogh and Edvard Munch, involved contending ideas
about politics, increasingly difficult social relations, and the loss of
certainty in science and culture. For the most part, the anxieties and
uncertainties of European life remained beneath the surface of that
life, only occasionally breaking through in the form of strike
movements in France or revolution in Russia or brilliant departures in
music and art in the Hapsburg empire and Germany. Until the
summer of 1914 Europe's dominant position appeared to most observers to be permanent and unassailable.

The Europe that so convincingly dominated the world actually
made up only a part of the geographic area commonly thought of as
Europe. This Europe, its industrial heartland, could be located by

using Essen, the center of the heavily industrialized Ruhr district and site of the Krupp steel works, as the center of a circle with a radius of five hundred miles. The resulting circle of industrialization and urbanization included most of the important industrial centers of Europe, a large number of the great European cities and the states with the greatest amount of urban population, and those areas in which the literacy rates were highest and death rates lowest. Outside the circle, to the south and the east, were areas in which industry was not as important a part of the national economy, in which most of the population lived in the countryside, and in which relatively low literacy and high mortality rates prevailed (See Map p. 3).

Included within the circle of industrialization and urbanization were Great Britain (but not Ireland), Germany, France, Belgium, the Netherlands, Denmark, the northern part of Italy, and the Austrian half of the dual monarchy of Austria-Hungary. Great Britain had long dominated this area, both in industrial production and in trade. By 1900, however, this dominance was beginning to fade. While Britain still led Europe in coal and pig iron production, she had lost the lead in steel to Germany. Furthermore, her share of world trade had decreased steadily in the twenty years before 1900 while Germany's share had increased. Germany was also moving ahead rapidly in the newer chemical and electrical industries.

Russia was outside the circle of industrialized nations. The strenuous efforts that she had made in the 1890s to encourage industrialization may stand for efforts made elsewhere in Europe to break into the circle. In 1900 industry in Russia was still confined to a few pockets of territory, the environs of St. Petersburg and Moscow, the portion of Poland controlled by Russia, and the Donbas in the south. In terms of territory and population, Russia was a great power, yet, as officials pointed out, she was little more than a colony of western Europe in terms of economic strength and industrial capacity.

Economic and Social Changes

Russia's efforts to draw even with those powers which had already industrialized were made more difficult by the fact that the processes of industrialization and urbanization were still continuing in western Europe. In the period around 1900 Europe was experiencing what has often been termed a second industrial revolution. Where the first had been based on textiles and, later, coal and iron, the second rested not only on important improvements in the production of steel but also on

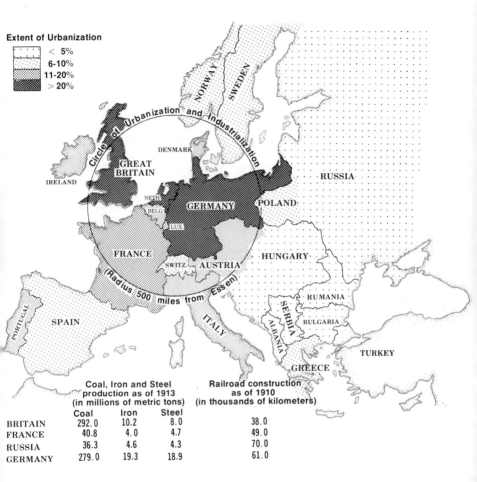

Extent of Urbanization

	< 5%
	6-10%
	11-20%
	> 20%

NORWAY

SWEDEN

Circle of Urbanization and Industrialization

DENMARK

GREAT BRITAIN

IRELAND

RUSSIA

NETH.

BELG.

LUX.

GERMANY

POLAND

FRANCE

SWITZ.

AUSTRIA

HUNGARY

(Radius 500 miles from Essen)

RUMANIA

PORTUGAL

SPAIN

ITALY

SERBIA

ALBANIA

BULGARIA

GREECE

TURKEY

	Coal, Iron and Steel production as of 1913 (in millions of metric tons)			Railroad construction as of 1910 (in thousands of kilometers)
	Coal	Iron	Steel	
BRITAIN	292.0	10.2	8.0	38.0
FRANCE	40.8	4.0	4.7	49.0
RUSSIA	36.3	4.6	4.3	70.0
GERMANY	279.0	19.3	18.9	61.0

The circle of urbanization and industrialization in Europe before World War I. Within this circle are those countries with extensive railroad networks, advanced industry as indicated by figures for the production of coal, iron, and steel, and a high percentage of people living in cities of 100,000 or more. Outside the circle are countries with much less extensive railroad networks, limited industrial development, and populations living largely in the countryside or in small towns.

the new chemical and electrical industries and on production for consumers.

Changes in the organization and management of industry had important consequences for the development of society. The size of industrial units grew enormously to take advantage of the economies of scale. In Germany, for example, two firms, the Allgemeine Elektrizitäts Gesellschaft and the Siemens concern, controlled over 90 percent of the electrical industry. Within such large industries, factory workers had a much more impersonal relationship with their employers than had been the case in the smaller, somewhat paternalistic firms that had predominated earlier. Workers also found that relations with fellow employees were different. Big business required vast numbers of clerical personnel and technicians, a requirement with significant social ramifications. These new elements within the middle class increased in number even more rapidly than did workers in the early part of the twentieth century.

Business, in its efforts to create and expand markets for its products, shaped the development of society in more subtle ways, also. Around 1900 business began making major efforts to reach the general public and convince it to buy certain products. An ad in the 1890s in a British paper such as the *Labour Leader* had typically been a small, somewhat didactic paragraph filled with print and requiring a considerable degree of literacy to read and understand. In the first decade of the twentieth century, ads became larger and easier to read. Illustrations were emphasized over print.

In addition to changes in the economy, society was also transformed by the continuing process of urbanization. While some thirty million Europeans emigrated abroad between 1890 and 1914, more than twice that number moved into urban and industrial areas in their own country in that same period.

A good part of the social tension before World War I came from the accelerating pace of change which, for many, replaced the familiar and the comfortable with the unknown. Within the circle of industrialization and urbanization, the pace of change, on the whole, was more rapid and the tensions greater. There were, however, few areas in Europe in this period where changes in the economy and in social relations were not taking place at a rapid rate. And every accommodation to change, no matter how apparently successful, was constantly undermined by the dynamic quality of life.

Peasants and Workers

Within European society, life was changing most rapidly for the peasantry. The spread of railroads and a commercial economy into the countryside, the development of a system of primary education in most countries, the introduction of universal male suffrage in many countries, and large-scale conscription of the peasantry for military service meant that an increasing number of peasants participated in various ways in the national life of their country. As they learned to speak the national language, to use its coinage and system of weights and measures, as they became aware of the ways in which other people lived, the traditions and customs of their own area became less meaningful to them. The process by which peasants became a part of the modern world was largely restricted in this period to Britain, France, Germany, northern Italy, the Low Countries, and Scandinavia. Peasants in Spain, southern Italy, eastern Europe, and Russia still found the gap extremely wide between their lives and the lives of those from urban areas.

In every rural society there were gradations. A *kulak* in Russia, for example, relatively well-to-do as the owner of land and animals and the employer of agricultural laborers, would have a better idea of changing circumstances than the ordinary *muzhik*, who might own some land but would most likely have to supplement his income by hiring out as a laborer. In Britain before the war, agricultural laborers lived in great poverty and restricted circumstances compared to those of tenant farmers. Peasants of all sorts had to deal with the fall of agricultural prices in the last part of the nineteenth century. Some met the challenge in ways other than the traditional method of acquiring more land. A number used new tools and machinery and tried new methods and techniques. There was also a limited effort to move away from grain farming to meat, dairy, and truck products. Danish farmers were the most successful at developing these new specializations.

For many peasants who left the land to work in a factory, life changed quite rapidly. However, by 1900 there were many third- and even fourth-generation workers who were accustomed to urban, industrial life. For them, adaptation to the maturing industrial system of the prewar period was relatively easy. Nevertheless, even for these "seasoned" workers attitudes toward work were ambiguous. It was not often that one could find employment that was satisfying in the way it sometimes had been for artisans in preindustrial society. Life

Oxford Street, London, 1909. Well-dressed men and women crowd the streets and sidewalks of London before World War I. (BBC Hulton Picture Library)

was now less defined by work than it had been, but efforts to find compensatory fulfillment outside work, in family life and leisure, were not always satisfactory. Still, a rich and complex working-class popular culture developed that was in large part an attempt to offset the realities of industrial life. But much of this culture—in Britain, fish-and-chips, the music hall, and cheap novels—was commercialized so that slowly rising or stagnant earning power restricted the development of sources of satisfaction outside work.

If the industrial system was not seen as completely satisfactory, it was, at least, accepted as the framework in which economic life took place. Anti-industrial attitudes were not widespread. Germany is a case in point. The German Social Democratic Party (SPD) was the strongest in Europe. It staunchly defended Marxist orthodoxy on the need for revolutionary overthrow of bourgeois society and the state. At the same time, many within the party worked for limited improvements by legislative action. This was undoubtedly the goal of the German trade union movement. Although acceptance of the industrial system was never made explicit by the SPD or the trade unions, there were numerous indications that it was tacitly accepted by large numbers within both groups.

The SPD and the German working class have been characterized as existing in a state of "negative integration" with German society in the early part of the twentieth century. Mutual hostility and suspicion prevailed; integration was only partial in that the SPD and the working class did not (and often were not allowed to) participate fully and positively in all aspects of German life. Yet the SPD was set firmly in the framework of German society and German workers participated in national life in many ways. Examples might include the veneration of the kaiser or working-class fascination with the growth of Germany as a world power. German workers, like the British, lived largely in a self-created little world of popular culture, but there were some bridges to the larger world around them.

It was not so for the Russian workers, whose cultural and social isolation was heightened by a physical isolation that kept them out of those parts of Russian cities used by the upper classes and confined to working-class districts. Protest against the industrial system in Russia was more radical and intransigent than in Britain, France, Belgium, or Germany. In Russia and elsewhere outside the circle of industrialization, the intensity of work, the greater degree of supervision and lessening of personal initiative, and the more extensive use of technology that characterized an industrial economy were particularly hard on a working class that generally had little experience in matters industrial and urban. It had fewer cultural resources with which to reach an accommodation with the new industrial order. Many felt overwhelmed by the experience, even more so perhaps than did British workers in the first part of the nineteenth century. A substantial number adopted radical viewpoints.

In general, the working class reacted to changing circumstances less according to national characteristics than according to the stage of industrialization reached in a particular area. Where experience was lacking, hostility and friction were vented in radical and often violent protest. Where experience with industrial life reached back over two or three generations, a durable if not always satisfying relationship between working class and industrial order emerged. For workers in Britain, France, Belgium, and Germany, the industrial system was becoming increasingly acceptable, even if expectations always seemed to race ahead of fulfillment.

The Middle Classes

In later decades, the middle classes were to view the era before 1914 largely as a golden age, *les bon vieux temps,* "the good old days." In retrospect it seemed that there had never been a better time for the well-to-do than in the two decades before the war. Economic opportunities abounded, political influence was increasing, and even social prominence was on the rise. The changing economic structure offered few opportunities for individuals or families to own and control their own enterprises, but this was compensated for by an expansion of positions within management. Wider educational opportunities also made it possible for many to enter the professions or the upper reaches of government bureaucracies. Possibilities, especially in western Europe, of achieving a comfortable income and a commensurate status were good.

The middle class was not a unified group. Views of businessmen often conflicted with those of professional men or another group of businessmen. The class was, nonetheless, a formidable political power in states where parliamentary government was well established. Politics was increasingly the preserve of professionals, both elected and unelected, and the middle class supplied more and more of these people. At the same time, the middle class furnished the leadership of most major European political parties. This was true even of some socialist parties, where renegade members of the middle class formulated most of the policies and interpreted doctrine for the rank-and-file. Governments were increasingly sympathetic to middle-class views, as demonstrated by the trend toward protective tariffs and other legislation favorable to business.

The middle class was beginning to set the tone for all of society. The activities of the aristocracy and, particularly, the royal families of Europe were still of great interest to many Europeans, but, more and more, standards were set by a new elite drawn from both the middle class and the aristocracy. The upper middle class with its vast wealth became an important source of patronage for the arts and a significant influence on fashion and style.

The lower middle class, like the middle class, was not a unified group. One component, the independent lower middle class of shop-keepers, merchants, and artisans, had long been a part of the European scene. It had emphasized familiar middle-class ideals of family, property, and respectability. A second component, largely dependent, was a product of recent structural changes in the economy. The expansion of distribution and sales, together with the increased complexity of organization, required vast numbers of clerks, salespeople, and technicians. Governments also began to require larger and larger numbers of clerical and technical personnel.

Both elements of the lower middle class had in common a sense that in terms of status and behavior they were distinct from the working class. In terms of income, the lower middle class no longer earned a great deal more than the working class. It spent its money differently, however, either buying or saving mainly for items connected with social status, such as a piano; the working class tended to spend on immediate pleasures. The intense consciousness of status was reflected not only in the behavior but also in the politics of the lower middle class, which was usually conservative, anti-socialist, and sometimes also anti-Semitic. In politics the lower middle class favored parties such as the Radical Party in France or the Christian Social Party in Austria, parties that catered to the "little man" and stressed the importance of order, property, and attachment to the nation.

Like the middle class, the lower middle class enjoyed the good times of the era before 1914 including prosperity, status, and political power. Living in close proximity to the lower classes, the lower middle class tended to take the good times less for granted than the middle class and to be more anxious about any developments that might threaten their position in society.

Other Groups

The aristocracy before World War I was already faced with a number of threats to its position in society. Its responses in part

Another side of life in London before World War I. A working-class family in 1912 faces an uncertain future. All the food in the house—a little butter, some sugar, and a nearly empty tin of milk—is on the table. (BBC Hulton Picture Library)

involved formation with the upper middle class of a new elite based on intermarriage, common patterns of education and consumption, and similar economic and political views. Other segments of the aristocracy simply ignored the outside world by restricting their activities and contacts to the confines of a small circle of peers. Such was the style of life described by Marcel Proust in *Remembrance of Things Past*. Others watched the bases of their life-style erode without doing anything effectual to stop the process, similar to the Russian aristocrats in Anton Chekhov's play *The Cherry Orchard*. For many in the aristocracy, however, especially those in Germany, Austria-Hungary, and areas to the east, the decline was relative, not absolute, and the need to reverse it not always perceived as pressing.

One other important group should be mentioned. Women were involved in a number of important developments at the turn of the century. Suffragettes in Britain mounted a major campaign in the years before the war to win the vote in national elections. Female socialists in Poland and Russia played major roles in the revolutionary movements of those countries. Most women, however, participated in rather limited ways in the activities around them. Most countries by 1900 allowed women to own property and control their earnings. Some, like Britain and France, permitted women to practice as lawyers and doctors. Both educational and employment opportunities were expanding rapidly. Still, women like Nora, in Henrik Ibsen's *A Doll's House*, were an exception: society tended rather to see women as Eliza Doolittles, the main character in George Bernard Shaw's *Pygmalion*, as objects to be manipulated and shaped according to the wishes of the husband and father.

Intellectual and Cultural Trends

By 1914, then, various groups within European society were contending in different ways with economic and social change. Part of the process of adjustment involved intellectual and cultural activities and beliefs. For many Europeans, life in the early twentieth century was made palatable by the belief that Europe was on the path of progress. The idea of progress had seemingly been proved correct beyond question by the achievements of science and technology. Other developments, such as the spread of civil liberties and parliamentary forms of government and rising standards of living, convinced many Europeans that Europe was on the right path and that whatever problems existed would be eventually solved.

Dressed in their holiday best, this crowd of well-to-do men and women are going by train on an excursion. (BBC Hulton Picture Library)

The idea of progress, of the perfectability of humanity, stemmed from the eighteenth century. But the *philosophes* of that century, commentators on the workings of society and government, had been cautious optimists. Much of the caution had been lost by the end of the nineteenth century. Science now seemed capable of explaining all that really needed explaining. A technology could apparently be devised for any problem.

There were warning voices, of course. Philosophers, novelists, and historians such as Friedrich Nietzsche, Fëdor Dostoevski, and Jakob Burckhardt had questioned the idea of progress, the possibility of humanity's freeing itself from error and sin, and the belief that Europe then enjoyed the best of all times. In the 1890s, T. H. Huxley, long a defender of Charles Darwin's theories of biological evolution, cautioned his readers against relying on the workings of the evolutionary process to provide progress automatically. Biological evolution, he pointed out, was painfully slow and uncertain. Humanity could continue to evolve culturally, as it had in the past, but it could not take progress for granted. One of Huxley's former pupils, H. G. Wells, provided a dramatic discussion of this thesis in *The Time Machine*.

In the last generation before the war, a full-scale "revolt against positivism" broke out. The term "positivism" was simply shorthand for a belief in progress and faith in the powers of science and technology. The "revolt" was led by men who had been educated in the tradition of positivism. Most of them had no intention of discarding scientific techniques or the gains of technology: they wanted only to probe more deeply behind the accepted truths of their time. An outstanding example of this generation of scientists and thinkers is Sigmund Freud, a Viennese Jew, physician, and founder of psychoanalysis. Freud's theories received a wide hearing only after World War I, but, even before the war, Freud became a major figure in scientific circles, gaining disciples and enemies. Perhaps the most important suggestion that he made was the contention that humans were not totally rational in their behavior. In fact, Freud suggested that the average person was driven by impulses, especially sexual, seldom recognized as being what they were and conditioned by experiences long since lost to his conscious mind. The implications of these ideas were staggering for anyone who believed in humanity's essential rationality as a basis for continuing progress.

Freud, in suggesting his theories, had wanted to confront the irrational and master it to whatever extent might be possible. Another representative of the "revolt," Henri Bergson, took a somewhat different approach. Bergson, an enormously popular intellectual figure in the prewar years, stressed the importance of intuition in intellectual matters. While not emphasizing irrationality, as some thinkers were doing, Bergson de-emphasized the importance of a scientific, strictly rational approach. This was perhaps a helpful antidote to scientific narrowness, but Bergson moved toward outright mysticism with his concept of *élan vital*, the vital spirit that humanity could tap in its creative efforts.

The period was rich in intellectual change. Freud and Bergson were only two of the many scientists and philosophers trying to free themselves from a world view that seemed unnecessarily limited and confining. This effort was reinforced by virtual revolutions in physics and in biology. The revolution in physics involved a series of discoveries that suggested that atoms were not irreducible bits of matter but, instead, small worlds within themselves. This was the beginnings of atomic physics, an entirely new area of investigation. Work by physicists, in particular that of Max Planck and Albert Einstein, began to call into question the universal validity of the Newtonian synthesis (Newton's suggestion that discoverable and uniform laws existed that covered the motion of all objects whether they be planets or objects on earth). In biology, the rediscovery of the Austrian monk

Gregor Mendel's work on genetics led to the first explanation of the process of evolution, a process that Darwin had described and documented but had not been able to account for satisfactorily. Both atomic physics and genetics had tremendously important potential, but at this point they raised more questions than they answered.

In the first decade of the twentieth century, educated persons with an interest in science would probably have noticed two differences from the situation that prevailed a generation before. First, there was no general agreement on how to explain various phenomena in scientific terms; an overall picture of the workings of the universe that would accurately reflect current scientific thinking seemed impossible. Secondly, these hypothetical persons would not have been able to understand or participate meaningfully in the scientific controversies that raged around them. Charles Smithson, the amateur paleontologist depicted by John Fowles in *The French Lieutenant's Woman*, a brilliant reconstruction of late Victorian Britain, simply could not have existed in 1905. For many, however, it would not have mattered. The wonders of technology provided suitable outlets for the scientifically inclined. One could follow the development of practical applications of electricity without worrying about whether the phenomenon should be explained in terms of the wave theory or the particle theory.

The arts, too, had broken loose from familiar nineteenth-century moorings. Painting had traveled farther than any other medium toward a modern style before World War I. As early as the 1870s, it left behind camera-like realism, although Impressionism, with its emphasis on capturing the play of light at a given moment, was in its own way a form of realism. The drift away from the concerns of realists with exact depiction of form and careful use of color accelerated in the 1880s and 1890s with the works of a Dutchman, Vincent van Gogh, and two Frenchmen, Paul Gauguin and Paul Cézanne.

Modern art received initial recognition in 1905 at the *Salon d'Automne* in which the painters exhibiting were labeled by a critic as *les fauves* ("wild beasts"). One of *les fauves,* Henri Matisse, led the way to cubism and abstract art in a number of paintings completed around this time. Modern art was not confined to Paris. It included important centers in Vienna and Munich and numbered in its ranks people such as Marc Chagall from Russia, Edvard Munch from Norway, James Ensor from Belgium, and Pablo Picasso from Spain.

Literature was somewhat behind art in terms of the movement toward a modern style. Here the realistic tradition, particularly strong in the novel, continued to prevail. Two areas of innovation, however, were poetry and drama, which were both introduced to new techniques and themes in the last part of the nineteenth century. Music was perhaps the most traditional of the arts. Richard Wagner's operas, despite his theories of art, differed in degree but not in kind from previous romantic efforts. Similarly, Gustav Mahler's symphonies expanded and extended the possibilities of the genre but did not break totally new ground. Music was on the verge of plunging into the modern, however. Igor Stravinsky's *Rites of Spring* stunned its audience at its premiere in 1913. Stravinsky, probably the most important figure in music in this century, enormously expanded the range of musical possibilities with his work.

Political Changes

As dramatic as some innovations in intellectual and cultural matters were, they were understood by only a small part of the public. No doubt they contributed to a tension that underlay the general satisfaction that many Europeans felt when they viewed their present circumstances and speculated about the future, but nowhere were these innovations as important in public life as the pressures exerted by incessant change in social and economic structures. The art of government was becoming a good deal more complex as governments sought ways in which to allow participation by new groups in politics, to perform a wider variety of services than previously, and to deal with a world that commerce and technology had made much smaller and more interdependent. In the realm of politics, the underlying tensions in European life occasionally broke through to the surface in the form of revolutions and assassinations, hard-fought election campaigns, and bitterly contested legislation.

In part, political tension was obscured by the apparent spread of parliamentary forms of government and universal male suffrage. Much of what passed for progress, however, was only "pseudo-constitutionalism" in which the formal political structure masked the way in which government functions were really carried out. In these cases, as seen in the German empire and the Russian empire (after 1905), political tension had largely been contained but not removed.

A bewildering variety of "isms" contributed to the problems of politics. In addition to conservatism, socialism, and liberalism, by the turn of the century there were other "isms" such as nationalism, racism, and imperialism, that cut across established political boundaries and often drastically changed the nature of politics. Of the older "isms," conservatism was headed in two directions at the beginning of the century. On the one hand, it showed itself on occasion to be aware of the need for reform and government intervention, if perhaps more inclined to limited government and freedom for individual initiative. On the other hand, many conservatives wanted to maintain the status quo or, if possible, undo some changes that had taken place and return to a simpler past. This type, especially prominent in Germany, Austria-Hungary, and Russia, turned before World War I to nationalism, militarism, and racism as means for preventing change.

Liberals followed a single line of evolution in the period. Increasingly they had to face the necessity of surrendering their most cherished principles from the nineteenth century, those of limited government and a laissez-faire approach to economic and social questions for a more interventionist stance by the government. The best example of this in the period before the war was the Liberal government in Britain after 1906. In some countries liberal parties were still struggling to obtain basic political rights. Such was the situation for the Progressive party in Germany and the Kadet (Constitutional Democratic) party in Russia. In these cases political reform took precedence over social reform.

Socialism was the most dynamic of the broad political movements in the period. Marxist socialism was the major variety, although there were important anarchist and populist movements as well. Marxism was hampered by its use of a rhetoric that was violently revolutionary and in stark contrast to a practice often reformist and conciliatory. Politicians from other parties on the left or left-center took Marxism at its word and ruled out the possibility of compromise and cooperation.

Britain

Britain in 1900 was the premier example of a parliamentary government. The locus of political power was the Parliament, from the ranks of which came the prime minister and members of his cabinet. The king possessed important responsibilities but little power. It was, however, only in 1910 and 1911 that the power of the House of Lords to veto legislation passed by the House of Commons was severely curtailed, making the House of Commons unequivocally the center of political affairs in Britain.

The Liberals remained in power between 1906 and 1914 partly through agreements with the Labour party and the Irish delegation to Parliament. By 1914 these agreements were fast becoming liabilities. The Labour party was increasingly dissatisfied with its alliance with the Liberals, despite the gains made. Even more important, working-class militancy grew enormously from 1911 to 1914. A series of strikes in 1911 and 1912 reflected the influence of the idea that change would come only through direct action. In the spring of 1914 a "triple industrial alliance" of the transport workers, railwaymen, and miners was formed. Beyond the control of the moderate union officials or the Labour party, it was watched nervously in the summer of 1914.

That same spring, the question of home rule for Ireland, promised to the Irish delegation in return for their support, came before the House for the third time and passed. Ireland was to receive home rule with no separate provision for northern Ireland (Ulster). Volunteer armies in northern and southern Ireland were already in existence. Many in the British army had indicated that they would not act to enforce home rule. Civil war seemed a possibility. A militant suffragette movement completed the forces, making for what has been described as "domestic anarchy" in 1914. Britain faced its worst crisis in decades in the summer of 1914.

France

By way of contrast, the French, who had entered the twentieth century in the midst of a grave political crisis, had managed by 1914 to repair their political system. France was fortunate in that it was subject to the fewest economic and social strains of any major power in the early years of the century. The Third Republic was designed to govern a country in which changes were taking place relatively slowly. The government largely ignored change that was taking place within the social structure and the economy, and if it could not be ignored, as was the case with labor militancy, the government repressed it.

Between 1906 and 1911, a period in which the Radicals (a left-center party devoted to the preservation of the French Republic and to the advancement of the interests of the "little man" in French society) were dominant, two developments unfurled. One was the emergence of a radical right movement centered on the newspaper *Action Française* and the writings of Charles Maurras and Léon Daudet. *Action Française* favored a return to strong government at

home and a highly nationalistic and aggressive policy abroad. Its
views were shared by many who were not royalists but still found the
Third Republic lacking. At the same time that a sizable opposition
arose on the right, labor militancy increased on the left. Strikes
among vineyard workers took place in 1907 and again in 1911. A
major strike by postal workers occurred in 1909 followed by a strike
of railroad workers in 1910. The premier, Aristide Briand, a former
socialist, called out the troops. The railroad workers pressed for a
general strike but the movement collapsed. The criticisms and
demands of neither the left nor the right had been met; they had only
been sidestepped. France in 1914 possessed a workable system of
government provided not too many demands were placed on it.

Italy

Italy followed a pattern similar to that of France in this period,
beginning the twentieth century in crisis, yet appearing by 1914 to
have achieved stability. Beginning with an abortive campaign for
empire in Abyssinia in 1896, the country rapidly fell into a domestic
crisis punctuated by strikes and food and tax riots. A wave of strikes
in the spring of 1898 led to clashes between workers and troops in
Milan in May. The following year the prime minister introduced
legislation restricting civil rights as a means of restoring order, and
threatened to rule by decree if necessary. The left bloc in parliament
eventually resorted to the tactic of walking out in protest to the prime
minister's threats. It was a dangerous gamble, as Mussolini's reaction
in 1925 to a similar tactic was to demonstrate, but this time it worked.
In the elections of 1900, the left bloc increased its representation and
preserved the idea of parliamentary government in Italy.

Emerging in 1900 as a prominent figure in politics was Giovanni
Giolitti. In the years that followed he dominated Italian politics by use
of a system that had long been customary in his country's politics,
trasformismo. This involved giving political groups at least some
things they wanted in return for their support on other matters. It was
the art of compromise and the possible. If it involved corruption, as it
did in dealings with politicians from southern Italy, *trasformismo* was
justified by the idea that it accustomed people to working through
parliamentary institutions and strengthened the concept of national
unity. If it created a large amount of cynicism about politics, that, in
Giolitti's opinion, was a price that had to be paid. As in France,
dissatisfaction with parliamentary government appeared both on the
increasingly militant left and the nationalistic and bellicose right.

Even more than the French, the Italian system of government concealed serious defects that times of crisis would reveal.

Austria-Hungary

The parliamentary governments of Europe, for all their flaws and inadequacies, seemed more likely to endure than the constitutional monarchies of Austria-Hungary, Germany, and Russia. The situation in Austria was, as the Viennese liked to put it, hopeless but not serious. The dual monarchy was a cumbersome form of government with separate parliaments for Austria and Hungary. Common to both halves of the empire were ministries for war, finance, and foreign affairs. Also holding the empire together were the emperor, who was emperor of Austria and king of Hungary; the army; and, more and more, an interdependent economy. Tearing the empire apart was nationalism. The Czech-German quarrel in Austria brought the activities of the Austrian parliament to a virtual standstill. The rise of the socialists, themselves divided along national lines, and the Christian Socialists, a party that emphasized concern for the "little man" and virulent anti-Semitism, added ideological obstacles to the functioning of parliament. One solution was a triple monarchy with the organization of an autonomous Yugoslav (South Slav) state from portions of Austria and Hungary. Another was a federal state composed of a number of largely autonomous units. The greatest obstacle to any of the various solutions proposed was Magyar intransigence. Magyar elites dominated Hungarian politics and opposed any reorganization of the empire. In 1914, Franz Joseph had been emperor for sixty-six years and was then eighty-four years old. Many believed that he was all that kept the empire together.

Russia

The century began badly in Russia with an economic recession, strikes, peasant disorders, and acts of terrorism. The government's difficulties increased after Russia became involved in war with Japan in 1904. Repeatedly defeated by the Japanese, the Russian government faced a rising tide of discontent at home among workers, peasants, intellectuals, and members of minority nationality groups. The Revolution of 1905 was triggered by "Bloody Sunday" in January of that year. It involved a peaceful procession to the Winter Palace in St. Petersburg, organized by a Russian Orthodox priest, to present a petition by workers to the tsar. The procession was fired on by troops and dispersed with great loss of life. The event touched off waves of strikes and disturbances that receded at times but always returned, generally larger than before. A series of strikes in September led to a general strike in October that paralyzed the country. Nicholas II was advised either to grant concessions or to establish a military dictatorship. The latter possibility was out of the question, given Nicholas' indecisiveness and the weakness of the military.

The October Manifesto, the document establishing the Duma or parliament, was seen by many as the beginning of a new era in Russian history. The revolutionary forces split. Most moderates and liberals were hopeful that a true parliamentary system would evolve. A party of moderates, the Octobrists, was founded on that hope. The major group of liberals, the Kadets, was more skeptical of the government, but it, too, hoped for the best. Some of the socialists, however, especially the Marxist revolutionaries, wanted to continue the revolution.

Liberal and moderate hopes were soon dashed. As the government regained confidence in 1906, it worked to limit the powers of the Duma and to repress any remaining signs of the revolution. Piotr Stolypin, the minister of the interior and a leading government figure between 1906 and 1911, was successful in destroying or forcing underground the various revolutionary groups. In what was virtually a coup in June, 1907, he changed the electoral laws to disfranchise many workers and those persons from non-Russian parts of the empire. The Third Duma was a much more manageable body than the First and Second had been.

Stolypin also carried through an important series of measures that allowed a peasant to claim his land from the village commune as a unified, independent holding. The idea behind the measure was that the peasants would be more conservative politically if they had property of their own. Furthermore, if they farmed as independent farmers free of the restrictions of the commune or *mir*, they would be more productive.

Some historians, in assessing Russia in 1914, point to the changes that the Stolypin land reforms were making, the spontaneous revival of the industrial economy, and the continued existence of institutions of parliamentary government, to justify an optimism about the solidity of the empire had it not then been wracked by war. Others, however, emphasize continuing problems in the countryside with low productivity and overpopulation, the precarious and generally fruitless existence of the Duma, the chasm between educated society and the government, and the hostility between urban workers and society, to buttress their case that collapse was inevitable. They also point to the lack of political leadership in Russia after the assassination of Stolypin in 1911. Nicholas II was not well suited to help Russia build on her past achievements and minimize her existing deficiencies.

Germany

Germany did not experience the same difficulties as Austria-Hungary and Russia. Its problems with minority groups were negligible in comparison to those of the other two states. It enjoyed an immensely strong economy. The Reichstag had functioned as a national parliamentary body since 1871. Despite Germany's apparent stability, however, many worried about her. Simply because she was so strong economically and militarily, Germany was a formidable force on the continent. Without responsible leadership, she could become a danger to other states. In the minds of many, responsible leadership was precisely what Germany lacked in the years before 1914. The Reichstag had little control over the government for, though it looked like a Western parliament, it did not name the cabinet ministers. Astute chancellors tried to maintain majorities and to manipulate opinion, but much government activity went on beyond the purview, much less control, of the Reichstag.

A strong chancellor, as Bismarck had been until his fall from power in 1890, could exercise considerable power. But Bismarck had based his power both on majorities in the Reichstag and on the loyalty of the kaiser. Neither chancellor in the years before the war, Bülow or Bethmann-Hollweg, was able to duplicate Bismarck's pattern of government. The kaiser, Wilhelm II, was not an effective source of power either. He was erratic, and when he intervened in governmental affairs it was often to the embarrassment of those in government. A case in point is the interview he granted to the London *Daily Telegraph*, which was published on October 28, 1908. In the interview, the kaiser made a number of statements that revealed his unsure grasp of government operations and also irritated the British.

Special-interest groups did achieve positions of influence in Germany. The Bülow tariff of 1902, a protective tariff, was brought about by the cooperation of industrialists from the Rhineland and Junker landowners from East Prussia. The combination of rye and steel was powerful in Germany. Similarly, the Navy League, composed of merchants, businessmen, and military, was able to launch a major campaign of naval construction. And the general staff of the army increasingly usurped the government's prerogatives in voicing opinions or making commitments.

In the 1912 elections both the SPD and the Catholic Center party made strong showings. If they had banded together with the Progressive Party, a majority on the left and left-center might have been created to press for a revision of the political system. Such a coalition was unthinkable, however, and Germany continued into 1914 without leadership except for that provided by nationalists and militarists.

The Coming of War

It has been suggested that several major states had reached a point of severe crisis in 1914 and that this was an important motive in their decisions to go to war. The heady experience of military success and the resulting surge in national pride would supposedly divert the population's attention from domestic problems. The thesis is intriguing, but it exaggerates domestic considerations. Only two of the states in question, Russia and Britain, were faced with acute crises in 1914. Each of the other powers had political systems that were flawed and burdened by numerous problems, but each was functioning and seemed likely to continue working in the foreseeable future. Britain faced her most severe challenge since 1830; one can only speculate on what might have been, but, given Britain's record of resolving crises short of civil war and revolution, chances seem good that Britain would have found a compromise in 1914, too. Russia was clearly headed toward revolution, if not in 1914, in a matter of a few more years. It was in Russia that some voices were heard calling for war as an easy solution to domestic difficulties.

Although domestic problems played a part in the coming of war, the major reason was a belief on the part of various governments that they had reached a point beyond which they dared not go if they wanted to continue to exist as major powers. Each major power was part of an alliance system, the maintenance of which seemed crucial to their status as a great power. Two powers, Germany and France, felt this particularly strongly. Germany thought it crucial to support her major ally in the Triple Alliance, Austria-Hungary (the other member of the alliance was Italy). Otherwise, Germany feared that she might be caught between two great land powers, France and Russia. France, having long suffered in diplomatic isolation after the Franco-Prussian War of 1870-1871, did not want to give up her alliance with Russia. At the same time, she hoped to draw Britain into a more definite alliance

and transform the Triple Entente of France, Russia, and Britain into a
real military partnership.

Ranged against the compelling desire to survive as nations were the
forces of international cooperation in such matters as postal and
telegraph services, economic interdependency, various pacifist
movements, and the international socialist movement organized as
the Second International. The arguments of Norman Angell's *The
Great Illusion* (1910) that war would lead to economic collapse were
widely read but not heeded in 1914. Neither international cooperation
nor economic interdependency were sufficient to stop war when it
came.

Strong forces worked toward war before 1914: militarism, nationalism, racism, and imperialism. Of these, imperialism was probably
the least important. Clashes over colonial territories increased
international tension, to be sure, but in the construction of empire
there was room for give-and-take. Colonial antagonism could be more
easily forgotten than disagreements over territory in Europe. The
Triple Entente, after all, was composed of ex-competitors in Africa
and Asia. Racism also did not play a vital role in the coming of war
although, like imperialism, it accustomed people to believing in their
superiority to others and in rights that supposedly were theirs by
virtue of that superiority.

Nationalism and militarism were the chief contributing factors in
the outbreak of World War I. Militarism in the first decade of the
twentieth century resulted in vast increases in the size of military
establishments and in the formulation of plans for mobilization and
deployment of troops that could take on lives of their own once a
crucial point had been reached. As nationalism became less and less
tolerant, viewing the world as a pie of limited size so that one nation
took what it needed at the expense of other, less important, nations,
the concern became greater to protect the national interest.

All the factors cited played a role in turning what has been called,
with good reason, the Third Balkan War into an international con-
flagration. The beginning of the crisis was the assassination of Franz
Ferdinand, heir to the Hapsburg throne, at Sarajevo, June 28, 1914.
Behind it lay more than a decade of frustration for two countries,
Austria-Hungary and Russia. Austria believed that its continuing
integrity as a state depended on using the assassination as an excuse
to crush Serbia and so remove an important source of support for the
nationalist agitation that was tearing it apart. Russia believed that its
influence in eastern Europe would not survive a diplomatic defeat of

the sort that Austrian humiliation of Serbia would represent. Even so, Russia might have stood by had Austria acted promptly. Europeans everywhere had been shocked by the assassination.

Austria did not act quickly, but went instead to Germany where on July 5 her representatives obtained the so-called "blank check." Germany believed that Austria was justified in taking strong action against Serbia and encouraged her because she feared for her own position in Europe should Austria decline as a power. She did, however, expect Austria to act while world opinion was still favorable. Austria delayed further, first to win over Stephen Tisza, the Hungarian premier, and then to investigate Serbia's role in the assassination. In the meantime, Russia's position had begun to harden and she warned Austria that she would not tolerate the humiliation of Serbia.

Austria ignored the warning and presented an ultimatum to Serbia on July 23. Serbia accepted all but one term which, by allowing the Austrians to take part in the Serbian investigation of the assassination plot, would have infringed on her sovereignty. Serbia's reply was seen by all the powers, Germany and Austria included, as remarkably conciliatory. Yet Austria went ahead with mobilization and a declaration of war on July 28. Germany was beginning to have second thoughts by this time, but she did not effectively apply pressure to halt Austrian preparations for war.

Also on July 28, the Russians ordered a partial mobilization and then, for technical reasons, on July 30 ordered full mobilization. Otherwise, it was felt, Russia would have no chance of influencing Austria. Russian mobilization made it imperative that Germany put the Schlieffen plan into effect. Since this plan called for Germany to deal with France first, then quickly turn back to the east, each day the Russians had to mobilize before the Germans launched their drive to the west jeopardized the success of the plan that much more. After Russia's mobilization, which was a military rather than a political decision, it was all a matter of railroad timetables. Germany attacked France, violating Belgian neutrality in the process. Britain came into the war to aid the French and to defend the principle of neutrality. Only Italy remained, for the time being, out of the conflict.

Some of the very elements that had made Europe master of the world worked in World War I to destroy her. Industrial productivity and the capacity to mobilize men and money made possible a carnage few Europeans could anticipate before 1914. The five years of war and revolution damaged the fabric of European life beyond repair.

24   Europe, 1900-1980

The contradictions of the prewar period, more or less successfully repressed at the time, emerged to challenge the old certainties. It was the end of one era and the beginning of another, and darker, one.

Suggested Readings

J. Kim Munholland, *Origins of Contemporary Europe, 1890-1914* (1970)

Edward R. Tannenbaum, *1900: The Generation Before the Great War* (1977)

Arno J. Mayer, *The Persistence of the Old Regime: Europe to the Great War* (1981)

Oron J. Hale, *The Great Illusion, 1900-1914** (1971)

Jan Romein, *The Watershed of Two Eras: Europe in 1900* (1978)

Robert K. Webb, *Modern England: From the Eighteenth Century to the Present** (1968)

Gordon Wright, *France in Modern Times: 1760 to the Present** (third edition, 1981)

Gordon A. Craig, *Germany: 1870-1945** (1978)

Michael Balfour, *The Kaiser and His Times** (1972)

Christopher Seton-Watson, *Italy from Liberalism to Fascism, 1870-1925* (1979)

Robert A. Kann, *The Multinational Empire: Nationalism and National Reform in the Hapsburg Monarchy, 1848-1914*, 2 vols. (1964)

Donald W. Treadgold, *Twentieth Century Russia** (fifth edition, 1981)

Guido de Ruggiero, *The History of European Liberalism** (1927)

Peter N. Stearns, *Lives of Labor: Work in a Maturing Industrial Society* (1975)

Carl E. Schorske, *German Social Democracy, 1905-1917* (1970)

Standish Meacham, *A Life Apart: The Engish Working Class, 1890-1914* (1977)

D. K. Fieldhouse, *Colonial Empires* (1971)

Heinz Gollwitzer, *Europe in the Age of Imperialism, 1880-1914** (1979)

Gerhard Masur, *Prophets of Yesterday* (1961)

H. Stuart Hughes, *Consciousness and Society** (1961)

Carl E. Schorske, *Fin-de-Siècle Vienna: Politics and Culture* (1979)

Laurence Lafore, *The Long Fuse** (second edition, 1971)

Vladimir Dedijer, *The Road to Sarajevo* (1966)

*indicates paperback edition available

2

War, 1914-1917

The summer of 1914 was exceptionally fine, with warm and sunny weather. The leisured went on picnics, had tea outdoors, played sports, walked, and swam. Even those without wealth and great stretches of leisure enjoyed an occasional excursion or afternoon in the park.

The declarations of war at the end of July and the beginning of August did little to dampen spirits. Men went off to war as if they were going on an outing with old schoolfriends, one that might sometimes be rough and uncomfortable but still great fun. The wives, sweethearts, sisters, and daughters who accompanied the soldiers to the railroad stations sometimes shed tears amid the enthusiasm. No one, however, least of all the military, anticipated the tragedy that Europe had stumbled into the summer of 1914.

The military in each country, while anxious about the details of the campaigns they had planned, were confident that their efforts would be swiftly successful. There was nearly universal agreement that the war would last about six weeks. Germans expected to be in Paris by the anniversary of the Prussian victory over the French at Sedan in 1870 (September 2); Russians thought they would be in Berlin about the same time. One Russian officer agonized over whether he should pack his dress uniform to take to the front or have it sent to him a few weeks later. No plans were made for wars of long duration, although both the French and German commanders had recognized the possibility of this. The lack of foresight is perhaps understandable. Wars in recent experience had been brief and had involved only a few decisive battles. The one major exception had been the British campaign against the Boer republics. Then, too, the strategies formulated by the rival commanders involved campaigns which, to be successful, had to end quickly. A long war simply meant the failure of one's strategy. No general staff cared to contemplate that possibility.

The Failure of the Schlieffen Plan

No set of campaign plans was more closely tied to the idea of a short, decisive war than the German, or the Schlieffen Plan. Based on the likelihood that war would mean a struggle on two fronts for Germany, the Schlieffen Plan became a rationale for war itself. Once Russia began mobilizing, the German military believed that the Schlieffen Plan had to be implemented or Germany would, in effect, abdicate its position as a world power. Putting the plan into effect necessarily involved war with France, for the plan envisioned sending German forces through Belgium to the north and west of Paris, in a sweeping arc that would encircle and crush the French armies. Once this had been accomplished, German forces would turn back to the eastern front in time to deal with the Russian armies, which would be then just completing mobilization according to German calculations. It was a daring scheme and one that came close to working. Several factors, however, intervened.

Perhaps the most important of all the factors that caused the German effort to go awry was British intervention on the side of the French which, together with unexpectedly stiff resistance by the Belgians to the invasion of their country, prevented the Germans from completing the sweep of the arc that they had originally planned. The Germans had gambled that the British would not enter the war or, if they did, would be ineffective in aiding the French. The invasion of Belgium, necessary to German plans for outflanking the French army but challenging the traditional English goal of guarding the Low Countries from great power control, decided Britain on intervention, or at least furnished the pretext. The British were able to land four divisions of infantry and one of cavalry in France by mid-August, the greater part of the British army not stationed around the world in colonial outposts.

Also crucial was an early Russian drive into East Prussia. The Germans, anxious about leaving the Prussian homeland exposed while they dealt with the French, panicked at the news of the Russian invasion and detached some forces in the west to reinforce troops in the east. The Russian initiative had thrown the Germans off balance, but at considerable sacrifice, for the Russian armies were soon separated and annihilated. Of even greater consequence, the German victories in the east at Tannenberg and the Masurian Lakes established the reputations of Generals Paul von Hindenburg and Erich Ludendorff as great leaders. Ludendorff emerged during the war as the virtual dictator of Germany. Hindenburg was also enormously powerful during the war and played a fateful role in the late 1920s and early 1930s in the rise of Nazism.

The German commander in the west, Helmuth von Moltke, nephew of the great Prussian general during the period of the unification of Germany, contributed to the failure of the plan not only by weakening his forces in response to the Russian threat but also by failing to exercise close supervision over his forces in the field. His counterpart in France, General Joseph Jacques Joffre, contributed significantly to French success by his calm example and his superior generalship in the Battle of the Marne, the battle that sealed the fate of the Schlieffen Plan.

French and German forces met east of Paris on the Marne River, beginning on September 5, for the first major battle of the war. The fact that the battle took place to the east of Paris, instead of to the west or south as had originally been planned, indicated that the various factors already mentioned, in particular the activities of the British Expeditionary Force, had necessitated a serious modification of the Schlieffen Plan. The French and British made good use of German confusion, in part by using the taxis of Paris to rush reinforcements to the front, but mainly through use of the railroad network to move men and material, to end any chance that the Schlieffen Plan had had of working. On the 8th, British and French troops nearly broke through, but by the 10th a stalemate had been reached. The German strategy had failed.

Trench Warfare

After the Battle of the Marne a so-called "race to the sea" took place. The sea was not the object; rather, each side hoped to turn the other's flank and break the stalemate. What developed instead was a line of trenches running from the English Channel to the borders of Switzerland, a distance of about four hundred miles. The trenches had been dug for shelter from artillery bombardments and enemy attacks, but it quickly became apparent that trenches combined with machine-gun fire and barbed-wire emplacements gave the defense a decided edge over the offense. The war in the west became a war in which movement was highly limited. Even more important, it became rapidly apparent that the war would be long and costly.

Siegfried Sassoon, a British infantry officer and war poet, once commented that "when all is said and done the war was mainly a matter of holes and ditches." The holes and ditches were enormously complicated. For example, the French system, with a frontage of about 270 miles, contained approximately 6250 miles of trenches of one sort or another. Trenches usually were arranged in three roughly parallel lines: first was the front-line trench; then several hundred yards behind this was the support trench; and finally, another few hundred yards behind the second line of trenches ran the reserve trench. In addition to the three parallel lines of trenches, the firing trenches from which attacks were launched and enemy attacks repulsed, there were various trenches running perpendicular to the firing trenches. Behind the front there were communication trenches along which came ammunition, reinforcements, and food. Running out from the front line into No Man's Land were "saps," shallow ditches leading to forward observation and listening posts, grenade-throwing and machine-gun posts. Dimensions of firing trenches varied, but they would almost always be deeper than a man was tall, with, on the enemy side, a parapet of earth or sandbags rising another two or three feet off the ground. Trenches were built in a zigzag fashion to minimize damage from shelling and to make it difficult for an attacking enemy to clear a trench. In the sides of the trenches were one- or two-man holes, "funk-holes," and deeper dugouts. There was something of a national style in trenches: German trenches tended to be deeper, drier, and more elaborate than the British or French systems; the British systems seemed the most provisional and least carefully worked out.

Life in the trenches, "the troglodyte world," was utterly different from civilian life or even from life in the rear. One example was the distortion of traditional concepts of time. Activity was greatest during the night when, hopefully, the enemy could not observe what was taking place. Under the cover of darkness, repairs and extensions were made to the trenches and the barbed-wire emplacements in front of them, supplies and reinforcements were brought up, scouting parties sent out. At dawn and again at dusk, men in the trenches stood-to and peered anxiously across No Man's Land. Dawn, especially, was the favorite time of attack. One of the many ironies of the

British soldiers in the trenches in 1918. The German trenches were so close that the British could hear the Germans talking while the photograph was being taken. The trench is uncharacteristically dry. (BBC Hulton Picture Library)

war was that sunrise and sunset, the one conventionally a symbol of hope, the other a symbol of calm and peace in lyric poetry, were times of anxiety and despair.

During the day the troops ate, cleaned their weapons, slept, wrote letters, and deloused themselves. When it rained, the trenches were filled with water and mud. In the winter it was bitterly cold. Rats—large, aggressive rats—were everywhere in every season. Just as constant was the boredom. The narrow band of sky above the trenches became a major source of diversion, especially when airplanes got into dogfights overhead.

Boredom and misery were preferable, however, to those times when an attack was imminent. If the enemy mounted an attack, then one could expect hours, sometimes days of intense shelling. The tension became almost unbearable. The narrator in Erich Maria Remarque's novel *All Quiet on the Western Front* explained:

> The front is a cage in which we must await fearfully whatever may happen. We lie under the network of arching shells and live in a suspense of uncertainty. Over us Chance hovers.

For those who were to go "over the top," the suspense was no less unbearable. At first some of the attacks had the quality of a game. There are stories of men kicking soccer balls before them as they advanced toward enemy lines. The idea was to be the first to kick a ball into the enemy trenches. Later attacks were mad dashes across lunar landscapes, past the carnage of previous battles, and on past the barbed wire and machine-gun nests to the first in a series of trenches. Attacks were seldom successful. If one trench was taken, there remained two or even more behind it. Massive mutual bloodletting was the only outcome of most offensives.

After a week or so in the front lines, troops were moved back to the rear and their places taken by others. It was not uncommon to have lost 50 or even 75 percent of one's outfit if fighting had been heavy. Even if a sector was quiet, people were killed and wounded daily. "Wastage" was the official term for it.

One of the characters in *All Quiet on the Western Front* says, in a discussion of what life will be like after the war, "Two years of shells and bombs—a man won't peel that off as easy as a sock." And, in fact, many of those who experienced the front were not able to shake off the experience. The sense of alienation and estrangement from civilian life and values was strongest during the war itself, but for many who had been on the front lines it endured after the war. The life that they had led before the war often seemed to them distant and unrecoverable. Those who had been in the front lines noticed with great bitterness that the officers and politicians who pressed aggressively for yet one more campaign lived in relative comfort and security. Soldiers fantasized how it would be if politicians and generals were brought to a great stadium and forced to fight it out among themselves, or how it might be to run amuck among well-meaning but ignorant civilians and show them what war was really like. Siegfried Sassoon described the latter fantasy in chilling terms in "Fight to the Finish." The soldiers, "who'd refrained from dying," had returned home victorious and were parading down the street before cheering civilians when suddenly they fixed bayonets and charged. The narrator, hearing "the Yellow-Pressmen grunt and squeal," turned with his "trusty bombers" to go clear out Parliament.

The distance in space between the front and home was never very great in World War I. An irony of the war was the fact that a soldier could be in London or Berlin on leave one day and at the front within the next day or two. The two worlds were separated not as much by space as by experiences that marked many men permanently, coloring their perceptions and shaping their actions in postwar years.

Men on the frontlines were preoccupied by details such as avoiding being blown to bits by incoming shells or bayoneted in the next attack; the generals took a larger view of things and believed, until 1917 at least, that a breakthrough could be achieved and victory gained if only the offensive were prepared with sufficient care. Each offensive called for a more intensive shelling of the enemy than previously, a greater concentration of troops on a wider sector of the front for the initial assault, and a larger contingent of reserves to exploit the breakthrough. Yet, somehow each offensive failed as did the previous ones, a few square miles gained at the cost of tens of thousands of dead.

There was an initial resistance to new technology, despite the obvious importance of the machine gun early in the war. Still, a number of new types of weapons were introduced in the course of the war. The British used tanks for the first time in 1916, but the potential was not recognized at the time and tanks became an effective weapon only in the campaigns of 1918. Poison gas had been introduced even earlier, in 1915, but it was difficult to use because it depended upon wind conditions, and never became a major factor. Airplanes were pressed into war service immediately and became a dramatic and glamorous part of the war. After the development of machine guns

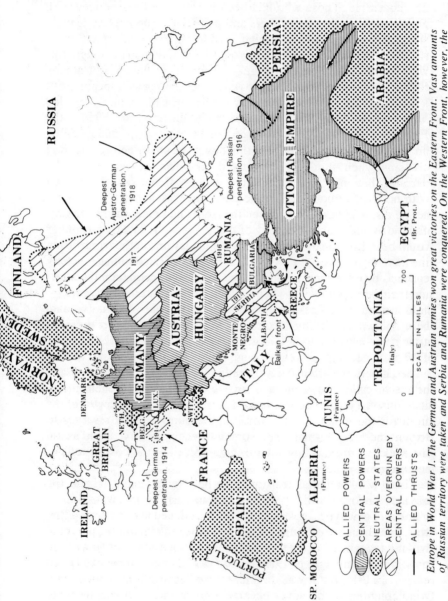

Europe in World War I. The German and Austrian armies won great victories on the Eastern Front. Vast amounts of Russian territory were taken and Serbia and Rumania were conquered. On the Western Front, however, the German army made little progress. The resulting stalemate cost millions their lives.

RUSSIA

FINLAND

NORWAY

SWEDEN

DENMARK

IRELAND

GREAT BRITAIN

NETH.

BELG.
LUX.
1914

GERMANY

AUSTRIA-HUNGARY

SWITZ.

FRANCE

SPAIN

PORTUGAL

SP. MOROCCO

ALGERIA
(France)

TUNIS
(France)

ITALY

TRIPOLITANIA
(Italy)

RUMANIA

1916

SERBIA

BULGARIA

1915

MONTE-NEGRO

ALBANIA

GREECE

Balkan front

OTTOMAN EMPIRE

PERSIA

ARABIA

EGYPT
(Br. Prot.)

Deepest Austro-German penetration, 1918

1917

Deepest Russian penetration, 1916

Deepest German penetration 1914

0   700

SCALE IN MILES

ALLIED POWERS

CENTRAL POWERS

NEUTRAL STATES

AREAS OVERRUN BY CENTRAL POWERS

ALLIED THRUSTS

synchronized to fire between the propeller blades, aerial combats became deadly games. Each country had its aces, the most famous being the German, Manfred von Richthofen, the "Red Baron." Much more crucial for the fortunes of war were the submarines, the German U-boats, with which Germany hoped to starve the British into surrender. After initial heavy losses of shipping, ways were found to counter the threat of U-boats. The major result of their unrestricted use in 1917 was to bring the United States into the war. It was the entry of the United States into the war—an event that tipped the balance of resources—rather than the introduction of a new weapon that finally brought the war to a close.

The Course of the War

After the Battle of the Marne in September 1914, and the "race to the sea," the western front remained stable throughout the remainder of the year and all of 1915. The action in 1915 was in the east, where an Austro-German campaign resulted in a general retreat by the Russians. By September, when the Austrians and Germans stopped to regroup, the Russians had retreated nearly three hundred miles, surrendered territory equivalent to all of France, and suffered enormous numbers of casualties. Yet Russia had not been knocked out of the war. In fact, reorganization of the government and war effort made it possible to hope that she would recover from the defeats of 1915.

The allied powers were encouraged in 1915 by the entry of Italy into the war on their side. Italy was regarded as a major addition to the allied forces even though she had a poorly equipped, poorly led army and a weak navy. Italy came into the war in 1915 in the belief that Britain and France would win and that she, in return for helping to gain victory, could expect important territorial gains from the dismemberment of the Austrian and Turkish empires. The British and the French, for their part, hoped that Italy would place significant military pressure on the Austrians and, indirectly, on the Germans.

The war involved fighting in the Middle East as well, where the Ottoman empire fought as an ally of Germany and Austria. The British, with the help of forces from India, Australia and New Zealand, were able to protect the Suez Canal and oil installations. In return, they worked to encourage Arab nationalism against the Ottoman empire. They and the French laid the basis for much of the present dilemma in the Middle East by making contradictory promises to Arab nationalists and to Zionist organizations seeking a national Jewish homeland. The involvement of other areas in the war effort was relatively minor, but colonial peoples everywhere were encouraged by the war to press more strongly for independence. The war showed them that Europeans were neither omniscient nor omnipotent, and therefore not necessarily destined to rule over them. Also, some, such as the Indians, had contributed to the war effort in the expectation of a reward of independence or greater self-government for their sacrifices. Unlike the impact of World War II, the result of World War I was not the dissolution of various colonial empires (except, of course, the German empire), but a visible weakening of the structures.

1916

In 1916 the western front exploded as commanders on both sides sought to prove that a breakthrough could be achieved. The most significant event of the year was the German attack on the French fortress of Verdun, the principal fortress facing Germany. Verdun had little strategic value and, in fact, the French had removed much of its armaments. The German commander, Erich von Falkenhayn, reasoned that the French would defend it vigorously, however, because of its symbolic value. His plan was to bleed France white by attacking something that they regarded as a symbol of their war effort. The German attack in February took the French by surprise and was successful in capturing one of the key outer defenses.

The French reacted just as Falkenhayn had believed they would. They rushed reinforcements to Verdun under the command of Philippe Pétain, who reorganized the French forces and conducted a successful defense. "They shall not pass" was the motto Pétain used. German efforts continued until December, but with little success. Falkenhayn forgot his original intentions and became as obsessed with taking Verdun as the French were with defending it. Verdun became closely associated with the French war effort because of Pétain's practice of rotation of troops. A large proportion of the French army went through the hell of Verdun at one point or another in 1916. It was a test for the French soldier and was his victory, just as the Marne had been a victory for the French generals. The cost to both armies was staggering. Both nations were bled white at Verdun; each suffered over 350,000 casualties.

In addition to the French soldier himself, one hero to emerge from Verdun was Pétain, the organizer of the defense. His reputation as the defender of Verdun led France to call him from retirement in 1940 when, shattered by the German *Blitzkrieg* in World War II, she looked to him for salvation. On that occasion, however, Pétain was not equal to the task. There were no heroes on the German side. Falkenhayn was discredited by Verdun with the result that the team of Hindenburg and Ludendorff became virtually all-powerful in Germany by the beginning of 1917.

The Battle of the Somme, which began in July 1916, was to be the supreme effort by the western allies to achieve breakthrough and victory. An intense bombardment of over one and one-half million shells from fifteen hundred guns prepared the way. On July 1 110,000 British went "over the top." Sixty thousand casualties were suffered that first day. Although the allies outnumbered the Germans two to one, they could not penetrate the German defense in depth. Tanks were used for the first time but, although effective, they broke down too easily and were too few in number. The struggle continued into November with little result except, once again, massive casualties. The British and Germans each lost over 400,000 men each, while the French lost 200,000.

In the east, the allies achieved considerable success in initial efforts in 1916. General Aleksei Brusilov, commander of the Russian forces along the southwestern front, launched an attack on June 4 that caught the Austrians entirely by surprise. The offensive quickly lost momentum, however, because of shortages of ammunition and problems with other supplies and reinforcements. At the same time, the Germans and Austrians brought in reinforcements from the Italian and western fronts. Still, the offensive had forced the Austrians to halt their drive against Italy and had weakened their offensive capability in the east. It had also disrupted German efforts at Verdun. Once again, at great sacrifice, Russia had provided a timely diversion. The sacrifice involved the loss of one million men and practically all available supplies. By the end of 1916 the country was on the verge of collapse.

As a matter of fact, all the belligerents were straining by the end of 1916 to maintain the war effort with its continuous demands on men and material. Before 1914 no one would have believed it possible for European nations to endure what they had already endured by the end of 1916. Russia was the most severely strained among the several countries, but all were showing signs of exhaustion.

The Home Front

Although only those at the front knew and were marked by the full horror of the war, even those on the home front witnessed a comprehensive transformation of their lives. Politics, economics, and social relations took on new forms and functions in the course of the war. After the war, life for most resumed normal outlines, but the memory of what had been changed to enable countries to bear the extraordinary burdens of World War I was kept alive and used as a guide when other seemingly extraordinary situations in the twenties and thirties apparently called once more for centrally directed and highly concentrated efforts. The temptation to resort to the comprehensive solutions provided by wartime experience was difficult to resist, even when situations were not so extraordinary.

During the war, every country came to be governed by a dictatorship, whether an obvious or a somewhat disguised one. In some countries, a struggle took place between the military and the civilian leaders for control. Elsewhere, strong figures came from the ranks of politicians and government leaders. In France, the military largely dominated the government in the first part of the war without, however, replacing it. In November 1917, Georges Clemenceau formed a cabinet in which he served as premier and minister of war. This government took France through the last, crucial year of war and into the initial efforts to construct a lasting peace. The military in Germany, having shown considerable autonomy even before the outbreak of war, increased their influence steadily in the course of war. At almost the same time that France was being brought back under the control of a civilian government, the military in Germany achieved a position of dominance. In July 1917, Theobald von Bethmann-Hollweg, chancellor since 1909, was forced out of office and replaced by a relative unknown who was primarily a front for General Ludendorff. The latter became the real source of authority in Germany and remained such until the fall of 1918. In Britain, civilian government continued throughout the war, although the role of Parliament and even that of the full cabinet was diminished in favor of the War Committee. Within this inner group David Lloyd George emerged as the major figure, eventually becoming prime minister in December 1916. In Russia the autocratic government continued largely as it had in the past. Unlike most other belligerents, Russia produced no strong figure from either the military or civilian government. The tsar, Nicholas II, attempted to play this role, even to the point of taking

Women workers on the Home Front. One of the most important developments of World War I involved thousands of women working in jobs that they would never have had before the war. These women are working on a truck in an engineering shop in 1917. (BBC Hulton Picture Library)

command of the Russian forces. After the February Revolution in 1917, Aleksandr Kerensky also attempted this role and failed. Ineffective, often incompetent leadership in Russia was especially unfortunate, given the severity of her problems with mobilization and distribution of resources.

Governments had been slow to realize the special demands that war now imposed, but by 1916 most governments were beginning to mobilize and control the allotment of resources, restrict the lives of civilians as well as soldiers by means of such activities as rationing and censorship, and to influence views and values through propaganda. Efforts along these lines were most extensive in Germany, not only because the authoritarian form of government was intensified by the dominance of the military, but also because of the serious shortage of raw materials that quickly appeared after Britain imposed a blockade. Some goods could be obtained by trading through neutrals. Not only the amount but the type of goods traded this way was surprising. Concrete for German blockhouses came from England through the Netherlands. There are other examples, but Germany was nonetheless forced early in the war to rely on a careful use of available resources and on technical ingenuity to manufacture what was lacking.

The most innovative figure in the organization and allotment of German resources was Walther Rathenau, head of the *Allgemeine Elektrizitäts Gesellschaft*, one of the largest and most important businesses in Germany before the war. In 1914 Rathenau organized each branch of production so that raw materials were allocated to producers who were the most efficient and involved with work of the highest priority. Rathenau also pushed efforts to develop substitute products and to manufacture some items synthetically. His *Kriegsrohstoffabteilung* (KRA or War Raw Materials Administration) became a model for state organization and regulation of the economy. It was not until the end of 1916, however, that a comprehensive attempt was made to mobilize the human resources of Germany through the Auxiliary Service Law. Before this, some men had been deferred from military duty because of their importance as skilled workers or farmers. Now all males between seventeen and sixty were committed to and at the disposal of the war effort. The organization and manipulation of the German economy and society served as a model for efforts by authoritarian governments on various occasions to mobilize their countries. The Bolshevik policies during the civil war in Russia after the October Revolution of 1917 furnish a good example of how the model was used.

Mobilization of men and material succeeded in maintaining the German war effort but could not avoid the imposition of considerable hardships on the civilian population. Beginning with the "turnip winter" of 1916-17, when turnips replaced potatoes as the basic food, civilians faced severe food shortages. Thousands died that winter of malnutrition and starvation. Other goods were in short supply, too. Civilian suffering in Germany in World War I was more intense and widespread than in any other country with the exception of Russia.

While Russian civilians, especially those living in the large cities, suffered greatly from shortages of food and fuel, from a military standpoint the shortages of raw materials for the factories were far more crucial. In Russia efforts similar to those undertaken by Rathenau in the KRA were attempted, but with little success. The organization of the War Industry Committees in 1915, plus other civilian attempts to bring together resources and solve the problems of supply and distribution plaguing the Russian war effort, met with a suspicious hostility on the part of the tsar and his officials. When a prominent leader of the Duma (the Russian parliament) brought up the possibility of civilian efforts to increase the supply of boots for the army, the minister of the interior accused him of using that to work toward a change in the constitution. Everywhere Russian officials saw civilian attempts to help as efforts to bring in reform and revolutionary change by the back door, thereby undermining the autocracy.

Austria-Hungary fared worse, if anything, in its efforts to organize for war. The two halves of the empire competed with each other for food. Various nationalities and ethnic groups did what they could to undermine the war effort. The last link holding the empire together, Emperor Franz Joseph, died in 1916. His heir, Karl, began trying at the end of 1916 to extricate Austria-Hungary from the war and somehow save the dynasty.

The British and French faced fewer problems than the three empires in the east, but still had to struggle to improvise means for conducting war on an unprecedented scale. Rumors of a shortage of shells led to a broadening of the Liberal cabinet in Britain into a nonpartisan regime in May 1915. Following this, in July 1915, a Ministry of Munitions was created, headed by David Lloyd George. He quickly turned the ministry into the British equivalent of the KRA, controlling the allocation of material and men and the level of profits. Through control of the munitions industry, Lloyd George was increasingly involved in the regulation of the entire economy.

On the whole, the British ran the most successful war effort of the European states. Unhampered by blockade, as was Germany, or by enemy occupation of important industrial areas, as was the case with France and Russia, and possessing a formidable industrial base, which Italy and Austria-Hungary lacked, Britain paid for more of the war effort by taxation than any other belligerent and distributed the burdens of conducting the war more equitably as well.

The Social Impact of the War

Even in the best-run war efforts, there was much dislocation and suffering among civilians, but one of the most important ways in which war changed social relations was to reduce the importance of class or status. The emphasis from the beginning had been on the cooperation of all layers of society in the war effort. Each country had its equivalent of the French *union sacrée* or the German *Burgfriede*. Governments erased many distinctions through rationing and other efforts to make the burdens of war equitable. Governments also erased distinctions by the first efforts toward the standardization of life, an example of which were the form postcards that civilians received from the front: on the card were only a few standard messages from which the soldier could choose. In a more positive manner, the comprehensive mobilization of each population during the war created a sense of participation in the affairs of the nation and a sense of individual self-respect that many had not felt before. Many were thrust into new responsibilities and discovered abilities and aspirations that had previously lain dormant. One such person was Rosina Whyatt, a household servant before the war, who went to work in a munitions plant and after the war became a labor organizer. Many felt that after the war they could not accept a return to the old society and that, in any case, they had earned a reward for their sacrifices. These feelings were reinforced by returning soldiers who, after living through the horrors of trench warfare, would not willingly stand mutely in awe of their "betters" again. Leonard Thompson, a farm worker from Suffolk, came back after serving in the war to organize a branch of the Agricultural Labourers Union. Others in Britain and on the continent followed similar paths.

One group in particular took on new roles during the war. Women found positions in industries that had traditionally been closed to them as well as expanded openings in areas in which they were already active. It became far more acceptable than ever before for women to have their own apartments, to go out unescorted, and, generally, to make their own decisions about their lives. In Britain and Germany, although not in France, it seemed impossible after the war to deny women the vote. Many people, of course, returned to an older concept of the place of women once the unusual situation created by the war had ended. Many others, however, found it impossible to give up the independence and responsibility to which they had become accustomed. The era of the flapper in the twenties would not have been possible without the changes in attitudes, in both males and females, caused by World War I.

While groups that had been subordinate and dependent before the war were gaining self-esteem and independence, many groups dominant before the war experienced a weakening of their positions and a loss of confidence. Many in those groups that had governed Europe before the war, both the aristocracy and the upper middle classes, could not help but question the values they had believed in so strongly, given the obvious and direct connection between those values and the calamity of a world war. A surprisingly large number managed to resist the need for a critical reexamination of values and assumptions, however. One of the greatest tragedies of the war was that it decimated the ranks of the leaders of the next generation. The most idealistic, the most likely to be able to deal with the new conditions that the war was creating, were also those who were most likely to volunteer for service and, because of their leadership abilities, to become lieutenants in charge of the forces on the frontlines. The casualty rate among lieutenants was higher than that for any other rank.

The psychological impact of the war is even more difficult to outline than the social impact. Obviously, wives without husbands and children without fathers were psychologically scarred by the war. Even more clearly, men in the trenches were burdened by their experiences. There has been speculation that various groups, even entire generations, never recovered psychologically from World War I and were doomed to succumb to the strain of the next severe crisis that they experienced. This assertion, which is difficult to pen down precisely, will be examined further. For now it may be enough to say that a collective experience of the magnitude of World War I was bound to have a significant psychological impact.

1917

By 1917 the war had produced difficult, sometimes desperate situations in each belligerent country. At the front, armies showed unmistakable signs of exhaustion. For each belligerent, 1917 was unquestionably the low point in the war. The allies were able to continue fighting in 1918 only because American entry into the war held promise of victory. Germany continued fighting and compelled its allies to continue, too, largely because a few powerful leaders, in particular Ludendorff, could not admit the possibility of defeat or forego the achievement of power and position that they sought for Germany.

In the year 1917 everything seemed to fall apart. The extreme example of collapse was Russia, where in March 1917 (February according to the calendar then in use in Russia) a revolution took place that resulted in the end of the Romanov dynasty, the first of several royal houses that fell because of war and revolution. Events in Russia in 1917 will be dealt with in the following chapter.

Almost as serious as revolution in Russia were the French army mutinies in April 1917. Generals and politicians tended to see revolutionary conspiracies and lack of patriotism as principal factors behind the mutinies. In fact, the mutineers, who numbered between thirty and forty thousand, were reacting to the disastrous spring offensive and to the string of failed offensives that had preceded it. Soldiers protested what appeared to be a callous disregard for lives on the part of officers who had persisted in employing the same tactics time after time despite repeated slaughters on the battlefield. General Pétain was called in to restore morale and to suppress the mutiny. His concern for the well-being of each soldier and his efforts to work out new methods of fighting helped to bring the mutinies to an end. About 10 percent of those actively involved in the mutiny were sentenced. Of those, 554 were sentenced to death but only 49 were actually executed.

The French army mutinies had been a political as well as a military problem. The government was afraid that the mutinies might turn civilian discontent into outright revolution. While these fears were probably exaggerated, there was growing discontent in France with the war, especially among workers. The strike movement, extremely limited in number of strikes and strikers in 1915 and not much larger in 1916, was larger in terms of numbers of strikers in 1917 than the previous two years and even larger than either 1913 or 1914. Revolution was not a serious danger in France in 1917, but everywhere there was dissatisfaction and discouragement.

Somewhat similar situations existed in Italy and Britain. Each country experienced military disaster in 1917 and widespread dissatisfaction on the home front. The British army did not experience a mutiny on the scale of the French mutiny, but discontent reached an unusually high level and some incidents occurred. At home the strike movement had never declined to the extent that the French and German movements had. In 1917, however, the numbers of strikers were larger than those for either of the troubled years of 1913 and 1914.

The Italians suffered a tremendous reversal in the Caporetto campaign at the end of 1917, in which 300,000 were taken prisoner and thousands deserted during the retreat; a description of this forms a major part of Ernest Hemingway's *A Farewell to Arms*. Caporetto strengthened the positions of those who wanted Italy to leave the war and those who believed that Italy's sacrifices in the war demanded suitable compensation at the end of the fighting.

The year 1917 was difficult for Germany as well. While she could hope that the Russian revolution would paralyze the Russian war effort, she had to contend with the entry of the United States into the war. The United States became involved partly because of German determination to resort to unrestricted submarine warfare and partly because of diplomatic blunders like the Zimmermann note, in which Mexico was offered American territory in return for joining Germany in a declaration of war. Time was quickly running out for the German military effort. Soldiers were beginning to feel that further fighting was hopeless in the face of an enemy better supplied and fed than they. At home there was increasing discontent, too. As in most countries, the strike movement increased considerably in 1917; it was five times as large in 1917 as in 1916. Open discussion of peace was another sign of war weariness. The Reichstag passed a resolution in favor of a peace of understanding on July 19.

In every country it was clear that the war effort could not be sustained much longer. For Britain and France, it was a question of holding on until the United States could send sufficient men and supplies to tip the balance. For Germany and her allies, victory depended on taking advantage of Russia's collapse and making a last effort to gain victory in the west.

War Aims

All countries, despite restiveness among soldiers and civilians and strong undercurrents of desire for "peace without annexations or indemnities," were committed to war aims which could only be accomplished by the achievement of a clear-cut victory. Some war aims had long been acknowledged publicly. The French desire to regain Alsace-Lorraine was well known. Most war aims, however, had been developed in the course of the war as opportunities presented themselves or as leaders sought to determine ways in which war could be justified once victory had been won. In several cases, secret treaties had been signed that detailed the distribution of territory after the war.

Germany's aspirations were undoubtedly the most unrealistic. Somewhat different versions were presented by different groups within Germany, but there was an essential consensus. Germany would dominate the European continent economically and politically. France would be weakened to the point where she could no longer function as a great power. Belgium and the Netherlands would become, in effect, satellites. Luxembourg and territory in the east would be annexed. Central Europe, *Mitteleuropa*, would be utterly dominated by Germany. In Asia and Africa, Germany planned to construct a large and powerful empire that would counter the British empire, which Germany saw as too strong for her to defeat. German war aims, even in their most ambitious manifestations, were seen as basically defensive. Their accomplishment would provide Germany with the resources and room that she required as a great and progressive nation. This, many Germans sincerely believed, would benefit all mankind in that Germany was the leading nation of the civilized world and the repository of the most important values and ideals. At the same time, Germany would be secure from threats by Britain, France, or Russia, threats that had caused the war in the first place, in Germany's estimation.

France wanted Alsace-Lorraine, of course, and also talked of taking areas along the Rhine that would add to her industrial strength and weaken Germany. She also had an interest in some territory controlled by Turkey and was willing to bargain with Russia over the latter's interest in Poland and the Straits. Even Britain had an interest in rounding out her colonial empire through the acquisition of German colonies and through a share in the partition of the Turkish empire.

For many political leaders a curious dilemma existed. Whatever their reasons for entering war, these leaders had entered into agreements about the shape of the postwar world which they believed had to be honored. At the same time, they could not tell their countries that these were the aims for which millions were dying. Furthermore, most leaders of the belligerent nations were not able to look beyond territorial gains to see what various groups within their own society expected to gain from the war. These groups, in particular women and the working class, hoped for political and socioeconomic reforms as rewards for their sacrifices in the war effort. Even before Woodrow Wilson and V. I. Lenin began, each in his own way, to turn the war into a crusade, large numbers of people in every country told themselves that war had to have as its result something more than just a rearrangement of political boundaries.

That many in Europe had come to expect a totally new era to be the result of the war is understandable, given what it had cost in loss of lives and property. The total number of casualties—killed, wounded, or missing—was more than thirty-seven million. More than eight million were killed. Millions of the wounded were left maimed for life. A large part of a generation had been left on the battlefield. The loss of property, particularly in northern France and in Belgium, was high. To this might be added the costs of paying pensions to the wounded and survivors' benefits to the widows of soldiers, costs that would continue long after the war ended. There were hidden losses as well.

The European states had become debtor nations in the course of the war. The United States emerged from the war as the major creditor nation and, increasingly, the financial center of the world. Germany lost its colonies and its assets outside Europe; other countries found it necessary to sell off much of their holdings abroad to pay for the war effort. European states, preoccupied by the war, also lost ground in the competition for international markets. Their home economies, naturally oriented toward production for the war, found it difficult to make the transition to a peacetime economy.

It is appropriate to consider here the impact of the war as a whole on European civilization. Jack J. Roth writes that the "war [was] no mere 'catalyst' accelerating prewar tendencies." It "not only facilitated change, it played a powerful role in molding its quality and strength." One or two examples here may help to clarify the point. Even before the war, there had been appeals to irrationalism and violence. War, by exposing millions to years of violence and irrationalism of the most incredible sort, not only reinforced the prewar ideas but also, for many, made these ideas seem entirely normal. Another example might be drawn from the development of increasingly powerful governmental bureaucracies before the war. Again, experience in war with economic planning and control and with extremely powerful governments convinced many that liberal, democratic governments and laissez-faire economies were impossible in the world of the twentieth century. It is no accident that millions of people in Europe in the 1920s and 1930s looked to comprehensive solutions for their problems by omnicompetent governments.

Roth concludes by pointing out that the war severely damaged but did not destroy the old order in Europe. Not all was swept away. In the 1920s and 1930s attempts were made everywhere to restore the old or some semblance of it. Old centers of power and old attitudes hung on, all the more defensive because of the challenges to their positions. Changes everywhere had been massive, but only in Russia did a successful revolution take place. This meant that embattled conservative forces faced forces for change almost everywhere. The next two decades were spent in trying, unsuccessfully, to come to terms with the impact of World War I.

Suggested Readings

Cyril Falls, *The Great War, 1914-1918** (1961)

Marc Ferro, *The Great War, 1914-1918** (1973)

Norman Stone, *The Eastern Front, 1914-1917* (1976)

Alistair Horne, *The Price of Glory: Verdun, 1916** (1979)

Richard Watt, *Dare Call It Treason* (1963)

Eric J. Leed, *No Man's Land: Combat and Identity in World War I* (1979)

Erich Maria Remarque, *All Quiet on the Western Front** (1929)

Henri Barbusse, *Under Fire** (1917)

Robert Graves, *Goodbye to All That** (rev. ed., 1960)

Jon Silkin, *Out of Battle: The Poetry of the Great War** (1978)

Paul Fussell, *The Great War and Modern Memory** (1975)

Fritz Fischer, *Germany's Aims in the First World War** (1968)

Jere C. King, *Generals and Politicians: Conflict between France's High Command, Parliament, and Government, 1914-1918* (1951)

Gerald D. Feldman, *Army, Industry and Labor in Germany, 1914-1918* (1966)

Arthur Marwick, *The Deluge: British Society and the First World War** (1970)

Jack J. Roth, ed., *World War I: A Turning Point in Modern History** (1967)

René Albrecht-Carrié, ed., *The Meaning of the First World War** (1965)

*indicates paperback edition available

3

Revolution and Peacemaking, 1917-1919

The Russian Revolution and the intervention of the United States in World War I were the two events of 1917 most responsible for the way in which the war ended and the postwar settlement developed. Rightly or wrongly, the latter was personified by Woodrow Wilson, President of the United States, and the former by V. I. Lenin, leader of the Bolshevik faction of the Russian Social Democratic Labor Party (RSDLP) and the leading figure in Russia in 1917. Each man spoke for a program of postwar change. Whereas most politicians talked only of the necessity of defeating the enemy and rearranging the map so that that enemy would never again be a menace, Wilson and Lenin, from quite different perspectives, proposed a world that would be entirely different from the world that Europeans had known before the war. The programs put forth by Wilson and Lenin made it possible for many to hope that the war might serve a purpose after all. For a time, at least, the despair and cynicism engendered by years of warfare were dispelled.

Of the two programs, Wilson's was the better known. Wilson, who had worked to keep the United States out of the war and who, as late as 1916, campaigned on his past record as an isolationist, was determined to make the entry of the United States into the war count for something. The peace settlement after the war would not be the product of secret diplomacy by a few great powers but rather a peace based on principles that had been stated before negotiations began. The "Fourteen Points," an address made by Wilson in January 1918 to a joint session of Congress, contained three main guidelines that Wilson wished to make the basis of the new international politics. The first, point one, called for "open covenants openly arrived at." The second, implicit in a number of the points, was the principle of national self-determination. The third, point fourteen, recommended the formation of a "general association of nations" in order to assure the political independence and territorial integrity of each nation. All three reflected Wilson's distrust of traditional diplomacy. In his opinion, the war had resulted from the tendency of the great powers to conduct diplomacy in secret and to make deals at the expense of those not represented in the negotiations.

Wilson was an idealist in that his vision of the postwar world bore little resemblance to most Europeans' memories of the prewar world. He was not a utopian dreamer, however, as demonstrated by the emphasis he placed on the importance of a "general association of nations." This organization was to mediate between the real world of human beings and the world that Wilson hoped to see, a world based on open diplomacy, national self-determination, disarmament, the lowering of economic barriers, and cooperation among nations. Wilson's vision of a different and better world was tempting and attractive not only to the allies of the United States but also to many Germans, who believed that Wilson's program would lead to a fairer, more equitable peace than that which they would likely get from the British and the French. To some extent, the appeal of Wilson's ideas was related to the course of the war. As the allies came closer and closer to victory over Germany in 1918, they began to think more about making Germany pay for the war and less about Wilson's version of a new and better world in the postwar era.

Lenin's program appealed to a segment of the population different from that which Wilson addressed. Whereas Wilson called for an end to aristocratic methods of diplomacy and their replacement by democratic methods, an appeal essentially to the middle classes, Lenin talked of the coming revolutionary transformation of the world that war would bring, an appeal mainly to the working class and, to some extent, the peasants. Lenin and the Bolshevik party fully expected revolution to break out in western Europe in 1918 not only as the result of the hardships brought on by the war, but also because of the manner in which war had revealed the bankruptcy of the bourgeois order. The Russian Revolution was merely a catalyst, an event that would ignite the fires of revolution elsewhere.

Lenin had in common with Wilson only a belief in the right of national self-determination. Diplomacy, however styled, was in Lenin's opinion merely a tool of oppression used by the state. None of Wilson's fourteen points dealt with Lenin's most pressing concern: the need for a new social order. Although Lenin's program appealed to millions, it was feared by millions more. His ideas were feared because behind them lay the fact of the Russian Revolution and the forces that it had unleashed. No one, Bolsehvik or bourgeois democrat, quite knew what might develop from the events of 1917 in Russia.

Russia in 1917

There were actually two revolutions in Russia in 1917. The first came in February.* The February Revolution involved an abdication of authority by the government in the face of increasing disorder rather than a revolutionary seizure of power. Crowds appeared on the streets of Petrograd (the *nom de guerre* of St. Petersburg) beginning on February 23, 1917, for a variety of reasons—food riots, a Woman's Day celebration organized by the socialists, and a lockout at the Putilov Works. Each day the crowds increased in size and by February 27 troops had begun to mix with the crowds.

On February 27 the Duma, with great reluctance, formed a Provisional Executive Committee which later established a Provisional Government. From the first, the Provisional Government shared power with the Soviet of Workers' and Soldiers' Deputies in Petrograd. The Soviet, modeled on a similar institution in the 1905 Revolution, saw itself as the watchdog of what it believed was a bourgeois revolution. It did not wish to take power, yet it could not avoid acting on occasion to protect the interests of the people. Whether it wished to or not, it possessed enormous power as the *de facto* representative of the people, not just of Petrograd but of all Russia. This power called into question the ability of the Provisional Government to lead the country.

The Provisional Government has often been characterized as being weak, unrealistic, and hypocritical. Its failure, the failure of liberalism in Russia, has been seen by some as leading directly to the Bolshevik takeover in October. These criticisms are valid but should be qualified by setting the Provisional Government's actions in the

---

*Dates used in the discussion of events in 1917 in Russia are according to the Julian calendar in use there at the time. In the twentieth century, it was thirteen days behind the Gregorian calendar in use in western Europe.

Provisional govt failed as it had the best intentions

context of the times. It failed precisely because it had the best of intentions, that is, it wanted to deal carefully and fairly with the three major problems facing Russia in 1917—the problems of peace, land for the cultivators, and a permanent form of government. The latter two problems were regarded, understandably, as complex questions requiring careful study. While war continued, the Provisional Government believed that these questions must be put aside. Hasty decisions or decisions prejudiced by the extraordinary demands of war would do more harm than good, in their opinion.

decision to continue war doomed P. Govt

It was the decision to continue the war that doomed the Provisional Government. In part, this was a matter of honor. Russia had obligations to fulfill with her allies. In any case, unilateral cessation of hostilities with Germany would not serve the cause of peace. Russia could only exert pressure on the allies to move as quickly as possible toward peace without annexations or indemnities. Behind these reasons, which involved honor and common sense, there were more selfish reasons for continuing the war. Some members of the government, especially Pavel Miliukov, Minister of Foreign Affairs and the major figure in the original Provisional Government, hoped to gain indemnities and the various territories promised Russia in secret treaties made during the war. Whatever the reasons, the Provisional Government failed to see the necessity of extricating Russia from the war, a hard reality that Lenin forced the Bolsheviks to accept in 1918.

The Gordian knot of war remained for the Provisional Government even after its reorganization in May, a reorganization in which several socialists accepted cabinet posts and Aleksandr Kerensky, a right-wing Socialist Revolutionary, became Minister of War. Kerensky, who had been the only socialist in the first government, was now the most prominent member of the reorganized government. Despite his apparent ability to deal with the vastly changed situation created by the February Revolution, he had no better idea of the relationship of the Provisional Government to the masses than nonsocialist politicians. He was committed to continuing the war effort and, in fact, was personally responsible for preparing the army for an offensive in June.

The effect of the reorganization of the government in May had not been to improve its relations with the masses but rather to discredit the socialists, in particular the Mensheviks, the more important faction of the Russian Social Democratic Labor Party (RSDLP) at that time, and the Socialist Revolutionaries (SR), the most influential group in the countryside. This left the Bolshevik faction of the RSDLP free to say what it pleased, unrestricted by participation in the government. The Bolsheviks, however, a group dominated by the ideas and personality of Lenin, had relatively little influence in Petrograd in the spring of 1917. Mensheviks and SRs controlled the Soviet. The Bolsheviks had an even smaller following in the countryside and among troops on the front lines at this time.

When the February Revolution took place, Lenin was in exile in Switzerland. It was not until several weeks later that he, with the help of the German government, was able to return to Russia. In a speech given shortly after his return, he established the Bolshevik position. There was to be no support given the Provisional Government. The second stage of the revolution, the proletarian stage, was at hand and it would be the task of the Bolsheviks to lead the transition to that second stage, at which time the Soviets would take power.

It was not easy for Lenin to convince the Bolsheviks that his "April Theses" were correct. The Bolsheviks in the spring of 1917 were still more like a debating society than the tightly organized, disciplined, revolutionary party that Lenin wanted. After accepting his ideas, however, they did become better organized, especially in comparison to the other political parties. They had clear ideas about what to expect in the future and about how they would deal with events. No other party could say that. With their radical slogans of Land, Bread, Peace and All Power to the Soviets, the Bolsheviks rapidly gained adherents.

The Bolsheviks grew rapidly in the spring and early summer of 1917, but in July they nearly lost everything. After the failure of the Kerensky offensive in June 1917, massive demonstrations in Petrograd threatened to topple the government. Both the Soviet and the Bolshevik faction faced difficult choices. Groups of demonstrators pleaded with the Petrograd Soviet, seen as the spokesman for the entire Soviet movement, to take power. The leaders of the Soviet refused, some unable to escape orthodox ideas about revolution, others afraid that they lacked ability to govern Russia or that they would not be accepted by all groups. The Bolsheviks, for their part, were tempted to take the lead in the demonstrations. If they did, they might find the movement insufficiently strong to seize power, which would leave them badly exposed. If they did not, the masses might desert them for more radical groups. Finally, they decided to attempt to control the demonstrations and use them for political propaganda purposes while avoiding actual revolution.

Crowds on the Nevsky Prospekt in Petrograd flee for cover during the disorders in July 1917. The July Days followed the failure of the Russian offensive in 1917. Soon after the July Days, the Provisional Government arrested many prominent Bolsheviks. Lenin went into hiding. Within a few months, however, the Bolsheviks were able to overthrow the Provisional Government in the October Revolution. (BBC Hulton Picture Library)

Just at this point, the government came out with "evidence" that Lenin and other prominent Bolsheviks were German agents. Lenin and some of his associates had, of course, been brought back to Russia courtesy of the German High Command and had been supplied with money by Germany. While Lenin's activities may have worked to the benefit of Germany, no evidence was presented showing that he or any other prominent Bolshevik had been acting on German orders. This kind of distinction was, of course, too subtle to be understood at the time. Helped by Joseph Stalin to shave off his goatee and disguise himself as a workman, Lenin then escaped into hiding in Finland. Several important figures, however, Lev Kemenev, Leon Trotsky, and others, were arrested. It seemed to be a death blow for the Bolsheviks.

Kerensky, now Premier of the Provisional Government, apparently had won. His position seemed to be reinforced by the failure of the right-wing coup attempted by General Lavr Kornilov in late August. Kornilov had hoped to seize power and eliminate the elements on the left, the Soviets and the socialist parties, that he believed were restricting the government.

In reality the Provisional Government was losing even the limited power that it had once had. The problem was no longer that of sharing power with the Soviet movement. Power was now diffuse. The Petrograd and Moscow Soviets still retained a great deal of power in that they were the leading spokesmen for the Soviet movement throughout Russia. Now, however, local Soviets all over the country were making decisions about basic matters in their locality without reference to what took place in Petrograd. Military units, especially those around Petrograd, also possessed some power, but, again, power tended to be effective only on a local basis. What existed by September 1917 was a kind of organized anarchy. An incredible variety of committees and organizations had appeared to deal with pressing problems. No single organization could really speak for all the people. A process of fermentation was working in Russia, within the armed forces, among the peasantry and the workers, and within various national and ethnic groups. The aspirations of these many different groups could not be adequately expressed in conventional political terms, as Kerensky was trying to do by patiently preparing for the election of a Constituent Assembly. The energies of the masses had been unleashed by the destruction of the traditional authorities. No government could succeed unless it tapped those energies or, at the least, managed to ride their currents.

Lenin sought to direct the raw energy of the masses to the goal of seizing power. While he probably did not understand the needs or aspirations of the various groups any better than other contemporaries, he did see the possibility of combining the anarchistic rebelliousness of the masses with the revolutionary efforts of the vanguard of the proletariat, the party. In mid-September, he wrote to the Central Committee (CC) of the Bolshevik faction to announce that "the Bolsheviks must take power at this very moment."

Lenin's proposal embarrassed the CC. It did not believe that the Bolsheviks were strong enough to seize power and, as diplomatically as possible, it tried to shelve Lenin's proposal. Only after he returned to Petrograd to plead his case in person did the CC agree to place "armed uprising on the order of the day." Lenin based his plan for the seizure of power on his interpretation of events in Russia. The Bolsheviks had majorities in the Soviets in Petrograd and Moscow, there were significant peasant movements in the countryside, and the opponents of the Bolsheviks were vacillating. Taken together, these developments created a favorable climate for the seizure of power, in Lenin's opinion. Not all shared his optimism and some voted against his plan. Trotsky voted yes, but sought ways to translate the theoretical possibility into a reality. First, he used his position as president of the Petrograd Soviet to establish a Military Revolutionary Committee (MRC). This organization was designed ostensibly to coordinate the defense of Petrograd, but the Bolsheviks used it to gain influence over the Petrograd garrison. Trotsky also worked to disguise the Bolshevik seizure of power as a defense of the revolution mounted in the name and for the benefit of the Soviet movement.

The seizure of power by the Bolsheviks took place on October 25, 1917. Actually "seizure of power" is too glorious a phrase to convey the reality of the confused situation in Petrograd. It would be more accurate to say that once the Provisional Government failed in its attempt to destroy the Bolsheviks and the MRC, power was dumped into the lap of the Bolshevik faction. Trotsky's preparations made it appear that power had been seized in the name of the Soviet movement. Not all members of the Second Congress of Soviets, meeting at that time in Petrograd, accepted that notion; but the delegates who remained at the meeting, although a minority, voted to accept a Bolshevik government. For the time being, it was also accepted in Moscow and other important cities. Perhaps more important, it was accepted in most areas at the front. In the provinces, distant from central authority in any case, a watchful attitude was adopted. At the same time, centers of resistance sprang up, but the Bolsheviks managed to retain power without great difficulty in the last months of 1917.

The situation became much graver in 1918. The revolutionary government faced several difficult situations. First, it had to contend with the Constituent Assembly, elected in November after the revolution. The Bolsheviks were badly outnumbered, notably by the Socialist Revolutionaries who had received strong peasant support. At the initial meeting of the Constituent Assembly in January 1918, delegates began immediately to criticize the government sharply. The government responded by dispersing the assembly at the end of the first day; there was not enough organized support for parliamentary rule to counter this move.

The second problem could not be dealt with so easily. It involved ending the war with Germany. Trotsky led the Russian delegation in negotiations with Germany and Austria beginning in December. He was not able to moderate the harsh demands laid down by the German general staff. Lenin, as he had so often in the past, used his powers of persuasion and his prestige to get the Bolsheviks to agree to accept the German terms. With great reluctance, Russia signed the Treaty of Brest-Litovsk on March 3, 1918, abandoning Poland, Lithuania, the Ukraine, the Baltic provinces, Finland and Transcaucasia. Russia lost major portions of her industrial capacity and food-raising capabilities, but she gained time in which to attend to internal problems without the demands of war impinging. It was a substantial but necessary sacrifice. Otherwise, it is difficult to imagine how the government could have survived the three years of civil war that followed.

As Russia left the war her former allies felt that they had been betrayed. Even more important, they feared Russia's revolutionary example and began to offer aid to the various counterrevolutionary forces in the Russian civil war, the third and last of the difficulties facing the Bolsheviks in 1918. They also contemplated possibilities for direct intervention, the possibility of mounting a crusade against Bolshevism. The threat of revolutionary infection from Russia remained on the minds of leaders of the allied governments in the last months of the war and during the efforts to reach a peace settlement as well.

The End of the War

For most of 1918, despite the attention given to the Russian situation, the major issue continued to be the war. At the beginning of the year the situation did not look good for the allies: the British and French armies had suffered greatly in campaigns in 1917, the Italian army had been routed at Caporetto, and the Russians had left the war on terms most advantageous to the Germans. Help was on the way, of course, in the form of American troops and supplies, but there was concern about the ability of the allies to hold out until that time.

Germany had problems, too. Time was running out for her. If victory could not be gained in one last offensive, then Germany would have to seek peace as quickly as possible. She was more vulnerable in 1918 than her opponents knew. The harvest of 1917 had been poor. There were shortages of everything. Labor unrest was indicated by large-scale strikes in January. Even Brest-Litovsk had not helped that much. Nearly a million German troops still remained in the east, in part to occupy the new territory Germany had gained.

On March 21, 1918, Ludendorff launched the last effort and struck first against the British. A small breakthrough was achieved. General

Ferdinand Foch was named to coordinate the allied defense and brought up French reinforcements to close the gap. The Germans tried again in April and in May. The attack in May against the French in Champagne was successful but not decisive. A final effort on July 15 was turned back by a French counterattack, supported by tanks and aircraft. In this, the second battle of the Marne, the Germans were forced to undertake a general retreat.

On August 8 the British achieved the first great breakthrough since 1914. It was, Ludendorff observed, "the black day of the German army." At the end of September, Ludendorff told the government that Germany could no longer win the war. An armistice must be signed immediately and peace sought on Wilsonian terms. On October 3, Prince Max of Baden, known as a liberal, became chancellor and included in his cabinet the Socialists Friedrich Ebert and Philipp Scheidemann. The next day Prince Max asked Wilson for an armistice to be followed by a peace conference based on Wilson's Fourteen Points. Three exchanges took place, with Wilson pressing for a change in the German governmental structure and the other allies balking at the idea of using the Fourteen Points as the basis for a peace treaty. In early November the allies agreed to base peace on the Points with two reservations: one was that the point concerning freedom of the seas be discussed at the peace conference; the other was that Germany would have to pay reparations. It became clear to the German government, if not to the kaiser, that an agreement on an armistice awaited only the kaiser's abdication. The armistice came finally on November 11 after Prince Max had announced unilaterally on November 9 that the kaiser had abdicated.

Revolution in Germany and Central Europe

A major reason for the German government's hasty efforts to end the war was the disintegration of its control over many military units and the development of a revolutionary atmosphere in several cities. The situation was much the same as it had been in Petrograd in the February Revolution: the old order was collapsing and creating the necessity of new political arrangements. The November Revolution in Germany had three foci: the naval base at Kiel in the northwest, Munich in the southeast, and the capital city of Berlin in the northeast. The mutiny of the navy at Kiel began after the arrival of several ships from the High Seas Fleet. The crews of these ships had been among those who at the end of October had refused to put to sea in the hopes of engaging the English fleet one last time. On November 3 a large meeting of sailors and workers took place in Kiel. After the meeting a group of demonstrators clashed with a detachment of armed sailors, resulting in several deaths. The next day a Soldiers' and Workers' Council was established, based on the Russian model. The demands of the Council included abdication of the kaiser, no military offensive by the High Seas Fleet, and release of all those previously imprisoned for mutiny. On November 5, Gustav Noske, a Majority Socialist,* worked out an agreement with the rebels. Troops sent to crush the mutiny would not be allowed into the town. Mutineers would not be punished. Political demands would be forwarded to Berlin. After this, groups of men spread out from Kiel across northwestern Germany, establishing Councils and in some areas taking over local governments. Shortly after the events at Kiel, on November 8, Kurt Eisner, an Independent Socialist, proclaimed a republic in Munich.

By November 9, then, much of Germany had experienced a revolution that included seizure of power on the local level and the articulation of political demands such as the abdication of the kaiser and a speedy end to the war. Attention now focused on Berlin where the chancellor, Prince Max, was attempting to convince the kaiser of the necessity of abdication in order to obtain an armistice. Prince Max was being pressed himself by the two Majority Socialist members of his government, Ebert and Scheidemann. They, in turn, doubted their ability to hold the workers in Berlin in check much longer. In fact, a mass demonstration had been called for November 9 after previously scheduled demonstrations had been postponed. Prince Max, as already noted, announced the kaiser's abdication on November 9 without the latter's approval. He also turned over the government to Ebert and Scheidemann. The essentially peaceful transfer of power in Berlin constituted the substance of revolution in that city and largely set the tone for the rest of Germany. Scheidemann did proclaim the existence of a democratic republic but only to head off any attempt to rally support for a socialist republic. Both he and Ebert agreed that radical action was not necessary. The required reforms could be achieved within the framework of a parliamentary democracy. A Council was established in Berlin but, unlike Russia in 1917, effective power remained in the hands of the joint Majority-Independent Socialist ministry. A meeting of representatives of

---

*Majority Socialists were members of the old German Social Democratic Party—the SPD; a splinter group, the Independent Socialists—the USPD, broke off in 1915 to protest against continuing support of the war by the SPD.

Councils from all over Germany in December voted full power to the new Socialist government.

That revolution in Germany came to so little can in part be attributed to the fact that war ended just after the revolutionary events of November. The strain of war had made it virtually impossible for the Provisional Government in Russia to deal with internal problems in 1917 and had contributed directly to political instability. Although the armistice entailed many disadvantages for Germany, it ended the war and left the government in a relatively strong position, especially after it had reached an accord with the army. The agreement with the army, later heavily criticized, had the effect of neutralizing the army in political affairs, but it also meant that the military establishment was maintained intact and unchanged.

The more radical forces in Germany found little sympathy for their demands among the Majority Socialists, who believed that the major demands of socialism had been met with the ending of war and the establishment of a government that was truly democratic. Other reforms could, they thought, be worked out gradually. Radicals in Germany also faced strong conservative forces. The army, if defeated, was still a formidable force in internal affairs. The bureaucracy was still functioning efficiently. Even though the old government had collapsed, most of the other institutions in Germany were still sound.

Finally, revolution in Germany lacked a mass base which the peasantry in Russia had furnished. The Spartacists, a small radical faction within the USPD led by Rosa Luxemburg and Karl Liebknecht, and other, even smaller radical groups found little support for their programs after November 1918. Disorder and sporadic insurrection continued in 1919. The Spartacist Revolt in Berlin in January, in the course of which Luxemburg and Liebknecht were murdered; further uprisings in February and March in Berlin, Munich, and other areas; and the proclamation of a Soviet Republic in Bavaria in the spring were all attempts to continue and to radicalize the November Revolution. None was in the least successful. The German Revolution stopped halfway.

Elsewhere in Central Europe, defeat in war, the disintegration of the old governments, and the powerful example of 1917 in Russia created potential revolutionary situations. In Austria there were disorders throughout 1919, but no revolutionary accomplishments. In Hungary the revolution in October 1918 had created a government of socialists and communists, but in March 1919 that government

The revolution in Germany in 1918 and 1919. Supporters of Spartacus, a radical group that wanted to continue the German Revolution of 1918, take to the street in Berlin early in 1919. (Katherine Young)

became a communist dictatorship under Béla Kun. Communist Hungary did not last long. Rumanian troops invaded in April. At the same time a counterrevolution began and by August 1 the leader of the dictatorship, Béla Kun, had fled the country.

Despite setbacks, by the end of 1919 the fate of world revolution was still undetermined. Revolutionaries were still optimistic but, as it developed, much of their optimism was unfounded. Success in Russia had been based on two factors, the utter collapse of the old regime and widespread rebellion among the lower classes in the city and especially in the countryside. Neither factor led to success in Germany, where the empire collapsed but the institutions and social classes undergirding it—bureaucracy, army, churches, great land-owners, and industrialists—remained. There was no German equivalent to the Russian peasantry on which the small, isolated radical groups could base their activity. In central Europe a large peasantry existed, but it was fragmented by ethnic and national differences and kept under control by great landowners, the aristocracy, and the military who, sometimes with difficulty (as in Hungary), managed to dominate politics after World War I in every central European state except Czechoslovakia. The only successful revolution outside

Russia in the immediate postwar period was in Turkey, where army officers and nationalists rallied in 1919 and 1920 to prevent the victorious allied powers from imposing peace terms on Turkey.

Revolution, if relatively unsuccessful by 1919, still had an enormous impact on postwar Europe. As in the United States, there was considerable and often irrational fear of a Bolshevik menace. A good deal of energy and time were spent at the Paris Peace Conference working out methods by which the Russian Revolution might be quarantined or possibly destroyed. An informal counterrevolutionary movement developed that led to dictatorship, initially in eastern and southeastern Europe, then in Italy and the Iberian peninsula, and finally in Germany.

Peacemaking, 1919

In the midst of this disorder and turmoil, when the threat of revolution looked a good deal more imposing than it did by the end of 1920, the victorious powers began meeting in Paris, not simply to end the war but also to reconstruct the world. Their task was a great deal more complicated than that which Metternich, Castlereagh, and Alexander I had faced in Vienna scarcely more than a hundred years earlier. As Arno J. Mayer has pointed out, negotiators at Paris met at the beginning of a revolutionary cycle, when much was still in flux, rather than at its end. Also, Europe in 1919 was far more disorganized than Europe had been in 1815. Four empires had disappeared: the Russian, German, Austro-Hungarian, and Ottoman empires. Various new states claimed to be in existence. In addition to political and diplomatic considerations, economic and even social and cultural factors now had to be considered.

Critics have often blamed the Paris Peace Conference and the various treaties it produced, principally the Versailles Treaty, for most of the difficulties Europe faced in the twenties and thirties. The peace treaties created problems rather than solved them, according to this view, because the peace conference was dominated by the three principal allies—France, Britain, and the United States—and did not consider sufficiently the views of two other nations, Germany and Russia, at the time temporarily powerless but obviously states that would have to be reckoned with in the future. A bad situation was further compounded, so this view goes, by the fact that the American viewpoint was expressed by Woodrow Wilson, an idealist who was all too often naively ignorant of the European scene. Of course, the fact is that Wilson, while idealistic, was quite well informed about the situation in Europe. Actually, both the British and the American delegations had made special efforts to secure expert opinion on various problems that the conference would deal with and to study the experience of the Congress of Vienna for mistakes to avoid and useful procedures to follow. The French delegation was much more dogmatic in its approach to peace, but even here it was tempered by the realism of Georges Clemenceau, who showed a subtlety of approach and understanding in diplomacy that he seldom if ever had shown in French domestic politics.

The Big Three—David Lloyd George of England, Clemenceau, and Wilson—did dominate the conference. Italy, represented by Vittorio Orlando, played a prominent role at first, but virtually withdrew when her demands for territorial compensation for her part in the war were not fully met. Russia was not represented because it was not clear at the time which of the several governments then active was the legitimate one. Even if the Bolshevik government had been recognized as a legal government, it is doubtful that it would have wanted to participate in the conference. In 1919 hope for the success of the world revolution was still high among the Bolsheviks in Russia. Paris was seen as a meaningless farce. That Germany was not represented turned out later to be a serious oversight. The intention had been for the allies to agree on peace terms which they would then present to Germany for negotiation. Unfortunately, allied discussions took so long that when the Versailles Treaty was finally prepared, it was presented to Germany as something that she must sign. By that time it was clear that people in the victorious countries were growing impatient and also clear that Germany had no possible chance of resistance.

On the one hand, the Versailles Treaty was too hastily drawn up, with several very complicated questions concerning boundaries decided by people acting mainly from political motives. On the other hand, the Treaty did not deal quickly enough with many questions and left others hanging, such as reparations. It was an imperfect document but not an impossible one. Its makers hoped that the imperfections might be worked out eventually through a system of postwar discussion, cooperation, and arbitration, and through the League of Nations.

Perhaps the only guiding principle at the Paris Peace Conference was that the allied nations would contain their differences of opinion and present a united front to the defeated powers. There would be no opportunity for a Talleyrand to repair the fortunes of a defeated nation as there had been in 1815. Italy, of course, violated this principle. The other three principal allies held fast even though Clemenceau was in considerable disagreement with Wilson on many issues. There was, however, no general basis for the peace that could be agreed upon, and without it even points of detail had to be worked out by the leaders on political grounds. Lack of a general basis for the peace also meant that decisions on one set of questions might not harmonize with decisions made in other areas. Germany, expecting a peace based on the Fourteen Points, could easily see where political realism had triumphed over idealism and resented the treaty even more for it.

Versailles was shaped by the tension between French demands for national security and American demands for a just peace. The French wanted to be certain that Germany would never again be strong enough militarily or economically to pose a threat. They believed as well that Germany should have to pay for a large part of the reconstruction efforts necessary to repair war damages in France. The United States emphasized the Fourteen Points. The British view was heavily influenced by the elections of December 1918, which Lloyd George had won by promising a harsh peace for Germany. His own inclination had been to work with Wilson but his campaign promises pushed him toward the French position. In practice, Clemenceau compromised considerably on French demands in order to secure Anglo-American cooperation in the postwar period. For his part, Wilson also compromised, often at Germany's expense, to secure precedents in matters like disarmament that might later become the basis for a general pattern and to bind the allies together in a cooperative effort which, in later years, might repair the defects of the treaty.

Germany was weakened by Versailles, although not fatally as the French had initially wanted. She lost little territory in the west. Alsace-Lorraine went to France. A part of Schleswig was ceded to Denmark after a plebiscite. A few border communities were transferred to Belgium (but restored to Germany in 1926). The coal mines of the Saar were placed under French control for fifteen years after which a plebiscite would determine the national status of the area. The Rhineland remained a part of Germany, despite extensive French efforts, but the area west of the Rhine and a strip fifty kilometers to the east were "demilitarized." Allied troops were to occupy the west bank for fifteen years. In the east, Germany lost a good deal more territory. A large part of Posen, West and East Prussia were ceded

NORTH

SEA

NORWAY

SWEDEN

FINLAND

BALTIC
SEA

RUSSIA

ESTONIA

LATVIA

DENMARK

Schleswig

Memel

LITHUANIA

Polish Corridor

Danzig

East
Prussia

NETH.

GERMANY

POLAND

BELG.

Posen

Eupen-Malmédy

Rhineland

Upper Silesia

Saar

FRANCE

CZECHOSLOVAKIA

Galicia

Alsace
Lorraine

SWITZ.

AUSTRIA

HUNGARY

Transylvania

S. Tyrol

Istria

Fiume

YUGOSLAVIA

RUMANIA

ITALY

ADRIATIC

SEA

ALBANIA

BULGARIA

BLACK

SEA

GREECE

TURKEY

MEDITERRANEAN

SEA

Territories lost by:

Germany

Russia

Austria-Hungary

Plebiscite area

Demilitarized Rhineland

0   400

SCALE IN MILES

Territorial transfers after World War I. The most significant changes took place in east Europe. The Austrian-Hungarian Empire disappeared. In its place were a much smaller Austria, a similarly reduced Hungary, and the enlarged states of Rumania and Yugoslavia (composed of the old Serbia and additional territory). In addition, two new states, Czechoslovakia and Poland (the latter included considerable territory taken from the old Russian Empire) were carved out.

to Poland. Danzig was declared a free city within the Polish customs union. Memel was ceded to the allies and later taken over by Lithuania. Upper Silesia's fate was to be determined by plebiscite. Germany also lost her colonies.

As a military power, Germany was much reduced in size. She was allowed an army of no more than 100,000 men with limitations on the types of weapons that they might have. Her navy was reduced in size and submarines were forbidden. Furthermore, Germany was not allowed to have an air force.

The most important issue involved in the treaty concerned neither territory nor the armed forces but rather reparations. In addition to deliveries of coal, construction of merchant ships, and payment of the cost of the armies of occupation, Germany was required to pay a sum of money as reparations. The amount was left unspecified in the treaty. Five billion dollars were to be paid by May 1, 1921, at which time a bill for the total would be presented. American experts believed that Germany had the capacity to pay for the "damages done to the civilian population of the Allies and their property." This was estimated to be between fifteen and twenty-five billion dollars. The British and the French wanted Germany to pay for the entire cost of the war, something that no nation could possibly do. The compromise reached involved German acceptance of responsibility for all war damages which, according to Article 231, were the result "of the war imposed upon them [the Allied and Associated Governments] by the aggression of Germany and her allies," and eventual agreement on a sum that Germany could pay. By leaving the total of reparations unspecified, the British and French hoped to gain the highest possible figure. The Americans, working through the reparations commission, hoped that a reasonable total, one within Germany's capacity to pay, might be reached once the tensions of the immediate postwar period had diminished.

The Treaty of Versailles was regarded by most Germans as extremely unfair and harsh. They had, of course, forgotten their own treaty-making efforts at Brest-Litovsk. The "war-guilt clause" (Article 231), reparations, unilateral disarmament, the loss of territory in Europe and colonies outside Europe—all furnished texts for German nationalists in the next decade.

Had the Treaty of Versailles been the only product of the Paris Peace Conference, Europe might have maintained political stability in the 1920s and 1930s. There were, however, four additional treaties and the League of Nations Covenant. The failure of several of these

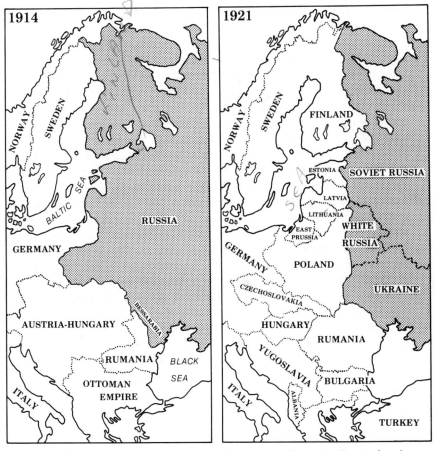

The Eastern Empires disappear. Not only the Austrian-Hungarian Empire but the Russian and the German Empires also disappeared in the wake of World War I.

agreements, combined with the limited success of the Treaty of Versailles, created an extremely volatile situation in the 1930s. Of the four treaties, two can be disregarded: the Treaty of Sèvres with Turkey never went into effect; the Treaty of Neuilly with Bulgaria had no important repercussions. The other two, the Treaty of St. Germain with Austria and Trianon with Hungary, created problems that were never fully resolved between World War I and World War II. Two different problems were created. First, Austria and Hungary, before World War I semiautonomous parts of the Hapsburg empire and each dominant in its own sphere, became small, relatively weak states. Austria particularly was an anomaly, a landlocked state of over six million, of whom two million lived in Vienna. The state was lopsided in every imaginable way, but especially lopsided econom- ically. Unfortunately, Austria was not allowed to join with Germany for fear that this would unduly strengthen Germany. The other problem involved the creation of a series of new or reconstituted states in central and eastern Europe and conflicting claims over territory and population. The idea of national self-determination was extremely difficult to apply in this area with any fairness. Czecho- slovakia, for example, included areas in which the majority of the population was German or Polish. These areas had been included for strategic reasons, as was Sudetenland with its majority of Germans, or for historic reasons, as was Teschen with its Polish majority. Poland included areas with German majorities. Rumania and Yugo- slavia had large concentrations of Magyars. Numerous other exam- ples could be cited of the impossibility of a simple, completely fair division of territory according to the principle of national self- determination.

The irony of the settlement in eastern Europe is that the frontiers established by the treaties and the quarrels arising from them had torn apart what had been an important economic unit. Factories were now in one state, their sources of raw material in a second, and their traditional markets in a third. This contributed to the weakness and instability of the area and nullified any possibility that the states of eastern Europe could serve as a proper counterbalance to either Germany or the Soviet Union.

The League of Nations

Each of the treaties just discussed had flaws. Each posed problems for Europeans in the next two decades. These problems might have been minimized or entirely avoided, however, had the League of Nations Covenant, a part of each treaty, been successfully imple- mented. The Covenant or constitution contained an adequate machinery for maintaining peace in the world. In Article X, members of the League agreed to "respect and preserve as against external aggression the territorial integrity and existing political independence of all Members of the League." Articles XII, XIII, XIV, and XV dealt with judicial settlement by the Permanent Court of International Justice of the Hague, submission of disputes to arbitration, and sub- mission of disputes to the Council or Assembly of the League. Article XI, in a rather general way, and Article XVI, in a more specific way, dealt with the courses of action that might be taken in case of war. The League could take such action as was necessary to resolve a dispute, including the use of military forces.

What made the League ineffective was, first, the absence of three major powers: the United States, Germany (which did join in 1926), and the Soviet Union (which joined in 1934, shortly after Germany had left). In the formative period Britain and France, each having a different idea of the way the League should be run, cancelled each other out. Later, in the early thirties, the League failed some crucial tests, perhaps because the issues involved were not seen as central to European politics. The failure of the League removed the major hope, perhaps from the beginning a utopian one, that the European postwar settlement could be made to work.

Europe was successful in the immediate postwar period in avoiding revolutionary upheaval in most states. For all the changes of war and revolution, Europe at the beginning of 1920 was not so different from the Europe of 1914. Or so it seemed. The two nations that in 1917 had introduced new perspectives into European life had for the moment largely retired from the scene. The new communist state in Russia continued as a source of inspiration for some and an object of hatred for others, but Russia faced enormous internal difficulties at the beginning of the twenties and had little time to spare for developments elsewhere, despite her internationalist rhetoric. The vast significance of the revolutionary events of 1917 in Russia would become apparent only over the next decade.

America was still deeply involved with Europe economically as a creditor nation, but for the most part had removed itself from European politics and diplomacy. The failure of Wilson to gain Senate ratification of the Treaty of Versailles and the League of Nations Covenant in 1919 and 1920 marked an end to Wilsonian efforts to reshape diplomatic relations. Although Wilson's stubborn refusal to compromise was an important factor in the defeat of the treaty, the defeat was mainly due to American reluctance to accept commitments that might impinge on national sovereignty. The French, who had counted not only on American participation in the League but also on American support of Anglo-American guarantees of French security, viewed the American failure to ratify the treaty as a betrayal of their vital interests. They entered the twenties even more determined to try to keep Germany weak.

The main object of many Europeans in the twenties was to return to "normalcy," as the Americans termed it. Both Europe and its relationship to the world had changed, but much of this was ignored. Scattered groups and individuals recognized the changes. Their voices were sometimes heard in the first troubled years of the twenties, but they were soon overwhelmed by the refusal of the majority to acknowledge the full extent of change in Europe.

Suggested Readings

E. H. Carr, *The Russian Revolution: From Lenin to Stalin* (1979)

William Henry Chamberlin, *The Russian Revolution**, 2 vols. (1965)

E. H. Carr, *The Bolshevik Revolution, 1917-1923**, 3 vols. (1951-1953)

Allan Wildman, *The End of the Russian Imperial Army: The Old Army and the Soldier's Revolt, March to April 1917* (1979)

Alexander Rabinowitch, *The Bolsheviks Come to Power: The Revolution of 1917 in Petrograd** (1976)

Marc Ferro, *October Nineteen Seventeen* (1980)

J. L. H. Keep, *The Russian Revolution: A Study in Mass Mobilization* (1977)

Isaac Deutscher, *The Prophet Armed: Trotsky, 1879-1921** (1954)

Adam B. Ulam, *The Bolsheviks** (1968)

Robert C. Tucker, *Stalin as Revolutionary, 1873-1929: A Study in History and Personality** (1973)

A. J. Ryder, *The German Revolution of 1918* (1967)

Richard A. Comfort, *Revolutionary Hamburg* (1966)

Allan Mitchell, *Revolution in Bavaria* (1965)

Francis L. Carsten, *Revolution in Central Europe* (1972)

Arthur J. May, *The Passing of the Hapsburg Monarchy*, 2 vols. (1966)

Paul Birdsall, *Versailles Twenty Years After* (1941, reprinted 1962)

Marc Trachtenberg, *Reparations in World Politics: France and European Economic Diplomacy, 1916-1923* (1980)

Charles L. Mee, Jr., *The End of Order: Versailles, 1919* (1980)

Harold Nicolson, *Peacemaking, 1919** (new ed., 1945)

John Maynard Keynes, *The Economic Consequences of the Peace** (1919, reprinted 1971)

Arno J. Mayer, *The Political Origins of the New Diplomacy, 1917-1918* (1959)

————————— , *The Politics and Diplomacy of Peacemaking: Containment and Counterrevolution at Versailles, 1918-1919* (1967)

*indicates paperback edition available

Overview: 1919-1939

The twenty years from 1919 to 1939 form a crucial period in the history of Europe. Despite the impact of war and revolution, many Europeans began the period under the assumption that the world would once again be like it was before 1914. Too much had changed, of course, since 1914 to permit a simple return to the old order. Much happened in the early 1920s to make return even more unlikely. Germany was wracked by repeated political and economic crises. Parliamentary government in Italy fell victim to a series of crises in that country and a new style of government, a fascist regime, emerged. Communism, despite the rigors of a civil war that left Russia in ruins, retained a base of operations in the Soviet Union and claims for the future in the Third or Communist International, the Comintern.

Yet by 1925 many Europeans had cause to believe that the worst was past. A rapprochement between France and Germany seemed to be in the making. The issue of reparations was dealt with in 1924 by the Dawes Plan; the question of common borders in the west was resolved in 1925 by the Locarno agreements. The specter of revolution had faded considerably by this time, too. The main element of stability, however, was the prosperity enjoyed by most countries and by a large portion of their populations. Of course, as some artists and social critics pointed out, the gap between the lives of the glamorously rich and those of the sordidly poor had, if anything, grown wider. Still, for many Europeans, the doubts that some had expressed in the immediate postwar period now seemed exaggerated.

The new prosperity was reflected in part in the great expansion of popular culture in the 1920s. The movies were a thriving institution. Radio in the 1920s became a means of communication and entertainment with a vast potential. A large number of cheap publications, newspapers, magazines, novels and popular reference works published in installments, were available. The department store began to offer serious competition to small shopkeepers. A mass culture was in the process of being created.

At the same time that a mass culture was developing, high culture continued to flourish. The many and conflicting currents of the twenties were, for the most part, efforts to work out the implications of the prewar modernist movement. Generally speaking, these currents involved one of three main emphases: a sometimes shrill protest against the ways of bourgeois society and a call for revolution, as was the case with the dadaist movement; or an effort to work with the forces of technology and industry for the public good and for the achievement of aesthetic goals, a good example here being the Bauhaus movement in Germany; or a determination to ignore social and political concerns for the compelling problems of art and literature, as was shown by the activities of some of the Bloomsbury group.

Much was changed by the Depression, which was a collapse of several important national economies, particularly that of the United States, aggravated by a breakdown in international economic cooperation. Most European countries contended also with political crises intimately connected with the economic difficulties. The German Republic fell apart in the early thirties, creating conditions which made it possible for Adolf Hitler and the Nazi Party to come to power. Other countries, France and Britain included, struggled with extremism on the left and the right. The appeal of authoritarian solutions, of an all-powerful government ordering society and the economy, was difficult to resist. Elsewhere, the gigantic experiments in social engineering in the Soviet Union turned the country almost overnight into an industrial power. Many, particularly those who did not examine the developments in the Soviet Union very closely, were impressed.

The major issue of the late thirties was the threat of war and how this threat might best be met. The League of Nations proved to be useless in this regard. Britain and France failed to meet Nazi Germany's challenges, even when the Soviet Union seemed to be offering its support, until after the destruction of Czechoslovakia at Munich in 1938. When Hitler early in 1939 broke promises he had made in Munich, the stage was set for the Polish crisis and the beginnings of World War II in September 1939.

In all the frenetic activity of the twenty years between 1919 and 1939, most Europeans failed to notice how the relationship of Europe to the rest of the world was changing. Other centers of power, both military and economic, had appeared in the United States, the Soviet Union, and Japan. Furthermore, the colonial world no longer automatically deferred to their European rulers. Desires for autonomy and independence were widespread. Western ideas about liberty and democracy were now being used against the colonial powers.

Changes in all areas of life had been extraordinarily rapid and pervasive in the period. As Europe entered World War II, many could not help but feel that Europe would not survive a second major conflict without drastic alteration. What most did not realize was the extent to which life had already changed.

4

Recovery, 1919-1924

The losses that Europe suffered in World War I were substantial. Millions were killed or maimed. Damage to property and goods, especially in parts of France, Belgium, Russia, and eastern Europe, was extensive. Yet perhaps more significant than these losses was what the French poet Paul Valéry meant when he said, "The Mind has . . . been cruelly wounded . . . It doubts itself profoundly." Many Europeans had lost something of their self-confidence and now viewed their civilization as fragile and mortal. Old political systems, social and economic arrangements, and cultural assumptions had been brought into question by the war. In the first years after that war, an unquestioning belief in progress through the expansion of industry and democracy no longer seemed possible.

Reactions to War and Revolution

Most Europeans recovered from the shock of war fairly quickly, at least on a superficial level, and returned as best they could to familiar routines. Some, however, either would not or could not simply pick up the pieces of their lives. Many turned to apocalyptical expectations or to a new, Marxist version of the doctrine of progress.

The idea that civilization would come to a sudden, catastrophic end had long been a main theme in the Western intellectual tradition. Whether humanity would then descend into the barbarism of a new "Dark Ages" or achieve a new and better form of life depended on the commentator's reactions to the circumstances in which he found himself. These kinds of ideas had been expressed before World War I, for example, in quite popular fashion by H. G. Wells in some of his novels. The experience of Europe in war and revolution made these ideas seem more substantial. Many sought explanations for recent developments in the wide spectrum of writings after the war that prophesied the end of European civilization. These ranged from bleak despair to cautious optimism. At one extreme, it would be difficult to find a more desparing statement than William Butler Yeats' "The Second Coming," in which he concluded, "And what rough beast, its hour come round at last/Slouches towards Bethlehem to be born?" Only slightly less chilling were the ideas expressed by Oswald Spengler in *The Decline of the West*, the most famous postwar prophecy of impending doom. Spengler spoke of European culture as passing through various stages of life toward an inexorable death, like other cultures before it. In the face of this prospect, he called Germans to be strong, heroic, and Prussian in a time of twilight. His views were often not fully understood, but they were widely discussed and cited. The popularity of his ideas or, more accurately, of slogans taken from his books, is an indication of the large numbers of Europeans who sought to make some sense of the experience of the war years.

Other writers used the theme of apocalypse to emphasize the possibility of renovating European civilization and preventing a collapse. Essentially, they offered a warning of what would come if nothing were changed—a collapse of civilization and a new Dark Age. This approach culminated in two remarkable books that appeared at the end of the 1920s: Sigmund Freud's *Civilization and Its Discontents* and José Ortega y Gasset's *The Revolt of the Masses*. Both men emphasized that civilization was an artificial product of human effort, maintained only by work and sacrifice. Freud, in line with his research before World War I, stressed the idea that civilization was based on the repression of natural instincts, so that one paid a psychic price for living in a civilized society. However, from his vantage point at the end of the 1920s, Freud saw the failure to maintain civilization exacting an even higher cost in the long run: the destruction of all human values.

While it was fashionable to assess the postwar situation in Europe in pessimistic terms, there were many intellectuals on the left and thousands of ordinary people who saw a new dawn breaking. For these people—many communists but also others only disillusioned with bourgeois Europe—the light in the east came from Bolshevik Russia. Artists and writers especially shared the Bolshevik belief that bourgeois society could not be redeemed and that only revolution offered hope. Poets, novelists, filmmakers, and artists saw 1917 as an epochal event in human history. The revolution aroused an expectation that utopia was at hand. There were difficulties, however, involved in being politically and artistically avant-garde at the same time. The communist movement in the 1920s increasingly demanded an art that appealed to the masses and taught them simple lessons. Artists, for their part, enjoyed the unparalleled freedom of creative experimentation that existed in the 1920s and were not always comprehensible in the works they produced. Those artists or writers who were radical in their politics seldom were satisfied with anything less than an unending revolution. Yevgeny Zamyatin, one of the leading literary figures in the Soviet Union in the early 1920s, wrote in his futuristic novel *We* that the proper question was always, What next? A revolution could never be finished.

Outside the Soviet Union, the surrealists in France came closer than any other artistic movement to full-scale cooperation with communism. Although some surrealists eventually joined the Communist party, most continued to work at shocking the middle classes out of their complacency and destroying artistic conventions as independent artists. For some, the communists themselves stood in the way of a true liberation of the mind and spirit through revolution. Other artists, particularly German expressionists like Georg Grosz, never joined a formal political movement but, nonetheless, condemned postwar society in savage and uncompromising terms.

Purely artistic and cultural experimentation was, in part, a third kind of reaction to the experience of war and revolution, an additional way of commenting on the nature of European civilization. Various experiments, especially in the realm of art, preceded World War I and in most cases the artist, musician, or writer was more concerned with the limitations of conventions and traditions in his particular area than with social or political issues. Nevertheless, the efforts to be innovative or at least to destroy old artistic conventions reflected and, of course, contributed to the sense of alienation that many felt as they examined postwar Europe. In the dadaist movement, for example, which began during the war, a playful but still serious revolt was mounted against culture and the society from which it derived.After the war, dadaism was transformed in Paris into surrealism, a simultaneous attempt to free the unconscious from the weight of culture and to overthrow bourgeois society. Dadaism, surrealism, and expressionism were each explicitly critical of postwar European so-

One of the great inventions of the nineteenth century, the train, is matched with one of the most important developments of the 20th century, the radio. A scene on a Grand National train in 1923. (BBC Hulton Picture Library)

ciety. A major part of art in the twenties, however, became less concerned with a social and political commentary and more intrigued with the play of line, form, color, and composition. The tendency to cool, detached, often geometrical abstraction was exemplified in the numerous paintings given the title *Composition* by Piet Mondrian in the twenties. The emphasis was increasingly on innovation, experimentation, and art detached from reality. This was in its own way a comment on that reality.

Literature was not as completely taken over by new forms and styles. In fact, fiction after the war consisted largely of traditional realistic novels. These could readily serve as vehicles of social commentary, but, as in the case of Thomas Mann's *The Magic Mountain*, the critique of postwar society was rather more subtle and less strident than that offered by the surrealists or expressionists. More likely the criticism implied in a work was lost on its audience, which accepted the depiction of reality as the way things were. Other works, such as James Joyce's *Ulysses* or T. S. Eliot's *The Waste Land*, were more innovative. Those two works drew a contrast between the inadequate present and the past strength of Western culture. Both are said to have encouraged Europeans to struggle anew, but the complexity of their form and use of symbol made it unlikely that many readers gained any clear messages from reading them.

Culture: High and Popular

Whatever the field of artistic or cultural endeavor, a major problem was created by the fact that many artists, writers, musicians, and others worked with the rather small, knowledgeable prewar audiences in mind. Yet a new, much larger and less knowledgeable audience existed in the twenties. This new audience attempted to understand and appreciate avant-garde culture, but it often lacked the necessary cultural resources, particularly as many artists became more boldly experimental. A product of improvements in the educational and communications systems, the spread of relative affluence to wider groups, and the growth of leisure time, the new audience could, in general, only follow enough of new developments in culture to become confused. Many people lacked the time and the extensive classical background necessary to appreciate fully or decisively reject, for example, the musical innovations of Arnold Schoenberg. A prewar audience would probably have had the cultural resources necessary for embracing or discarding them. In the postwar period, many people felt compelled to expose themselves to the avant-garde without being able to come to terms with it. Yet there was some correspondence between popular and formal culture.

An example was the popularization of Freud. To a great extent, people in the postwar period were absorbed by themselves, their own needs and problems. It was no accident that Freud became so widely known in the twenties after decades of writing and research; he only gave names to what preoccupied many Europeans in the twenties. Men and women in great numbers accepted the importance of irrational motivation, myths, the sex drive, and the unconscious in their lives. Their ideas about morality and standards of behavior took shape for different reasons, but Freud made it possible to talk about and, to an extent, explain such matters. War and revolution led many to question accepted beliefs and standards. Much of this was superficial and pertained to fashions more than anything else. But beyond the concern with short skirts, bobbed hair, movies, and American jazz, there was considerable debate about more substantive issues such as the new role of women and the extent to which the old class structure of society should be permitted to continue.

In one major way the popular and the artistic moods did differ. Intellectuals and artists continued to challenge prewar assumptions, but most Europeans attempted essentially to pick up where they had left off in 1914. This was especially true after the immediate postwar period of 1919-20, in which the conversion of industry from wartime to peacetime production and demobilization of the armies had caused considerable dislocation. Europeans wanted to eat and dress well and to live comfortably. Depending on their position within society, they might hope to advance socially or, at least, create the possibility for social mobility for their children. In this context, "normalcy" simply meant a concentration on the mundane but vital aspects of life: the family and the home, security and well-being. Understandably, many Europeans turned away from a direct confrontation with those defects of their heritage that war had revealed. They shunned even more emphatically the challenge of a Marxist utopia which some thought communism offered in Russia. Political issues continued to spark controversy, of course. Commentators assessed the impact of the Versailles Treaty and other postwar settlements, discussed the meaning of the Russian Revolution, and, from the fall of 1922 on, discussed the merits of fascism in comparison with liberal democratic systems which, even in Britain and France, had numerous detractors. Commitment, however, to a broad program of political and social change declined noticeably in the early 1920s. Even within the working class, two tense years of strikes and agitations gave way to greater calm in 1920.

Reconstruction

Europeans naturally became involved in the tasks of dealing with the destruction of the past several years. Some problems, however, could not be easily solved. One such problem was caused by the number of people killed and wounded in the war. More significant than the absolute loss was the creation of a "hollow generation." The twenty- to forty-year-olds, who should have provided most postwar leadership, were the group that had suffered the heaviest losses in the war. It was often those who had the most to offer society who sustained the highest casualty rates. The fact that the British army was a volunteer army until 1916 undoubtedly increased the proportion of British aristocrats, intellectuals, and professional men killed in the war, but the experience everywhere was roughly the same. These groups furnished most of the officers. While the higher-ranking officers had a comparatively easy time, captains and especially lieutenants died in large numbers. In this way, the very groups that could have contributed most to a re-examination of European values and institutions were depleted by the event that seemed to make such a re-examination necessary.

Harbingers of future developments were several massive transfers of population that resulted from territorial settlements at the end of the war. Perhaps the most dramatic exchange occurred in 1923, involving more than a million Greeks and Turks. Another harbinger was the massacre of more than one million Armenians by the Turks in 1915. In addition to the various demographic developments that can be documented readily and expressed statistically, there was also the important loss of confidence and drive among the millions who had experienced malnutrition, hardship, and stress. Alongside the physically maimed were many who were spiritually or psychologically hurt. This kind of loss cannot be easily measured. Many people simply had no reserves left; a crisis of almost any dimension tended to overwhelm them and leave them prey for those who promised easy solutions to difficult problems.

A problem that could be dealt with rather easily was the damage done to factories, mines, farmland, and other components of the economy. Reparations, government aid, and private loans contributed to a rapid recovery in western Europe at least. After a brief depression right after the war, the European economy quickly reached levels it would have reached had the war not interrupted economic growth. Some countries—France, Belgium, and Germany, for example—became even stronger economically than before the war through the modernization of equipment and processes. Productivity was increased considerably in some areas in the 1920s through the introduction of the assembly-line system and overall technological improvements. Rationalization and concentration, evident before the war, continued. New areas such as electronics were greatly expanded. Consumer goods industries became increasingly important.

There were, however, several underlying problems in the generally rapid recovery of the European economy. First, not every area in Europe recovered fully. Eastern Europe's difficulties were compounded by the breakup of the large market that the Austro-Hungarian empire had formed. Britain, long the leader of the industrial world, never completely recovered after World War I. Its industrial base consisted to a large extent of older types of industry such as coal and textiles, which in the 1920s experienced severe difficulties from international competition for markets and from the shifts to new products. Secondly, agriculture everywhere found it hard to maintain price levels after World War I. In the war, with fewer people on the land, prices had been high and farmers had cultivated all the land that they could. Some went into debt to purchase land and equipment. After the war, agricultural production in Europe returned to normal levels while outside Europe it stayed at wartime levels. The resulting surplus of agricultural products drove prices down.

The situation in agriculture is indicative of a third problem. Europeans had lost many of their overseas markets and even within their home markets faced stiff competition from abroad. Added to this was a reversal of the prewar credit situation, with Europe becoming a debtor to the United States.

Inflation was a final economic problem that most countries had to deal with after the war. With the exception of Britain, European states had financed the war largely by printing new money and by loans. After the war, the tendency was to increase the amount of money in circulation. This resulted in an inflationary trend in the twenties that became particularly severe in Germany. Inflationary pressures affected the middle and lower middle classes most severely. The value of savings accounts and investments was reduced. People living on fixed incomes found it extremely difficult to maintain old standards of living. Only a few could take advantage of the opportunity to borrow inexpensively for speculative investments. The experience of the early twenties left many economies relatively weak and unstable. It also left various social groups psychologically badly prepared for any future economic difficulties. On the whole, however, the European economy recovered successfully from the dislocations of war despite the existence of important areas and social groups that did not share fully in the recovery.

The Democracies in the 1920s

After a war in which the authoritarian governments had played a major role, the initial success of constitutional and democratic governments was a hopeful sign. There were some developments pointing in other directions, to be sure. Fascist Italy, for example, emerged as an alternative system, although it was not clear until 1924 and 1925 the extent to which it was incompatible with parliamentary and constitutional government. It was imitated in varying degrees in eastern Europe and the Iberian peninsula in the latter part of the 1920s. In countries like France where democratic forms of government seemed strongly entrenched, right-wing authoritarian movements like the *Action Française* carried over from the prewar period. New organizations hostile to parliamentary government were formed in the postwar era. In nearly every country, a communist party emerged from the old social democratic and trade union movements to challenge what communists termed "bourgeois democracy." And the various communist parties were connected with one another in an organization called the Communist International (the Comintern), which seemed, potentially at least, very dangerous to democracy. Nevertheless, it would be more accurate to emphasize the apparent success of experiments in democracy in Weimar Germany and Czechoslovakia by the mid-twenties and democracy's continued strength in northwestern Europe. A constitutional and parliamentary government, republican more often than monarchical, was the norm by the mid-twenties. Universal male suffrage was generally accepted; some nations had adopted female suffrage as well after the war. On the continent, socialist parties had to face the question of active participation in government. In Germany, the Social Democrats (SPD) formed a major component of the coalition government. In France, the Socialists backed away from full participation. Everywhere the centrist parties formed the backbone of the ministries. The extremist parties declined in strength after the immediate postwar period, although they retained organizations that allowed them to continue to question democratic institutions and to pose alternatives. It was still nearly a decade before Yeats' prophetic line "Things fall apart; the centre cannot hold" would come true.

Weimar Germany

Germany appeared by the mid-twenties to be the major European success story and a primary reason for emphasizing the continuing strength of democratic forms of government at that time. The first years, however, were difficult. Both the extreme left and right found an echo in Germany immediately after the war. The Spartacist revolt and subsequent disorders of 1919 gave way to the rightist Kapp Putsch in 1920 in which the *Freikorps*, paramilitary groups of war veterans, attempted a coup against the Republic. The army remained neutral and only a general strike by the trade unions prevented the coup from succeeding. Difficulties with both the left and the right continued until 1923; first an abortive Communist uprising sponsored by the Comintern took place in the Ruhr, and then Adolf Hitler's

National Socialist German Workers' Party (NSDAP, the Nazis) attempted a coup, the "Beer-Hall Putsch," in Munich. The slightly ludicrous nature of both of these events indicated that in spite of the extraordinary inflation racking the economy and the severe pressure by the French government on the German government, there was by 1923 a relative lack of strength among extremist groups.

Reparations were the main sticking point in Franco-German relations and also the foremost issue in German domestic politics in the early 1920s. France believed that Germany could pay enough in reparations to finance the reconstruction of France and other costs related to the war. The Germans doubted this. In January 1923 the French and the Belgians occupied the heartland of Germany's industry, the Ruhr, in order to force Germany to pay. The German government encouraged a program of passive resistance which it tried to finance by printing more and more money. Currency quickly lost all value other than the value of the paper for pulping. Finally, the government reorganized as a coalition of the People's Party (the old National Liberal Party), the Democratic Party (the old Progressive Party), the Center Party, and the SPD. The leader of the coalition, Gustav Stresemann, led the way to an acceptance of the policy of "fulfillment." Stresemann and many other leaders in government and business recognized that Germany could not continue to exist without good relations with France, Britain, and the United States. Exactly what Stresemann hoped to be able to do for Germany is still a matter of controversy. A strong supporter of the monarchy until 1919, he appeared to accept the Weimar Republic as a political necessity. If it was not the ideal political structure, it was nonetheless one within which much could be accomplished for Germany. That Stresemann remained a German nationalist committed to the revision of Versailles seems clear, but his methods were to avoid open confrontation and to work with existing possibilities. In 1924 this approach resulted in the Dawes Plan, which called for a restructuring of the reparations obligations and large foreign loans. These measures enabled the German economy to recover rather rapidly and to present the appearance of economic health in the middle of the 1920s.

The Weimar Republic was still vulnerable. Coalitions depended on the cooperation of the three middle-class parties—the People's, Democratic, and Center parties—with the SPD. The SPD, however, was resented by the middle-class parties. In addition, there were important differences of opinion on both economic and political questions that were only papered over. Perhaps the major weakness of the

Children playing with stacks of German currency made worthless by the runaway inflation of 1923 in Germany. The inflation of 1923 left many Germans badly prepared for the next great economic crisis, the Depression of the 1930s. (Katherine Young)

Weimar Republic was that no group supported it passionately and totally. At best, as Peter Gay has pointed out, some groups gave it a cold, intellectual kind of support, saying that it was better than the alternatives. Others, including most of the large number of civil servants taken over from the old imperial bureaucracy, plus the great landowners of East Prussia, many industrialists in the Rhineland, the army, and nationalists all over Germany, put up with the Republic because an alternative did not then seem possible. Symptomatic of German feeling toward the Republic was the election in 1925 of Paul von Hindenburg, war hero and supporter of the monarchy, as president. In 1925 the German version of fascism could not have been further from power, but the Weimar Republic, despite success at economic and political stabilization, was almost equally far from being firmly established as the form of government in Germany.

France

France in the immediate postwar period followed political trends similar to those prevalent elsewhere in Europe. The Socialist party, known as the S.F.I.O., split in 1920 at the Tours Congress with a majority voting to join the Comintern. Léon Blum, left with the remnants of Jean Jaurès' great party, worked over the next decade to rebuild it. The split on the left weakened the political influence of the working class. The French Communist party would have nothing to do with parliamentary politics. The S.F.I.O., since the 1890s ambivalent about participating in bourgeois politics, refused to enter the government in 1924 when the left won a majority. As a result, the left-center government of Édouard Herriot lasted only a short time. Conservatives dominated the decade. And the major figure among the conservatives was Raymond Poincaré, president of France during the war years. Poincaré disregarded French political conventions by returning to parliamentary politics after his term as president. Early in 1922 he formed a cabinet whose program focused on forcing Germany to meet the schedule of payments for reparations. France had suffered greater proportional losses than any other country in the war. Poincaré and many other Frenchmen believed that Germany had to pay for the reconstruction of the areas where fighting had been concentrated.

French efforts to force Germany to comply failed, as just noted. With the German economy on the verge of collapse, even the French could see that a policy of coercion was fruitless. The increased importance of Stresemann and his policy of "fulfillment" in Germany was matched to a large extent by the growing influence of Aristide Briand in France. Briand, who had begun politics as a socialist, had long been a careerist in the republican ranks. In the 1920s he became the spokesman for the French side for rapprochement with Germany. He and Stresemann seemed to trust each other. Together they created an atmosphere of conciliation and cooperation in the latter part of the twenties.

Germany appeared to be a political success by the mid-twenties. France, at least after Poincaré's successful efforts in the late twenties in dealing with inflation, also appeared to have achieved a good recovery from the dislocation of World War I. Great Britain, however, while it retained its basic political and socioeconomic arrangements, never fully recovered what it had lost in the war.

Great Britain

On the eve of World War I, three major problems had threatened to overwhelm the British government: 1) the question of Irish home rule, 2) the vote for women, and 3) a broad-based dissatisfaction among workers. At the end of the war, the first two issues were resolved, although not to everyone's complete satisfaction. Agreements in 1920 and 1921 resulted in the division of Ireland into Northern Ireland, which remained attached to Great Britain as an autonomous area, and the Irish Free State, which gained Dominion status. It was a far-from-definitive solution, but one which largely removed the Irish problem from British politics for the first time in over a century. The second issue was resolved when women over thirty were given the vote in 1918 (ten years later women received the vote on the same terms as men).

The third issue was more intractable if less potentially dangerous after the war than it had seemed in 1914. Workers' demands were not met, by and large, in the 1920s despite the growth in influence and power of the Trades Union Council (TUC) and the Labour Party. Labour replaced the Liberal Party as one of two major parties in British politics. In fact, although the Conservatives dominated politics in the 1920s, Labour did briefly form a ministry under Ramsay MacDonald in 1924. Increased influence in governmental and economic matters was not sufficient, however, to enable the working class to deal with Britain's declining economic position. In the course of the war Britain had exchanged its position of creditor for that of debtor. Perhaps even more important, it had lost important markets to countries such as Japan and the United States. In some important ways, Britain had become less competitive industrially. She had not participated to the same extent as Germany in the rapid development of electrical and chemical industries. A large part of her industrial base consisted of the older coal, iron, and steel industries. The coal industry, in particular, was a troubled industry in the twenties, with periodic strikes by miners leading to a large-scale confrontation with the state in 1926.

Despite Britain's problems, there was never any real question of changing the political and social system in any substantial way. Neither fascism nor communism made much headway in the 1920s even though Britain's recovery was the least satisfactory of all the major west European states. Britain had managed to do well in previous decades without radical alterations. Most of the population in the 1920s believed that Britain would continue to survive in good fashion without adopting extreme measures.

Fascism in Italy

Italy also experienced difficulty in adjusting to postwar circumstances and eventually turned to an alternative system of government. Italy's problems stemmed in part, somewhat paradoxically, from the fact that she had been among the victors in the war. Many Italians were dissatisfied with the provisions of the peace settlement as they affected Italy. Italy had been promised a great deal more in the Treaty of London (1915) than she had actually received at the end of the war. It appeared that she had sacrificed some 600,000 men and incurred a substantial war debt for relatively little in return.

Injured national feelings and an economy that was suffering from the effects of postwar adjustment and inflation were only two elements in Italy's difficulties. Another important element was political. Italian political life before the war had been based on the concept of *trasformismo*, in which coalitions were put together by parliamentarians who avoided controversial issues and met the needs of each party to the agreement to some extent. In the postwar period, universal male suffrage was firmly established and political parties tried to reach the masses on the basis of detailed programs. Politics also tended to become polarized, with parties taking firm stances that did not easily allow concessions to other points of view. In the elections in the fall of 1919 the two largest parties were the Socialists, soon to split into a socialist and a communist faction, and the newly formed *Partito Popolare*, a Catholic party. Neither could imagine governing with the other, which left the relatively small Liberal and Radical groups to attempt coalitions in the old style.

Old-style parliamentary government, even when strengthened by the results of the elections of 1921, which gave the Liberals and Democrats a working majority, was unable to deal with the political and social crisis of 1920-1922. The crisis involved the possibility of a "Bolshevik" revolution in Italy. In 1920 peasants in the south attempted to take land from the great landowners. A wave of factory occupations by workers took place in the fall of that year. The Italian Socialist Party split early in 1921, with one faction becoming the Italian Communist Party (PCI). Businessmen, wealthy landowners, government officials, and the middle class in general all thought that Italy was in danger of being overwhelmed by "Reds."

Into this situation stepped the small Fascist party, formed in 1919 by Benito Mussolini, a former socialist who had backed Italian intervention in World War I. The Fascists combined nationalism and patriotism. Inflamed by the poet Gabriel D'Annunzio's attempt to take over Fiume on the Dalmation coast for Italy, and fearing social unrest and what appeared to be the government's inability to protect Italian interests and preserve order, the Fascists took the law into their own hands. They protected the estates of large landowners from the peasants, broke up meetings of Socialists, Communists, and trade unionists, and even seized control of some municipal governments. In fact, while much of the disorder caused by workers and peasants ended by 1921, the Fascists continued their work and became in that year the actual source of the largest part of the continuing unrest. They were perceived by many, however, as saving Italy from Bolshevism.

Matters came to a head in October 1922. Mussolini demanded that a Fascist cabinet be formed. The premier refused and wanted to declare martial law. King Victor Emmanuel III would not agree to this, evidently fearing the power of the Fascists and believing also that they might govern responsibly if given the opportunity. The premier resigned and Mussolini was asked to form a government. The "March on Rome" that the Fascists had threatened against the government turned out to be only a train ride into the capital for Mussolini and some of his colleagues.

In the course of the next few years, Mussolini and the Fascists moved rather slowly to gain control of the government. The elections of 1924, held on the basis of the 1923 Acerbo election law which gave the party with the largest number of votes two-thirds of the seats, gave the Fascists an overwhelming position in the Chamber of Deputies. It was not, however, until the murder in 1924 of Giacomo Matteotti, a socialist deputy who had strongly criticized the Fascists, that the party broke with parliamentary and constitutional government in a decisive way. Shortly after the murder, most of the non-Fascist minority of the chamber left in the Aventine Secession. For several months, it appeared that Mussolini did not know how to handle the situation. Finally, early in January 1925, apparently prodded by more daring party lieutenants who controlled regional and municipal branches of the party, Mussolini took responsibility for the murder of Matteotti and announced the end of the old system of government.

To be sure, the introduction of fascism as a basis for the reorganization of politics and society altered more the form than the substance of Italian life. *Il Duce* (Mussolini) was a necessary symbol to hold the party together, but he had relatively few ideas that he wished to implement and little administrative ability. His forte was propaganda, the art of creating illusions, and no one was more deluded by Fascist Italy than Mussolini himself. Nonetheless, Fascist Italy did exist, whatever the nature of its reality, and it provided for some a more attractive alternative to liberal democracy than communism did.

The Soviet Union

Communism, of course, was the political system used by the Soviet Union, the nation that faced the most difficult tasks in bringing about recovery from the war. And interest among Europeans in its fate was probably greater than interest in any other country except Germany. In 1919 there had been, in fact, considerable discussion among the allies of the wisdom of intervention in Russia.

Opportunities for intervention abounded in the Civil War that raged in Russia between 1918 and 1921. The new Communist government was seriously challenged by several counterrevolutionary armies made up of conservatives and moderates. The White armies were only gradually defeated by the Red army constructed during the war by Trotsky.

The Communists fought the war largely without allies from the other socialist parties in Russia. Individual Mensheviks and Socialist Revolutionaries sided with the Bolsheviks, but attempts at coalition government floundered early in 1918 after the Left Socialist Revolutionaries left the government. By the last year of the war, oppositional socialist parties found it impossible to carry on their work. Even more crucial, the Bolsheviks began to lose their allies among the trade unionists and the peasantry. The peasants, the bulk of the population, represented a great danger. Without their support or at least passive acceptance, the Bolsheviks had no chance of survival. By 1921, as the Civil War with the middle class and aristocratic opponents of the regime was ending, peasant Russia was once again in ferment; several serious rebellions took place in this period in protest against the policies of "War Communism." The latter had involved forcible requisitioning of what was considered to be the surplus produce of the peasantry. War Communism also entailed strict control of industry and commerce, often at the expense of the working class, in whose name the revolution had been carried out in the first place.

That the Communist Party (as the Bolsheviks were known after March 1918) and its government survived was due in large part to astute leadership. Lenin, of course, played an extremely important role in the first years. Not only did he get the party to accept the Treaty of Brest-Litovsk, which removed Russia from the war, but he convinced members of the party to accept other difficult decisions, such as those implemented in War Communism, and provided a great deal of latitude for subordinates such as Grigori Zinoviev, head of the Comintern; Feliks Dzerzhinski, creator of the Cheka (the secret police); Stalin, Commissar of Nationalities; and Trotsky, Commissar for War. As organizer of the Red Army and director of the campaigns of the Civil War, Trotsky came to be second only to Lenin within the Communist leadership. Although the efforts of the leaders and the dedication and sacrifice of party followers were important, it still may be more accurate to say that, overall, the Soviet Union owed its survival mainly to the lack of unity among the various White armies and the collective failures of these armies to appeal to the peasantry or any other large group beyond the aristocracy.

The Kronstadt revolt in 1921, a mutiny of sailors at the naval base just outside Petrograd, dramatized the need for a revised economic policy after the Civil War. The sailors, once the most radical supporters of the regime, were protesting against the harsh economic policies that had been followed in the Civil War. Debate as to whether War Communism was an emergency response to the Civil War or a shortcut to socialism ceased as delegates to the tenth party congress realized the necessity of what was later termed a "temporary retreat" from radical policies. The New Economic Policy (NEP), sponsored by Lenin and accepted at the congress in 1921, allowed peasants to sell their surplus grain on the open market after payment of tax. Retail trade and private enterprise were partially restored while what Lenin called the "commanding heights" of the economy—banking, large industry, transport, and foreign trade—remained under government control.

NEP did not come quickly enough to prevent a severe famine in 1921-1922, but it did result in fairly rapid economic recovery over the next few years. By the mid-twenties, progress had been made in improving standards of living and in reducing illiteracy. By this time, however, Lenin was dead. He had first suffered a stroke in 1922 and by early 1923 was largely incapacitated. His death in 1924 marked the beginnings of a struggle for power, which by 1929 resulted in the emergence of Stalin as the most powerful figure in the party and government, and also in a turn to new experiments with the society and economy of the Soviet Union.

During most of the 1920s, the Soviet Union existed in diplomatic isolation. It was feared as a center of world revolution; France and Britain still had bitter memories of the way in which it had left the war in 1918 and of its refusal to honor the obligations and debts of the tsarist government. The Soviet Union tried various more or less conventional measures to strengthen its position diplomatically. It was successful in the early twenties in taking advantage of Germany's status as a pariah nation to conclude several agreements, including some that aided the German military in evading the restrictions of the Versailles Treaty. It was less successful in establishing trade relations with Britain, where negotiations collapsed by the late twenties.

In addition to the standard diplomatic apparatus, the Soviet Union could also call on the Comintern, an organization founded in 1919 to succeed the old social-democratic Second International, regarded by the Bolsheviks as bankrupt by 1919. Because the Soviet Union was the only socialist country in the world at that time, its prestige within the Comintern was immense. In fact, the Communist Party of the Soviet Union soon controlled the machinery of the Comintern and through it exerted a great deal of influence on important communist parties like those of France and Germany as well as on other communist movements. The difficulty that most Western observers had in separating the activities of the Soviet Commissariat of Foreign Affairs from those of the Comintern increased the hostility toward the Soviet Union that other European nations felt.

Diplomatic Relations

Although much attention was focused on the Soviet Union and the danger of a world revolution, Germany was the major diplomatic concern of the 1920s. The French attempts to coerce Germany into paying reparations in 1923, already described, were a policy of desperation. It was due, first, to the failure of the United States and Britain to ratify the treaty of mutual assistance concluded with France after the war. France felt alone on the continent. One stop-gap measure involved a series of treaties with small powers, principally Poland (1921) and Czechoslovakia (1924). Agreements with these countries, and later agreements with the "Little Entente" (Czecho-slovakia, Yugoslavia, and Rumania) never were an adequate sub-stitute for the prewar alliance between France and Russia. France tried to achieve security more directly by keeping Germany weak and France relatively strong through reparations. They were meant to be punitive not as much because of any war guilt that the Germans should have felt but more because France feared a revived Germany would quickly dominate the continent.

The League of Nations, which officially began in 1920, proved largely ineffective in dealing with problems inside and outside Europe. Within Europe the basic antagonism between France and Germany was resolved first on a bilateral basis and then strengthened by a series of agreements concluded outside the League. Major problems, such as the existence of the Soviet Union, were not dealt with at all by the League. Important efforts between 1923 and 1925 to strengthen and improve the League, namely, the draft treaty of mutual assistance and the Geneva Protocol, were not adopted, mostly because of the opposition of the British Dominions and Great Britain. The improve-ment of diplomatic relations by 1925 in Europe and the apparent resolution of the most serious problems helped to hide the ineffec-tiveness of the League, which, however, was beginning to accom-plish much of value in other, more technical matters.

Despite all the failures and continuing problems, many Europeans could, by 1924, feel a certain satisfaction with life. Germany and France were making visible progress toward a settlement of out-standing differences. The Soviet Union was still not integrated into European affairs, but the panicky fear of Bolshevism had abated considerably. Domestically, most nations had achieved a degree of political and economic stability. With the decline of political tensions and the increase in material well-being, the popular mood was one of optimism.

The new-found equilibrium was fragile, a condition which most preferred to ignore. The frenetic activity and pursuit of pleasure that marked the lives of many in the mid-twenties was perhaps a means of avoiding a close examination of the bases of economic and political equilibriums. Certainly the serenity and intellectual certainty that characterized prewar Europe had vanished. Some Europeans saw their age as materialistic and soulless. For them neither the deep despair nor the limitless idealism of the immediate postwar period was possible, only a conviction that something was not right what-ever the appearances might be.

Appearances were everything for so many. The brilliance of Europe's recovery from the war hid the ways in which both Europe and its relationship to the rest of the world had altered. The next several years were ones of peace, prosperity, and illusion.

Suggested Readings

Raymond J. Sontag, *A Broken World, 1919-1939** (1971)

Charles S. Maier, *Recasting Bourgeois Europe: Stabilization in France, Italy, and Germany in the Decade after World War I** (1975)

C. L. Mowat, *Britain Between the Wars** (1955)

A. J. P. Taylor, *English History, 1914-1945* (1965)

Nathanael Greene, *From Versailles to Vichy** (1970)

Rudolph Binion, *Defeated Leaders* (1976)

Edward R. Tannenbaum, *The Fascist Experience: Italian Society and Culture, 1922-1945* (1972)

Ivone Kirkpatrick, *Mussolini: A Study in Power* (1964)

A. J. Nicholls, *Weimar and the Rise of Hitler** (2nd ed., 1980)

Walter Laqueur, *Weimar** (1976)

Peter Gay, *Weimar Culture: The Outsider as Insider** (1970)

Henry A. Turner, Jr., *Stresemann and the Politics of the Weimar Republic* (1963)

Hans W. Gatzke, *Stresemann and the Rearmament of Germany** (1969)

Harold J. Gordon, *Hitler and the Beer Hall Putsch** (1972)

Francis L. Carstens, *The Reichswehr and Politics, 1919-1933** (1966)

Leonard Schapiro, *The Origins of the Communist Autocracy* (1977)

Moshe Lewin, *Lenin's Last Struggle** (1978)

Stephen F. Cohen, *Bukharin and the Bolshevik Revolution: A Political Biography, 1888-1938** (1973)

E. H. Carr, *The Twenty Years' Crisis** (3rd ed., 1946)

Arnold Wolfers, *Britain and France Between Two Wars** (1966)

Stephen A. Schuker, *The End of French Predominance in Europe: The Financial Crisis of 1924 and the Adoption of the Dawes Plan* (1976)

Sigmund Freud, *Civilization and Its Discontents** (1962)

José Ortega y Gasset, *The Revolt of the Masses** (1932)

*indicates paperback edition available

5

Prosperity, 1924-1929

The years from 1924 to 1929 were years of prosperity and peace but also years of illusion. The foundations of both prosperity and peace proved to be considerably weaker than Europeans in the halcyon days of the mid-twenties could have imagined. Prosperity was lost in the Depression that began unmistakably with the collapse of the American economy in 1929. To a large extent, its loss caused peace to slip away in the 1930s. In 1924 and 1925, however, reality seemed otherwise. The nightmare of war and the difficult experience of recovery appeared by then to be over.

Undoubtedly the major reason for the change in the atmosphere in Europe was the Franco-German reconciliation. The French and Germans had each pushed their respective policies of suspicion and antagonism to the limit by 1923. Cooperation between the two became an inescapable necessity. Gustav Stresemann, leader of the German People's Party, took the initiative in acting on this realization. His efforts in the latter part of 1923 ended the inflation in Germany. An international committee of experts, chaired by Charles G. Dawes, an American banker, began work shortly afterwards to reorganize the international economic context. In April 1924, a series of interdependent proposals, calling for an international loan for Germany and a rescheduling of reparations payments, was presented. France accepted the Dawes Plan and with it the necessity of cooperating in the rebuilding of German economic strength. As Raymond Sontag has pointed out, France was forced to choose between a weak

Germany that could not pay reparations and a Germany strong enough to pay. She chose the latter.

The measures included in the Dawes Plan did little more than defuse the explosive situation of 1923. What created an entirely different atmosphere was the series of agreements reached in 1925, the Locarno Treaties. These grew somewhat haphazardly out of the French search for security, British fear of involvement, and German yearning for recovery of her status as a major power. Britain and France had tried unsuccessfully in 1923 and 1924 to strengthen the collective security provisions of the League of Nations Covenant. In 1925, Sir Austin Chamberlain, foreign secretary in the Conservative government, turned to a proposal that Stresemann had made. It called for British and Italian guarantees of the existing frontier between Germany and France. By reassuring France, Stresemann hoped to prevent any revival of an Anglo-French alliance. Chamberlain, citing the vital importance of the area for British interests, supported the proposal in place of the more comprehensive military alliance that France preferred. Aristide Briand, who became the French foreign minister in April 1925, had reservations about the proposal, but agreed to it. His acceptance was apparently based on two lines of reasoning. One held that Germany could not be forever restricted by Versailles. This being the case, timely concessions might prevent Germany from risking war to achieve a revision of Versailles. The second held that French security depended on British support and that support depended to some extent on French efforts at conciliation.

Actually, neither Briand's nor Stresemann's motives can be assessed with any real certainty. Both spoke and wrote differently in different circumstances. Each appears to have acted from an enlightened sense of the national interests of his own country. Briand may have been more the visionary than Stresemann but each was moved to cooperation and conciliation by the hard realities of the 1920s.

The western statesmen met in Locarno in October 1925, and in the resulting Locarno Pact, France, Belgium, and Germany accepted their existing mutual frontiers and the demilitarization of the Rhineland. Britain and Italy pledged their guarantee. There was no Locarno in eastern Europe, but Germany did sign arbitration agreements with Poland and Czechoslovakia, which stipulated the settlement of disputes by peaceful means. At the same time, France concluded military agreements with Poland and Czechoslovakia. All this was to come into force when Germany joined the League, which she did in 1926.

Locarno was a beginning. Most problems produced by World War I remained to be resolved. In particular, there was considerable debate about the sincerity of Germany's involvement in the Locarno Pact. Germany's eastern boundaries had neither been recognized as definitive nor guaranteed by outside powers, and it was in the east that Germany had suffered the greatest territorial losses under the terms of the treaties constructed during the Paris Peace Conference. Still, if problems remained, at least frameworks for their resolution now existed and tensions were eased. The League was greatly strengthened by Germany's admittance. The fact that the Soviet Union and the United States remained outside cast doubts on its effectiveness beyond Europe, but within Europe there seemed no reason why it should not work in support of peace and stability.

In the era when the spirit of Locarno prevailed, there was continued discussion of disarmament. Discussion floundered, however, in part because of the difficulty of measuring the extent of a nation's armaments and comparing it with that of other nations. Lack of progress was also due to the unwillingness of the French to disarm without firm guarantees against potential German aggression. The Kellogg-Briand Pact for the renunciation of war, although widely acclaimed when it was signed in 1928, did nothing to alter the situation. Countries renounced the use of war except in self-defense, but did not disarm. When the Disarmament Conference, long prepared for, finally opened in 1932, Europe was preoccupied by the Depression. It did not have the energy to seek a creative alternative to the French call for security leading to disarmament. To the sound of arguments by then long familiar, the conference ended in July 1932. By that time the spirit of Locarno had almost completely disappeared.

Urban Life and the "Masses"

In the late 1920s the hopes that were dashed by 1932 were still high. In particular, international peace was reinforced by political stability in Europe and widespread prosperity. The prosperity that was the hallmark of this period was most evident in the cities. Here large, modern buildings, expensive new cars, great department stores and fashionable boutiques, scintillating nightlife, and a brilliant culture all expressed the affluence of European society. The wealthy lived in the cities, at least during "the season." But principally the cities were inhabited by the "masses." These included, of course, the working class and those members of the lower middle class—shopkeepers, tradesmen, and artisans—who lived and worked in close proximity to the working class. The masses, as defined by José Ortega y Gasset in *The Revolt of the Masses*, also included managers, technicians, clerical employees and white-collar workers whose education, dress, and attitudes set them apart from the working class and whose skills and abilities made possible the smooth functioning of modern industry and commerce. From his vantage point at the end of the 1920s Ortega, a Spanish essayist and philosopher, found the new, technically educated masses a frightening group. Each member of this group was competent within his or her own narrow sphere of activity, but not broadly educated or capable of understanding the complex and delicate nature of European civilization. Yet, because they understood one area, the masses believed that they understood and could pass judgment on practically any area of endeavor from politics to art. Ortega predicted that thirty years of domination by this group would be sufficient to cause the ruin of European civilization.

The disaster that befell Europe only a decade after the appearance of Ortega's book was in no way solely the responsibility of the managers, technicians, and white-collar workers. Still, their role in most European societies became a crucial one by the late twenties. Quite naturally, by virtue of their specialized education and skills, they played an increasingly important role in the economy. They also influenced the development of culture, primarily as consumers but also as transmitters of some aspects of high culture and as packagers of popular culture. Most important, they were vitally concerned with politics and demanded from it a continuation of those conditions that afforded them comfort and status. In the late twenties they voted primarily for middle-of-the-road parties, but they were susceptible to demagoguery and vulnerable to economic or social pressure.

The middle classes as a whole, while generally in favor of parliamentary, constitutional government and industrial capitalism, had anxieties, submerged during the good years of the late twenties, that differed from group to group. Businessmen, for example, tended to believe that parliamentary democracy was a weak and ineffectual means of government. A strong national state required a more authoritarian kind of leadership and, in any case, one sympathetic to business interests. Members of the ''old'' lower-middle class, retail shopkeepers and tradesmen, suspected that the enemy really was big business. Those who lived in small towns and provincial centers identified Europe's problems with the increase of urbanization. It was the city, especially Berlin in Germany and Paris in France, where all that was wrong and dangerous was spawned. For the middle classes, the late 1920s were good times, but, having experienced war, revolution, depression, and inflation in recent memory, this segment of the population was wary and somewhat insecure.

The working class's political challenge in the twenties also served to increase the insecurity of the middle classes. In the 1920s the organized working class was stronger and more influential than it had been before the war, but, paradoxically, not as strong as it might have been. The paradox was produced by two related developments. First, as has already been noted, the organized working class split in the immediate postwar period into a communist movement that centered on the Comintern and a socialist movement that continued the policies of the old Second International. The German Social Democratic Party, the SPD, faced competition from the left in the German Communist Party (KPD); and there were similar divisions elsewhere in Western Europe. The split was also reflected in the trade union movement and many other specialized organizations. Precisely because the communist and the socialist parties referred to the same heritage (Marxism) to interpret political and social events and because both appealed to the same social group (the working class), they were bitter rivals. The communists in particular thought the socialists were leading the working class astray and betraying Marxism. In addition to dividing the working class movement into mutually hostile groups, the split also made it difficult for social democratic parties to moderate their stance toward bourgeois society and government. Even in Germany, where the SPD was often a crucial element in coalition governments, the official line was unremitting hostility to the existing order. Any serious compromise of the Marxism doctrine might have driven even more of the working class into the communist party.

Although a united working class would have been stronger than a divided one, a divided one was still impressive. Socialists were not only represented in large numbers on the national level; they also played important roles in municipal and provincial governments in Italy (until the Fascists came to power), Germany, and France. Unfortunately, despite generally responsible attitudes and actions, working class representatives never gained the trust and full cooperation of their middle-class counterparts. Particularly in Germany, most members of the middle class resented the new political power of the workers on the local and state levels.

Organized labor faced even stronger resistance to its influence in the economic sphere. At the end of the war the labor movement had pushed hard for economic changes, including higher wages, better working conditions, shorter hours, and worker participation in the management of industry. The deterioration of the position of the working class caused by the war, the determination of returning veterans to gain what they believed was fairly theirs, and promises of a better life by politicians and business leaders fueled the strike movements in 1919 and 1920 in France, Britain, Germany, and Italy.

Efforts to resolve these economic and social problems in the immediate postwar period met with little success. In part this failure was due to the short depression that Europe experienced at the beginnings of the 1920s. The split within the labor movement at the same time also weakened it. Employers rapidly organized groups in the early twenties to influence the government and to provide mutual aid against strikes; the rate of defeat of strikes went up. Governments became less sympathetic to labor goals and in some cases, notably that of Fascist Italy, obviously hostile. Still, by 1924 and 1925 general prosperity led to better conditions for most groups of workers. Many worked eight-hour days with Saturday half-holidays. Real wages rose between 1924 and 1929. Workers participated with other groups in the new possibilities for entertainment and recreation. The major exception to the general labor peace in the latter part of the twenties was the British General Strike in 1926, but Britain was plagued by high levels of unemployment in the twenties and by a particularly troubled but important sector of the economy, the coal mining industry. Perhaps the main result of the resounding defeat of the coal miners, who had stayed out on strike after other groups involved in the General Strike had gone back to work, was the reduction of overt labor unrest in Britain despite the troubled economy.

Peasants and Agriculture

Peasants did not share in the general prosperity of the latter twenties. Food prices were low throughout the twenties and competition from abroad was stiff. Many peasants in western Europe had borrowed either during or right after the war to purchase land or equipment. These debts were difficult to repay in the later 1920s.

Many peasants had served in the army or had in other ways become more aware of the nature of life beyond their own region. They expected more in the 1920s and in some cases were willing to work in new and different ways to obtain their demands. In Britain many agricultural laborers joined organizations to improve pay and working conditions. The interwar period was one of bitter struggle as organized agricultural laborers tried to persuade their fellow laborers to join and fight to gain recognition from tenant farmers. In Italy an attempt in the early 1920s to reform landholding patterns was defeated in the postwar violence that led to Fascism. In Germany many peasants left the land for the cities, but they also began to support movements such as the Nazi Party, which promised to protect the farmer and the small agricultural enterprise. Although some French and German peasants resorted to lobbying groups, cooperative movements, and technical improvements, little changed in terms of agricultural practices and life-styles. Peasants continued to lead largely isolated, family-centered existences. The peasants in western Europe had been brought into contact with the modern world before World War I through the development of the market economy, the spread of public education, expansion of national institutions like the army, and the improvement of transportation and communication facilities, but their contact was still slight and episodic even in the late twenties.

In eastern Europe, the process of rural adaptation that had taken place in the west before World War I had barely begun by the end of the 1920s. The power of the landed elites and traditional aristocracies was still formidable. In some countries, Bulgaria for example, the small peasant landholders remained an important group. In most countries, Hungary being perhaps the best example, the large estate dominated agriculture. In every case, rural populations continued to grow, placing additional pressure on the agricultural economy. In much of eastern Europe, poverty, superstition, ignorance, and isolation were the rule among the peasantry. Some new ideas circulated as a result of service in the war, the impact of the Russian Revolution, and the work of peasant political movements, but most peasants lived in ways scarcely different from those of their ancestors in the early 1800s. Only in the Soviet Union was a large-scale effort made to introduce the peasant to the modern world, an effort that took on revolutionary proportions in the early thirties.

Popular Culture

While peasant culture in eastern Europe had scarcely changed and in western Europe was changing only slowly, many Europeans from the lower and middle classes participated after World War I in an urban-based, commercialized popular culture that made national populations far more homogeneous and even created in some cases the elements of international styles. It was in the 1920s, and the last half of the 1920s in particular, that popular culture as we know it today began to develop. This was based, of course, on many trends of the late nineteenth and early twentieth centuries: among them were the spread of literacy; the creation of mass circulation, inexpensive newspapers emphasizing the coverage of crime, sex, and sports; the publication of cheap magazines and books; the growing popularity of professional sports; and the appearance of a variety of forms of commercialized entertainment and leisure activities including the music hall and the movie theater. In addition to the printed media and the extremely popular movie industry, radio became a significant means of shaping culture and entertaining people in the 1920s. Mass production of shoes and clothing and the first use of synthetic material made it increasingly difficult to determine a person's occupation or social level by what he or she wore. The growing use of cosmetics also affected people's appearance. Popular culture, in sum, had become by the late twenties largely a matter of entertainment, recreation, fashions, and fads which, for a short period of time, might bind people from different social backgrounds together and blur the still significant differences that existed. No longer did it emphasize strategies for survival in crucial areas such as work, marriage, family and community life, strategies which once had been so vital to the well-being of people from the peasantry and the working class. Instead, one way or another, generally indirectly, it offered a conflicting hodgepodge of ideas on all kinds of subjects and left it up to the individual to construct his or her own standards of behavior. Similarly, popular culture no longer offered a clear sense of identity for lower-class groups as readily as it once had. Where it had once reinforced people's sense of their role in the family or community, it now presented a multitude of possible roles.

Furthermore, some people in interwar Europe viewed popular culture as a threat. In the first place, it tended to standardize national populations. Some degree of increased homogeneity was seen as necessary and beneficial, as opposed to harsh class antagonism, but thoughtful observers worried about the possibilities of manipulation of the masses. Radio and motion pictures were both powerful instruments of persuasion. It had become clear by the late 1920s that it was easy to sway public opinion, whether through advertising to encourage increased consumption of goods or through political slogans to gain support for various actions or groups. Not only were the masses in danger of being corrupted; the elites were faced with the same situation. Moral values, manners, and high culture seemed in danger of being undermined by a commercialized culture that was popular with nearly every group, especially with the younger elements of each group.

Whether good or bad, popular culture in the affluent and vital late twenties developed most of the attributes familiar in today's society. Entertainment became increasingly commercialized and built on changing fashions. New songs, new dance steps, new movie stars followed one another at an accelerating pace. The growth of spectator sports was only one example of the trend toward passive involvement in popular culture. In all areas, the lowest common denominator was sought in order to attract as wide an audience as possible.

High Culture

In the realm of high culture just the opposite was the case. After the initial postwar enthusiasm about the possibilities of using art to aid the birth of revolution, artists had worked mostly without attempting to reach a large audience. The emphasis was on art for art's sake and on experimentation and innovation. Concepts that had been shocking before 1914 were accepted in the 1920s by large numbers of those who followed closely developments in high culture. Modernism in art had clearly triumphed by the mid-twenties. New techniques in literature and music were gaining acceptance although they were still strongly resisted by many whose cultural sensibilities had been shaped by the modes and forms of the late nineteenth century. Those who did not follow developments in high culture very closely found nearly all aspects of modernism in the arts incomprehensible or uninteresting.

One characteristic of artistic and cultural life in the 1920s was the number of places where exciting and interesting work was being done. Britain, Spain, Austria, Italy, and Czechoslovakia each contributed. The major centers, however, were Germany and France. France, or rather Paris, became a mecca for expatriates. Spaniards, Italians, Russians, Irishmen, and especially Americans created a Paris of the mind and spirit. This Paris, described by Ernest Hemingway in *A Moveable Feast,* was not that of most Frenchmen, but nevertheless nurtured many great artists of this century and their creations. James Joyce, recognized by the expatriates as a commanding genius, wrote *Ulysses,* the masterful recreation of one day in Dublin, and published it in Paris in 1922. Picasso continued his experiments in painting, moving rapidly from one style to another. Igor Stravinsky, whose *Rites of Spring* had caused a scandal at its premiere in 1913, found a wider audience even though his music continued to be demanding and innovative. These three illustrate the paradox just mentioned, of artists and writers largely ignoring the needs of their audiences but nevertheless finding increasing acceptance and understanding.

Foremost among the Frenchmen who contributed to the vitality of cultural life in Paris was André Gide. Gide was recognized in the 1920s as a superb literary craftsman, although he was already in his fifties and had been writing for many years. In *The Counterfeiters* (1926) he dealt with a problem of great personal interest to him: a homosexual, he had long worried over the means of reconciling individual drives and needs with social conventions.

Whereas one may think of Paris in the 1920s as being romantic, bathed in soft light and warm spring rains, Berlin—the other focus of European cultural life—was harsh, glittering, and lighted by neon. Life was a cabaret. The contrasts between the lives of the poor and the newly rich were startling and were captured in uncompromising fashion by George Grosz and in a somewhat more sentimental manner by Käthe Kollwitz. In Berlin, as nowhere else in the 1920s, rage and anger, sometimes made more effective by the addition of humor and genius, continued to attack the social and political system. Perhaps the best example is *The Threepenny Opera,* a collaborative effort of the left-wing playwright Bertolt Brecht and the avant-garde composer Kurt Weill. The dominant note in Berlin, however, was the frenetic and cynical quality of lives based on jazz, nightclubs, drugs, drink, and prostitution. Life was lived very fast because the past indicated that what existed in the present might disappear in the future. The Weimar Republic, which many thought Berlin symbolized, was an object of much skepticism and disapproval.

Not all of Weimar culture was contained in Berlin, of course. One figure who dominated that culture while remaining outside Berlin was Thomas Mann, a famous and respected author even before World War I. In 1924 Mann published his most famous novel, *The Magic Mountain.* The novel operates on several levels: first, it is the story of Hans Castorp, who visits his cousin at a sanatorium, contracts tuberculosis, and has to stay on; second, it is a novel of education (in the German tradition of the *Bildungsroman*) in which Hans comes to understand something about life and death; and finally, it is a discussion of the nature of European civilization. Through the novel Mann expressed an acceptance of and commitment to the Weimar Republic. His commitment and that of many others were not sufficient, however, to offset the widespread skepticism, cynicism, and frank hostility.

Perhaps the most promising and positive artistic and cultural development of the 1920s transcended not only Berlin but also Weimar Gemany. This was the Bauhaus movement, an attempt to join the artist and the artisan in the creation of items that were both beautiful and useful. Bauhaus began in 1919 in Weimar as a kind of laboratory and missionary society as well as a school. Students were not made into disciples of the masters but all worked together, almost like a family, in a cooperative enterprise in which creativity and invention were encouraged and prized. While the foremost concern of the Bauhaus movement was architecture, the creation of a building as an artistic unity, the range of activity was broad and included typography, furniture design, lamps, rugs, pottery, bookbinding, dance, drawing, and painting. Ideally beauty and utility were to be combined, but much of the work produced by Paul Klee, Wassily Kandinsky, and Lyonel Feininger—three famous painters associated with Bauhaus—was done from aesthetic considerations alone.

In 1925 Bauhaus moved to Dessau, where Walter Gropius built his best-known buildings and much of the work in other areas associated with the movement took place. That same year, for example, Marcel Breuer designed the first tubular chair, a striking and influential piece of work that helped to form the basis for modern furniture design. It was the period in which Bauhaus achieved its greatest success out-side Germany and came closest to realizing its underlying goal, the elimination of "every drawback of the machine without sacrificing any one of its real advantages."

The Bauhaus movement had been deliberately unpolitical in an attempt to offset the implicitly liberal, democratic nature of its concepts and activities. Many other artists, writers, and cultural figures in the twenties avoided politics not out of necessity, as was the case with Bauhaus, but out of disinterest. By the end of the decade, however, it was becoming clear that cultural life and politics could not always be kept separate. Fascist Italy had already provided one example of the incompatibility of some kinds of politics and modern culture. The Soviet Union provided another, more complex example. In the early 1920s there had been a good deal of enthusiasm for the new revolutionary state among intellectuals and artists. By the late 1920s, even though most opponents of Communism had emigrated, there was an increasing amount of pressure being placed on culture in the Soviet Union. Socialist realism was put forward as the guideline in a much more forceful way than previously. The results began to show first in literature, where both the satirical short piece and poetry that had flourished earlier were replaced by lead-footed realistic fiction and doggerel, and in painting, where the greatest Russian painters were in exile and those still living in Russia were reduced more and more to realistic and artistically uninteresting renditions of themes favored by the Communist Party: happy peasants, vigorous workers, and benevolent leaders. Films remained a vital art form throughout the twenties. Russian filmmakers, as individuals and as a group, dominated the European film artistically in the twenties. Chief among them were Sergei Eisenstein, V. I. Pudovkin, Aleksandr Dovzhenko, and Dziga Vertov. Eisenstein was the best known. In the 1920s he directed *Strike* (1924), *Battleship Potemkin* (1925) with its famous sequence of the massacre on the steps of a park in Odessa, and *October* (1928), among others.

In the realm of high culture, despite ominous developments in Italy and the Soviet Union, the 1920s were a period of vigorous creativity. Artists were for the most part uncompromising in their demands on audiences, even in film where a mass audience might well be expected. They were also concerned with eliminating boundaries between various arts and in utilizing several different talents, as exemplified by the Bauhaus movement and the collaboration of Stravinsky and Picasso with Dhiagilev and others in the productions of the Ballet Russe. There was a growing tendency to remove art from the discussion of political and social questions, a tendency perhaps noticeable only because of the marked commitment of art and culture in the 1930s to the resolution of these questions.

Perhaps even more exciting than artistic and cultural developments and certainly less understood were scientific advances. Achievements in physics, the center of this advance, rested on work done in the 1890s and the decade before the war, work that had produced the atomic theory of matter. The idea that the atom was the basic unit of matter, in fact a miniature solar system of electrons, neutrons, and protons, was modified first by Max Planck in 1901 when he postulated in his "quantum theory" that change did not take place in continuous waves but in jumps. It was further qualified by Albert Einstein, who suggested in 1905 that both time and space were relative to the person measuring them. In the 1920s Werner Heisenberg put forth the theory of indeterminacy, the idea that the location of a particular electron could be predicted only within a range of probabilities. At least on the level of the very small, it now appeared difficult to find immutable laws that would explain the various phenomena; it seemed more profitable to examine the relations among phenomena. The exploration of the nature of the atom, while stressing the elements of discontinuity and indeterminacy, laid the foundations for further work in the 1930s which, in turn, made possible the production of the atomic bomb, one use of nuclear energy, in World War II.

More important for the twenties, scientific discussion of the ideas of discontinuity, relativity, and indeterminacy corresponded with an emphasis on subjectivism, with a lack of agreement on clear-cut standards of behavior, with a belief that many political or social problems were beyond solution, and even with the feeling of many that they had been irretrievably cut off from past traditions. As had been the case in the latter part of the nineteenth century with Darwin's theories of evolution, concepts used in physics in the twenties were misapplied to a variety of social, political and cultural phenomena. Einstein, like Freud, became a household name.

Domestic Politics: England and France

Contrasting strangely with the vitality and innovation in art and science and with the less dramatic but still apparent social and economic changes was the political conservatism of Europe. Despite Briand's interest in a united Europe and despite the large degree of cooperation among European nations brought on by economic necessity and diplomatic arrangement, Europeans were primarily occupied with the problems of their own nation and determined to resolve them in conservative fashion. Nowhere was this more evident than in Britain, where the general election of 1924 led to the replacement of the short-lived Labour government by that of the Conservative Stanley Baldwin, the dominant figure for the rest of the 1920s and most of the 1930s. The major test of the Baldwin government was the 1926 General Strike which grew out of a strike by coal miners on May 1. The General Strike lasted from May 3 to May 12, and involved more than one-third of the trade unionists in Britain. At issue was a government report calling for a reorganization of the mining industry and a reduction in wages. The owners rejected any reorganization and called not only for a reduction in wages but also for an increase in hours. The miners' reply was "Not a penny off the pay, not a minute on the day." The General Strike was intended to push the government to negotiation. The government did agree that wage reductions would be imposed only after reorganization measures had been adopted. The miners, however, would not compromise at that point, sparing the government the awkward task of getting industry to agree. After the General Strike had ended, the miners continued to strike for another six months until starvation forced them to return and to accept lower wages and longer hours. The General Strike was a genuine if also brief and relatively polite expression of class conflict. Ironically, it brought to the fore union leaders who favored conciliation rather than conflict. Industrialists also took note of the event and avoided the wage-reduction tactics of the coal mine owners. The Baldwin government survived the test of the General Strike and Britain passed the last years of the 1920s peacefully. Her fundamental economic and political maladjustments, both demonstrated by the issues involved in the General Strike, continued unresolved.

France, like Britain, returned to conservative government in the late twenties. Here the major figure was Raymond Poincaré who, unsuccessful in foreign affairs in the early twenties, restored financial stability to France in the later years. The problems of France revolved around the French expectation that German reparations would pay war debts and reconstruction costs. By the mid-twenties it could be seen that this was not going to be the case. Still, the government resisted the obvious—balanced budgets, increased taxation, currency controls, and devaluation of the franc. Only when Poincaré formed a government in 1926 was financial stability achieved. In large part this reflected the confidence of business in Poincaré. He contributed as well by traditional practices of reduced budgets and careful management. In 1928, with the franc worth about one-fifth its prewar value (as opposed to one-tenth at its low point two years before), France went on the international gold standard. The devaluation of the franc was a disguised repudiation of much of the national debt, which had been contracted in terms of the prewar franc. It was a difficult blow for many in the middle classes, the value of whose savings and investments had been undermined. The determination grew never to allow the franc to be touched again. Devaluation brought financial stability, however, and "normalcy" to France. In fact, mainly because of Poincaré's measures France was better prepared than most European countries for the worldwide economic difficulties that began in 1929.

Weimar Germany

Weimar Germany, in contrast to its own early years of strife and turmoil, passed the last half of the decade in relative tranquillity. Hitler, following his attempted *putsch,* spent a year in prison writing his political credo, *Mein Kampf* (1925); after his release he was able to rebuild the Nazi Party so as to make it stronger organizationally and more intensely loyal to him personally. Yet he was not able to make much headway in the late 1920s. He was the best-known figure of the extreme right, but not a major politician until cooperation with the German Nationalist Party, in the 1929 referendum on the Young Plan for the reorganization of reparations, brought him into national prominence. The Nationalist Party, based on the hostility of the aristocratic large landowners and some industrialists toward Weimar, seemed a much more substantial threat to Weimar than any group on the extreme right.

The major danger to Weimar in the late twenties was not without but within. The army had achieved a position of almost complete autonomy and was even more isolated from the mainstream of life in Weimar than the Imperial army had been before World War I. The civil service remained largely composed of people technically competent but uncommitted and often actively disloyal to the Republic. Business interests combined and organized to the point where they possessed enormous powers that the government could not begin to control. The 1925 election of Paul von Hindenburg as president—a man unsympathetic to parliamentary control of government—created another problem for Weimar. A republic with such a president and with so many groups antagonistic to it could hope to survive only if it avoided the necessity of dealing with serious problems.

The Smaller States

Outside the three major democracies of Britain, France, and Germany, democracy was also firmly established in the Lowlands (Belgium, Luxembourg, and the Netherlands), the Scandinavian countries (Denmark, Sweden, Norway, and Finland), and Czechoslovakia in eastern Europe. Belgium had been severely affected by World War I, but managed a rapid recovery under the popular King Albert (1909-1934). The most troublesome question concerned the division of the country between the French-speaking Walloons in the south and the Dutch-speaking Flemish in the north. Concessions in the twenties made Flemish the language of administration and instruction in the Flemish areas, and the regime in Brussels bilingual. The Dutch largely escaped the problem of postwar adjustment that most nations experienced. Under Queen Wilhelmina (1890-1948), the Netherlands enjoyed considerable prosperity in the twenties, much of it based on the great empire of the Dutch East Indies. Like the Belgian Congo, Dutch colonies continued to exist primarily for the benefit of the home country.

In the Scandinavian countries, the 1920s and 1930s were times in which not only parliamentary governments and universal suffrage but also the welfare state became firmly rooted. Each country instituted a range of social services including various plans to provide for old age, illness, accident, and unemployment. Another characteristic of the Scandinavian societies was the mixed economy, in which some government-run enterprises coexisted with many privately owned businesses and a few others in which both government and capital cooperated. Many developments in the Scandinavian countries between the wars foreshadowed general trends after World War II.

Neither the Scandinavian nor the Lowland countries were strong enough, individually or collectively, to affect the course of European developments in the interwar period. In eastern Europe, however, there were some states which had an important effect on European affairs in the 1920s and 1930s. In general, the eastern European states began the 1920s with constitutional and parliamentary governments. With the exception of Czechoslovakia, all had turned to authoritarian government by 1930. Each had been plagued by a combination of lack of experience with parliamentary forms of government, severe economic problems stemming from largely agrarian economies no longer in touch with prewar markets and resources, and problems with ethnic minorities.

Poland, perhaps the most important state in the area in terms of potential influence, experienced all the difficulties typical of the eastern European state following World War I. Caught between Bolshevik Russia and a resentful Germany, Poland struggled to achieve the borders that it had last possessed in 1772. It was partially successful in this, but in the process it aroused considerable hostility among Russians, Germans, and Lithuanians. A constitution adopted in 1921 established a republic modeled on the French system. The republic never functioned well, however. A parliamentary majority was virtually impossible to create in a political situation in which fifty-nine parties contended for the vote. Some fourteen ministries appeared between 1918 and 1926, most unable to deal effectively with economic problems and with the minority question. In May 1926, Józef Pilsudski, a long-time socialist-patriot regarded by many as the father of liberated Poland, led a coup that abolished the republic for all practical purposes. Pilsudski, with the backing of the military, remained in power behind the facade of a constitutional system until his death in 1935.

Hungary had a very brief experience with a republican form of government. The republic, declared in 1918, was transformed by Béla Kun in 1919 into a communist dictatorship which, in turn, was destroyed by the Rumanian invasion and the appearance of a counter-revolution. In 1920 Admiral Miklós Horthy, commander-in-chief, became regent and head of state. He declared Hungary a monarchy with the throne vacant. Principal efforts in the 1920s were devoted to maintaining the status quo, which meant reinforcing the power of the great landowners over the peasantry and that of the Magyars over the ethnic minorities.

In Yugoslavia, Rumania, and Bulgaria, authoritarian monarchies were in power by 1930. In the case of Bulgaria, a country with a large peasant majority and land divided mostly into small holdings, the period immediately after the war had been dominated by the Bulgarian Peasant Union headed by Aleksandr Stamboliski. Stamboliski attempted to establish a populist government that was anti-urban. At the same time, he attempted to counter communist influence through the establishment of the "Green International," a union of peasant interests against the red International (the Comintern) of the workers. He was overthrown in 1923 in a coup and killed. Elsewhere peasants' parties often had substantial followings but were unable to translate these into political power.

Czechoslovakia was the major exception to the rather sad tales of eastern Europe in the twenties. Tolerant of its ethnic minorities, heavily industrialized and possessing a large urban population in comparison to other states in the area, Czechoslovakia was the only nation with a deeply-rooted liberal tradition in eastern Europe. It was clearly a success by the end of the twenties and entered the thirties able to withstand the rigors of the Depression. In large part, its success was due to the constant efforts of the liberal Tomaś Masaryk and to the enormous prestige and respect he had acquired within the nation.

On the whole, the instability of the east European states stemmed from the strength of the older forces—the landholding aristocracy, the military, and the dominant ethnic groups—when confronted by some newer forces for democratic forms of government and more modern social and economic arrangements. Exacerbating this were economic problems caused by the breakup of the old economic unit formed by the Hapsburg empire and diplomatic tensions brought on by a location between two rival powers, Germany and the Soviet Union.

The Soviet Union

In the late 1920s, all Europe continued to watch experiments taking place even further to the east, in the Soviet Union. For most of the decade the Soviet Union followed the New Economic Policy (NEP) adopted in 1921. The level of experimentation was fairly low although much was being attempted in the spheres of education and cultural work. From late 1922 until 1928, however, the major preoccupation of members of the Communist party was who would dominate Russian politics. The issue had first been raised by Lenin's stroke in 1922. A second stroke in 1923 made it clear that some reorganization of the ruling group was needed. A *troika* (named after a vehicle pulled by three horses) emerged in 1923 and 1924 to carry on the work of Lenin and to prevent Trotsky, regarded by some as the Russian Revolution's equivalent to Napoleon, from becoming a dictator. The more prominent members of the *troika* were Zinoviev, head of the Comintern, party boss in Leningrad, and longtime close associate of Lenin, and Kamenev, also a close associate of Lenin and party boss in Moscow. Stalin, the third member of the group, seemed rather obscure and without much power. In fact, he had acquired considerable power through a series of bureaucratic posts, chief of which was the position of General Secretary of the party. Lenin had recognized Stalin's growing power. In his "Testament," a document discussing various important leaders of the party, which he dictated in December 1922, Lenin commented that he was not sure that Stalin knew how to use wisely the enormous power concentrated in his hands. In a postscript added early in January 1923, he recommended that Stalin be removed from his post of General Secretary to the Party. After Lenin's death, his "Testament" was read to the Central Committee of the Party. Stalin remained cool and calm considering the damning nature of the remarks. Trotsky remained silent. Kamenev rushed to Stalin's defense and in the end Lenin's recommendation went unheeded.

Although Stalin did not at first have pronounced views on the future of Russia, he soon began to favor the "right" position in the debate over industrialization. In 1924 he put forth the idea of "Socialism in One Country." According to this concept, the Soviet Union could create the conditions for socialism, an industrial economy, by itself without the aid of revolutionary states elsewhere in Europe. This was contrary to Trotsky's ideas about "Permanent Revolution," which called for aid from other centers of revolution, and contrary as well to the international revolutionary position taken by Zinoviev and

Kamenev. Eventually Zinoviev and Kamenev realized that they agreed in some rather fundamental ways with Trotsky. They also began to feel that Stalin could not be trusted. By the time they reached these conclusions, in 1925, they had helped Stalin strip Trotsky of much of his power. In addition, Trotsky and Zinoviev had conducted mudslinging campaigns that left both discredited but Stalin virtually unscathed.

By 1925 Stalin had moved into alliance with the "right" group, the most important of whom was Nikolai Bukharin, an eminent theoretician, editor of *Pravda*, and protégé of Lenin in the latter's last years. Stalin also used his positions to bring to key posts in the government and party a number of people personally loyal to him. In 1928, having completely crushed the left opposition of Trotsky, Zinoviev, and Kamenev the year before, Stalin broke with the right. He then adopted some of the ideas long associated with the left, ideas concerning economic planning and rapid industrialization based on the control of agriculture. Essentially, Stalin believed that the Soviet Union had to accomplish two tasks simultaneously. The state had to gain control of agricultural production and to destroy the possibility that the peasants would withhold that production in order to bring about the collapse of the state. Collectivization, establishing the peasants on large-scale agricultural enterprises where they worked together on the main crops, was one way of doing this. Collectivization, by enabling agriculture to become more productive and by making it easier to tap production according to the dictates of the state, would lay the groundwork for industrialization, the second major task.

At this point, Stalin was extremely powerful but far from all-powerful. His ideas were accepted because they appeared to meet the needs of the Soviet Union as the Communist party perceived them. The first five-year plan, in its original form, was ambitious but not unrealistic. Only later, through Stalin's arbitrary modifications, did the five-year plan and collectivization become overly ambitious and even utopian. In 1929 and 1930, then, Stalin and his colleagues implemented plans that would change drastically the lives of four-fifths of the population, those living in the country, and make the Soviet Union into a major industrial and military power.

Fascist Italy

At almost the same time, Fascist Italy was settling into a comfortable relationship with the most significant foci of power in the country

—the church, the great landowners, the military, and business. Mussolini had done away with parliamentary government in 1925 in what has sometimes been called the "second wave" of the Fascist revolution. In reality the new stage of consolidation involved a deal with business (the Palazzo Vidoni agreement in 1925, which resulted in the subordination of the labor movement) and a reconciliation with the Papacy in the Lateran Treaty of 1929. After 1929 Mussolini devoted most of his time to foreign affairs with occasional grandiose ventures in domestic policy, the various "battles" to increase population and grain production being the best known, and some feckless experimentation with the idea that politics should be based on representation of occupations and sectors of the economy, a corporatist political structure, on the side. Italian fascism, respected by many statesmen and politicians in Europe, from the liberal center to the radical right, had lost most of its dynamism.

Conclusions

Taken as a whole, the late twenties were times of economic prosperity and political stability for large parts of Europe. The liberal, parliamentary governments of the period were, however, seldom more than modestly successful. The experiences of Weimar Germany were a good measure of the lack of strength and popularity of parliamentary government. There were also some resounding failures in eastern and southern Europe where authoritarian regimes came into power. Two important tendencies, which became much more influential in the early thirties, were the decline of the liberal center in politics and, quite closely related, the growth of extremist movements on the margins of parliamentary life. These extremist movements, intriguing as they were, remained political novelties in the late twenties. In the early thirties, though, they became crucial factors in politics.

Much of the tone of the latter part of the decade was set by developments in both high and popular culture. While many remained interested in social issues and politics, the emphases were more likely to be on experimentation and innovation in high culture ("art for the sake of art") and on the creation of a new, mass culture based on city life, commercialized entertainment and leisure, and rapidly changing fads and fashions.

The glittering but somewhat shallow material culture owed much to an ever-expanding prosperity. That prosperity was already showing signs of faltering before the spectacular crash of the American stock market in 1929. Continuing low prices for raw materials and agricultural products were one indicator in the late 1920s of problems ahead. Rampant speculation and the creation of paper fortunes were other indicators. Particularly important was the precarious base for the credit structure in Germany and other areas in central Europe, dependent as it was on American loans. There were indications, even in 1928, that Europeans might have to face a period of economic readjustment. That readjustment turned out to be more severe than anyone had predicted, and involved political and cultural ramifications of great significance. The resources for meeting such a serious crisis were lacking. Beneath the glitter lay areas of great vulnerability. Europe entered a time of trial that would extend for the better part of two decades and shatter the illusions that had carried it through the 1920s.

Suggested Readings

Quentin Bell, *Bloomsbury* (1968)

Germaine Bree, *20th Century French Literature** (1962)

Herbert S. Gershman, *The Surrealist Revolution in France* (1973)

Nigel Hamilton, *The Brothers Mann: The Lives of Heinrich and Thomas Mann* (1979)

Edward J. Brown, *Mayahovsky: A Poet in the Revolution* (1973)

Robert A. Maguire, *Red Virgin Soil: Soviet Literature in the Late 1920s* (1968)

Wilfrid Mellers, *Caliban Reborn: Renewal in Twentieth Century Music* (1967)

Werner Hofman, *Turning Points in Twentieth Century Art* (1969)

Jon Jacobson, *Locarno Diplomacy* (1972)

Judith M. Hughes, *To the Maginot Line: The Politics of French Military Preparations in the 1920s* (1971)

Sean Glynn and John Oxborrow, *Interwar Britain: A Social and Economic History** (1976)

Robert Graves and Alan Hodge, *The Long Week-End: A Social History of Great Britain, 1918-1939** (1963)

Keith Middleman and John Barnes, *Baldwin, a Biography* (1970)

Paul Fussell, *Abroad: British Literary Traveling Between the Wars* (1980)

Erich Eyck, *A History of the Weimar Republic** (2 vols., 1970)

Andreas Dorpalen, *Hindenburg and the Weimar Republic* (1964)

O. Friedrich, *Before the Deluge: A Portrait of Berlin in the 1920s* (1972)

Karl J. Newman, *European Democracy Between the Wars* (1971)

Joseph Rothschild, *East Central Europe Between the Two Wars** (1974)

Hugh Seton-Watson, *Eastern Europe Between the Wars, 1918-1941* (2nd ed., 1967)

Peter F. Sugar and Ivo Lederer, eds., *Nationalism in Eastern Europe* (1969)

Joseph Rothschild, *Pilsudski's Coup d'Etat* (1966)

Richard B. Day, *Leon Trotsky and the Politics of Economic Isolation* (1973)

Stephen F. Cohen, *Bukharin and the Bolshevik Revolution: A Political Biography, 1888-1938** (1980)

Robert C. Tucker, *Stalin as Revolutionary, 1873-1929: A Study in History and Personality** (1973)

Isaac Deutscher, *The Prophet Unarmed: Trotsky, 1921-1929** (1980)

Alexander Erlich, *The Soviet Industrialization Debate* (1960)

E. H. Carr and R. W. Davis, *Foundations of a Planned Economy, 1926-1929** (2 parts, 1971)

Alan Cassels, *Fascist Italy** (1968)

*indicates paperback edition

6

Depression, 1929-1934

The period from 1929 to 1934 was a time of testing for Europe. The rapid economic decline in most countries brought into question social structures and political systems as well as economic policies. Even basic cultural assumptions were subjected to a re-examination. It has been argued that the Depression, not only in Europe but all over the world, had an even more pervasive impact than the two world wars of this century; nearly every nation and social group experienced it in a direct and immediate fashion. And from it, at least in large part, proceeded a whole chain of consequences which, added to other developments, did not stop until well into the 1950s. From the experience of the Depression came an increased dissatisfaction with parliamentary politics and liberal economics. To a great extent, this dissatisfaction was mirrored in the increased willingness to adopt more extreme measures, those embodied in communism and, especially, fascism. From there the distance to World War II and its consequences was not very far.

The Depression was unique not only because it was a phenomenon that most Europeans experienced firsthand and because it led to two decades of trials and tribulations; it was also unique in that for many persons it reconfirmed some lessons that had been drawn from World War I. The war had exposed the weaknesses of both conventional political wisdom and orthodox economic ideas. It had also hinted that Europe's position of dominance vis-à-vis the rest of the world might not be permanent. The Depression helped to bring these same issues to the fore again.

There had been other depressions in twentieth-century Europe before the Great Depression of the thirties, but these depressions had lasted only a year or two before prices reached a point low enough to encourage people to start buying goods again. Increased purchases would then lead to increased production and eventually to the creation of new jobs and a decline in unemployment. The economies involved in the Great Depression did not quickly recover. They continued to be characterized by low production and high unemployment throughout most of the 1930s.

For many Europeans, then, the shock of hard times and massive unemployment was heightened by the sense that there seemed no end in sight and no reason to believe that the situation would change. The working classes of the various countries were hardest hit by unemployment. For a worker, even one who could turn to some kind of welfare payment or dole, the most difficult part of the Depression was the inability to find any kind of work. Work was for many a way of defining themselves, and without work, especially when months of unemployment stretched into years, some began to lose their self-confidence and their sense of independence. It was also difficult for a young man or woman to start out in times that seemed so bleak. Many had to postpone plans for education or to settle for situations that were less attractive than what they or their parents had once anticipated. For the young, naturally inclined to idealism and high hopes, Europe in the thirties seemed mean and constricted. Many turned eagerly to movements that promised a way out.

Among the middle classes there was not quite as much risk of unemployment as among workers. Somehow, though, the stakes seemed higher. Workers had always known periods of unemployment, times when things were tight. For the middle classes, unemployment meant a loss of status, of respectability. One had to accept restricted circumstances, which meant, in effect, an entirely different style of life. It was a fearful and anxious time for this group.

The individual governments did little to help. In ways reminiscent of their early responses to World War I, they followed policies that had been used in the past with no attempt to ascertain their appropriateness for the present; they overlooked the needs and problems of large groups within their own countries; and they failed to cooperate with one another at almost every turn in arriving at international solutions.

Overlying the particular crisis of the Depression were unresolved problems and frustrations from the recent past. These included national aspirations that had never been successfully dealt with, past experiences with economic crises of one kind or another, criticisms of political institutions or social relations that had lain dormant until the Depression, and yearnings for a better and more satisfying life. All of these made the Depression more than just a time of economic hardship. It became in addition an explosive situation in which almost anything might happen.

America and Europe

One striking way that the Depression recalled the experiences of World War I was the extent to which it linked the destinies of Europe to those of countries outside it, particularly that of the United States of America. America's destiny, of course, had always been intertwined with that of Europe. The United States had become a factor of great significance in world politics by the early years of the twentieth century, and its entry into World War I clearly tipped the balance, psychologically as well as materially. Its refusal to adhere to the League or to enter into binding agreements guaranteeing French security and the status quo in Europe obscured the prominent role that it continued to play in world affairs after World War I. American sponsorship of the Washington Naval Conference in 1922, one of the few efforts at disarmament of any substance between the wars, is one example of its continued importance in world affairs. The United States naturally tended to work mostly in areas where it perceived vital interests to be at stake. Its largest contributions to the maintenance of European stability came through the Dawes and the Young Plans, attempts to reach satisfactory settlement of the reparations questions. Settlement of this affected the ability of other countries to repay war debts to the United States and the general health of the European economy. A healthy European economy, one in which capital flowed freely, opened important opportunities for investment and trade. Actually, this was America's greatest contribution in the 1920s to European and world affairs, a great outpouring of capital, agricultural and manufactured products, and techniques and methods. The United States had, in fact, assumed a vital role in the European and world economies. Europe no longer dominated the world economically. But this development and the somewhat less obvious but still significant challenges to political and cultural domination were partially hidden by European success in reconstructing a large part of prewar institutions and outlooks.

The event that clearly showed the changed relationship between the United States and Europe and contributed significantly to the collapse of postwar efforts in Europe to reconstruct a semblance of the prewar world was the crash of the New York Stock Exchange in October 1929. Even before the crash, however, the European economy was experiencing difficulties. In 1928 some American loans to Germany were recalled in order to take advantage of the high yields possible on American investments at the time. The difficulties created by the recall of these loans was an indication of the precarious foundations of German and central European credit structures. Other signs of trouble ahead might have been seen in the highly speculative ventures favored by many European investors and in the fact that many financial and commercial empires existed largely on paper. The continuing low prices paid for agricultural products were a source of problems, especially in eastern Europe. By 1928, then, signs of a slowdown in the economy were already visible in Germany. In addition, Britain had never fully recovered in the 1920s and many areas in eastern Europe were already suffering from a depressed economy.

While the American stock market crash was the single most important factor in the beginning of the Depression, it was, curiously enough, not a surprise to knowledgeable investors. They realized that prices paid for stocks no longer reflected the value of the assets of the companies involved. Speculation logically had to end somewhere. Sooner or later people would stop buying simply because they expected prices to continue to rise, thereby providing a windfall profit. In the context of the times, however, and given the naiveté of many investors, it is understandable that people continued to speculate. The crash, while not a surprise to some, was much more serious than anyone had anticipated. Stock prices fell farther than anyone had thought would be the case and the reaction to this was more pessimistic than had been predicted. Expenditures for new plants and equipment were curtailed in view of the uncertain economic future so that production of investment goods—items such as machinery, steel, and cement—dropped in 1930 by a quarter from the previous year's level. Added to this was a drop in the price of agricultural produce and raw materials because of the pressure of world surpluses in these areas. In 1931 and 1932, with the supply of money and credit reduced by accelerating bank failures, production of investment goods dropped even farther. Production declined in other sectors while unemployment increased. By a process that was as much psychological as it was economic, the United States fell into a severe depression by 1932.

The repercussions of American developments quickly spread to other parts of the world where, some contend, the policies followed and attitudes taken turned American difficulties into a worldwide catastrophe. It is easy to see how this could happen if one considers that American industrial production counted for about 40 percent of the world total. In addition, American investments had come to form a vital component of the European economies in the 1920s. After the crash, American investors withdrew funds from European banks in great quantities. Hardest hit were banks in Germany and central Europe. The decline in American industrial productivity, the withdrawal of American capital from the world market, and low prices paid for agricultural products and raw materials combined to reduce production, trade, and the movement of capital everywhere.

The crisis was international, but not much was done at that level to deal with the problem. In 1931 President Herbert Hoover of the United States proposed a moratorium of one year on all intergovernmental debts, in recognition of the problems of transferring sums of money for payment of reparations or war debts. This was accepted by European leaders and regarded as an acknowledgment of the connection between reparations and war debts, i.e., the latter would not be paid unless the former were paid. That this was not the American understanding became all too clear the following year, when America refused to tie a plan for setting aside reparations to an agreement on war debts. The question was never resolved by agreement. In the next few years, Germany repudiated reparations and most European states owing money to the United States made only token payments. In 1933 a third international effort floundered when the United States, by then set on a path of economic nationalism, declined to cooperate. Most other countries had already begun their own efforts to find a way out also.

Great Britain and the Depression

For the British, the Depression was an odd time. They had never fully recovered from the war. Unemployment had remained high throughout the 1920s. Several major industries—cotton textiles, coal, and shipbuilding, had experienced considerable difficulty before 1930. In addition to these problems, Britain had fixed the rate of exchange between the pound sterling and gold at too high a level in 1925. Because of this, British products were not always competitive on the world market. As the market began to collapse under the weight of falling prices for raw materials and the decline of the American economy, Britain found the level of its exports dropping as well. Since production for export was a vital part of the British economy, a downturn in that sector soon affected the entire economy.

Britain experienced a severe banking crisis in 1931, as did most other European nations. Contrary to the experience of Germany, some other central European states, and the United States, British banking got through the crisis without major failures. In fact, the crisis was probably beneficial in the long run in that Britain went off the gold standard as a result. This meant simply that the pound was freed to find its real value in relation to other currencies. It dropped about 30 percent, from a pound equaling $4.86 to a pound equaling about $3.40. This made British goods about 30 percent cheaper in the world market than they had been previously, and therefore made her more competitive. Many other countries followed Britain off the gold standard.

In statistical terms at least, the British experience in the Depression was not disastrous. Since it had never fully recovered economically from the war, the downturn in the early thirties was not that great. The volume of exports, never up to the prewar level in the twenties, dropped 37 percent from 1929 to 1932. Industrial production, however, fell only 12 percent and by 1932 was starting to revive.

Recovery had little to do with what the government did, although it had enacted a moderate protective tariff on manufactured goods and tried to encourage investment by establishing low interest rates. Rather, recovery seemed to come from within the workings of the economy itself and was based on two related developments. One was the expansion of some newer industries such as automobile manufacturing and chemicals. The other was connected with a housing boom in the 1930s. The two were related in that expansion of industry, particularly in the southeast, created a need for housing and, at the same time, supplied people with jobs so that they could afford to buy housing. For a number of different reasons, including lower interest rates, decreased costs of construction, and more money available from wages for housing because of the drop in the cost of food and clothing, housing was less expensive than it had been. For those who had work, the same applied to the purchase of items such as radios, phonographs, and refrigerators. Employment rose rapidly not only in the automobile industry but also in electrical manufacturing, where British research efforts led, among other things, to television, which the British Broadcasting Corporation introduced in 1936, and to the development of radar, an invention that played an important role in

A group of unemployed men entertain a theatre queue in 1932. The hatless man slightly to the right of the center of the photograph appears to be holding a hat or cap into which people might drop money. (BBC Hulton Picture Library)

the early part of World War II. British recovery, then, came largely through a boom in consumer durable goods—automobiles, ranges, and housing, among other items.

One problem with the British recovery in the 1930s was that there never was a real sense that the Depression was over. The decade remained for the average Briton a time of inactivity and decline, the period of the "Great Slump." A large part of the reason for this continuing feeling of national malaise was unemployment. In 1929 the rate had been 10 percent; by 1932 it had risen to 22 percent. The government acted to relieve unemployment and, in fact, extended and improved the support system in the 1930s. It also attempted to deal with the heart of the matter, the stagnant export industries—cotton textiles, coal mining, iron and steel manufacture, and shipbuilding in the north and west. Efforts were made to encourage the movement of labor to the more prosperous southeast. Subsidies were made available to manufacturers who located plants in the depressed areas.

Despite the various attempts by the government to deal with unemployment, it remained a major problem. In part this was simply because Britain was experiencing a fundamental adjustment of her economy, involving a transition from an emphasis on heavy industry to a new prominence for the consumer goods industries. This sort of transition took time. In large part, however, the government compounded the problem through unimaginative leadership. It relieved umemployment through the dole—a welfare payment system. Existing on the dole was not only economically unproductive but also psychologically damaging. The British working class had always stood apart from the middle and upper classes in British society, but in the 1930s a renewed bitterness overlay its relationship with other groups. Working-class experience in the 1930s also created a deep distrust of Conservative government, and helps to explain the otherwise inexplicable 1945 defeat of a Conservative government that had effectively led Britain through World War II.

France

Whereas Britain had suffered because it was vulnerable to changes in the international economic situation, France, not overly dependent on world trade and enjoying a competitive edge anyway because of the devaluation of her currency in the late 1920s, appeared at first invulnerable to the effects of the Depression. This apparent invulnerability caused France to be generally uncooperative in international efforts to deal with the Depression. Also an important factor here was French foreign policy. Germany had to be kept down, in the opinion of French policymakers. This meant that France was extremely reluctant to free Germany of her obligations to pay reparations and was suspicious of anything that might unduly strengthen Germany, such as the German-Austrian customs union proposed in 1931 as a means of dealing with the banking crisis in central Europe.

French success in avoiding the worst effects of the first part of the Depression was due to several anomalous features of the economy. For contemporaries, the most striking and significant factor was the balance in the French economy between industry and agriculture. French commentators liked to point to this in their assessments of French economic stability early in the thirties. Naturally, there was something to this. An economy less dependent on industry will not be as badly hurt by a decline in production, investment, and trade as one that is more dependent. Perhaps more important was the relatively low level of unemployment in France, compared to that of other countries. Officially, no more than 600,000 were out of work, even during the worst of the Depression. While the number of jobs shrank, as in other countries, the French labor pool also shrank. The generation coming into the pool in the thirties was very small because of the unusually low birth rate during World War I. In addition, young people remained longer in school. Many industrial workers went back to family farms or retired early. Approximately one-half million foreign workers left the country after becoming unemployed.

Although the Depression came more slowly to France than other countries, it nevertheless came and, once entrenched, was difficult to remove. France had already experienced a decline in the economy in 1930 and 1931. The devaluation of the British pound, which removed much of the edge enjoyed by the French franc in the late 1920s, led to a further decline in industrial production. A low point was reached in the spring of 1932 when industrial production totaled only a little over three quarters of the 1928 figures. After a slight improvement French industry declined again, probably because of the devaluation of the American dollar in 1933, an action that made French prices about 20 percent higher than world prices.

The government did almost nothing in the first half of the 1930s to remedy the situation. It followed an orthodox policy of deflation, primarily one of balancing the budget through a reduction of public spending. This only further depressed the economy. The obvious answer, one suggested by Paul Reynaud, was devaluation of the franc. This was politically impossible. Poincaré had devalued the franc in the 1920s because it seemed the only solution to inflation. But at that time, various promises had been made that it would be the one and only time. French national honor, and the balance of opinion within the propertied middle class, somehow required that the franc remain the Poincaré franc.

The election of a left-center government in 1932 made little difference in the policy used to deal with the Depression. The government, led by the Radical Socialist (Republican) Édouard Herriot and supported by socialist votes (although it included no socialists in the cabinet), continued to follow traditional economic patterns of response. The two years after the left's electoral victory were years of political instability, an economic situation growing steadily worse despite the brief respite caused by the revival of production between 1932 and 1933, and, after 1933, fear of Nazi Germany. For many Frenchmen, the viability of the Third Republic had become a serious question. Events in 1934 only underlined the seriousness of that question. One was the "Stavisky Scandal." Sergei Stavisky, a figure from the Parisian underworld, had in the 1920s moved from drug peddling, living off women, and other similar activities to more or less legitimate dealing. Indicted for fraud in the late 1920s, he had managed to gain repeated postponement of his trial, thanks to the help of friends in high places. After the collapse of his financial empire in 1933, the press demanded that Stavisky stand trial. Soon after this, it was reported that he had committed suicide before he could be captured by the police. The scandal, one of several calling into question the honesty of politicians and officials, led to a series of riots in January and February 1934. Efforts by the government to end the riots only produced a decision by rightist groups to stage a massive demonstration on February 6.

It is slightly ironic that the demonstration centered on the Place de la Concorde, across the Seine from the Chamber of Deputies. Not all the rioters were members of right-wing groups (some, for example, were communists). In any case, there is not much evidence pointing to a serious attempt at a coup or an insurrection. One bit of evidence pointing the other way is that shortly after midnight the rioters rushed off to catch the last subway trains home. Still, the police held the bridge with difficulty. Fifteen people died and fifteen hundred were injured. Had the crowd stormed the Chamber, a coup might have resulted.

The riots of February 6 were indicative of a deep dissatisfaction with the Third Republic in France and with parliamentary government. French politics were becoming polarized between right and left. The new right consisted of a number of groups modeled after the Italian Fascists. Several proto-fascist parties had formed by the end of 1934, the most important being the *Parti populaire français* led by the ex-Communist, Jacques Doriot. In addition, there were authoritarian movements such as the veterans' movement, the *Croix de feu*, which had a massive membership, along with the older right movement, the *Action française*. By the mid-thirties, politics was coming out onto the streets and France in some ways was beginning to resemble Italy in the early twenties. In reaction to this and out of fear of fascism both in France and elsewhere, Socialists, Communists, and Radicals organized the Popular Front movement during 1934-1935, a political coalition to combat fascism and to reform the Third Republic. Politics was becoming deadly serious and highly chaotic. Each side used all means at its disposal to gain support.

France in 1934 was no closer to a solution to the problems of the Depression than in 1932. She was, however, now somewhat distracted by the threat of fascism, a threat that had some basis in French developments but one that took on especially ominous proportions mainly because Hitler and the Nazis had taken power in Germany.

The Depression in Germany: The Nazis Come to Power

The Depression was the single most important factor in the Nazi "seizure of power" in 1933. Germany was particularly vulnerable to the economic dislocation in the United States because of the important role played by American capital in the German economy. When the market collapsed in 1929, American creditors called in loans. As the German economy slowed, unemployment rose. The coalition government in power in 1929 floundered on the question of unemployment payments. A government of experts succeeded it. Headed by Heinrich Brüning, it managed German affairs from March 1930 to May 1932. Brüning, like most other European politicians in the 1930s, approached economic problems from an orthodox standpoint. His policy emphasized balancing the budget by raising taxes and reducing governmental expenditures, chiefly by reducing unemployment benefits and civil servants' salaries. The policy was harmful in that it reduced economic demand and further depressed the economy.

In the European banking crisis of 1931, the German government intervened to save German banks from collapse. Although the British were forced to abandon the gold standard by the banking crisis, Germany stayed on. The government tried to remain competitive by a policy of deflation in which all prices were forced down about 10 percent. The German government's budget and monetary policies reflected the shock of the inflation of the early 1920s; property owners pressed the officials to avoid any radical experiments.

If the government missed one obvious opportunity by maintaining the gold standard, others were denied it. Brüning attempted to negotiate a customs union with Austria in 1931, a move that might have helped the economic situation of both nations and one that certainly would have created a psychological boost. France objected and the project was stopped. France also postponed the question of setting aside reparations payments until it was too late to do any good, economically or politically.

Germany by 1932 was experiencing serious economic difficulties. Production was down by 42 percent from 1928 and this had resulted in massive unemployment, around six million people. Economic difficulties were transformed into political difficulties in 1932 and

1933. Brüning had governed without a majority in the Reichstag, using the emergency powers granted the president by the Weimar Constitution. In an effort to resolve the political deadlock, Germany went to the polls in national elections no fewer than four times in 1932. Twice in 1932, Germany elected delegates to the Reichstag, in July and again in November. The results of both elections were similar. Of the old Weimar coalition parties, the Democratic and the People's Parties did badly. From a total of nearly 14 percent of the vote in 1928, they declined to under 3 percent in 1932. The Center Party largely maintained its electorate, but the Socialists, while remaining a major party, lost heavily. They dropped from nearly 30 percent of the vote in 1928 to just over 20 percent in 1932. The center of the political spectrum had won about 55 percent in 1928 but only around 35 percent in 1932. Yeats' line, "The centre cannot hold," had come true in an ominous fashion.

The extremes gained at the expense of the middle. On the left, the Communists had steadily increased their share of the vote from about 10 percent in 1928 to nearly 17 percent in 1932. On the right, the Nazis became a major political force, rising from under 3 percent in 1928 to 37 percent in the July Reichstag election. In the elections for president, their candidate, Adolf Hitler, forced the incumbent, President Hindenburg, into a runoff election before being defeated.

Throughout the twenties the Nazis had never been anything other than a minor right-wing party. Like others of its sort, it was vehemently opposed to the Versailles Treaty, fervently nationalistic, racist, anti-Semitic, and slightly socialistic. It had achieved some national prominence in the campaign in 1929 against the Young Plan to reorganize the payment of reparations. The main reasons for the rapid rise of the Nazis to the status of the largest political party in Germany by 1932, however, were the Depression and the party leader, Adolf Hitler.

Hitler had made himself into the indispensable figure in the Nazi party. In addition to a party hierarchy and a bureaucracy which ran party affairs, each member of the party owed personal loyalty to Hitler. In return, Hitler took responsibility for the affairs of the party. His political instincts were keen. An effective speaker both in public and on the radio, he understood the principles of mass psychology and modern propaganda techniques. Assisted by Paul Joseph Goebbels, Hitler utilized mass rallies, pageantry, radio, motion pictures, newspapers, and the airplane to sell his image and that of the party to as many Germans as possible.

Despite his undeniable political genius, Hitler's success as a politician was still dependent on circumstances. The Depression created the proper atmosphere within which he and the Nazis could work. As William Sheridan Allen makes clear in his study of the Nazi rise to power on the local level, Nazi efforts were only partially responsible for their success. The party gave the impression of being energetic, young, and fresh by the endless series of rallies, demonstrations, speeches, and campaigns that it sponsored. It reinforced the fears of particular groups and promised specific advantages to members of the centrist parties which were much more appealing than the platitudes these parties offered. In particular, the Nazis played on the hostility felt toward the Socialists who, after World War I, had become prominent in German politics on all levels.

One of the most remarkable aspects of the Nazi rise to power was their ability to say simultaneously the things that different groups wanted to hear. Despite the anticapitalist features of the 1920 "Twenty-Five Points" of the Nazi party, Hitler was able to convince big business and the industrialists in the early 1930s that his plans for economic recovery included a substantial role for business. There were also indications that an expansive and militarily strong Germany would offer greatly increased opportunities. Business support of the Nazis was crucial in 1932 and 1933. Somehow, at the same time, Hitler assured small shopkeepers and small businessmen that he would work to protect their interests and save them from economic ruin. The Germany of the little man and the small town would not be allowed to disappear. Hitler struck an even more traditionalist note in talking about farmers and women. The soil was of sacred importance to the Nazis, and small farmers would be helped in their efforts to remain on the land. Women would be encouraged to remain at home to raise the new generation of German *Volk* (people). For the middle classes, Hitler promised a stable economic order and firm government. Even workers could expect something, a job and a share in the national destiny. It was, of course, the idea that Germany under Hitler would regain its natural place in the world order that helped to hide the otherwise somewhat contradictory statements and promises. This attracted the military, too, which in the early thirties had the power to crush the Nazis but instead remained neutral.

Neither of the two governments that followed Brüning's government in 1932 was able to put together a majority in the Reichstag or to institute policies that would alleviate Germany's economic distress. The policies put into effect by Franz von Papen, which included a public works program and an expansion of credit, were just beginning to take effect by early 1933 when Hitler was named chancellor. The fact that Germany was emerging from the Depression was not perceived, and it was thought necessary to bring Hitler into the government in order to use his following to gain support for government policy. Hindenburg was convinced by von Papen that, as vice-chancellor, the latter could manipulate Hitler. This expectation, like a number of others, proved false.

Hitler continued policies begun in 1932, but increased the scope and the vigor of activities. The public works program was expanded, as were programs of labor service. The government tried to stimulate private investment as well. Perhaps as important as anything was the feeling among many Germans that now the government was finally doing something. The cause of the Depression had largely been psychological; the cure was also largely psychological. Unemployment dropped from 6 million when the Nazis took power to 2.5 million in June 1934. Production rose considerably in the period, reaching more than 80 percent of 1928 levels in 1934. By then military spending was beginning to have an impact on the German economy, but it was not the major reason for the improvement of economic conditions. Rearmament accelerated rather than brought about recovery.

In 1933 and 1934, as Germany began to recover from the Depression, the Nazis worked to consolidate political power through a process that Karl Dietrich Bracher, a leading German expert on the period, had labeled the "legal revolution." Essentially, it involved using the powers granted by the Weimar Constitution to the President and also to the Reichstag in order to undermine the Constitution itself. In the first several months of 1933, legal fictions were used to disguise questionable and quite obviously illegal actions by the Nazis. This made it possible, on the one hand, for civil servants, members of the judiciary, and millions of ordinary Germans to acquiesce in the Nazi seizure of power from above because it was carried out within a framework of legality. On the other hand, it made resistance by such groups as the Social Democrats difficult because they would seem to be defying the agencies of law and order in the state.

The first step in the process was based on goals Hitler had long since made clear, but also responded to the tactical possibilities open at the time; it involved yet another electoral campaign. This time the Nazis had the cooperation of the police in their harassment of communists and socialists. The communists were blamed for the Reichstag fire on February 27, 1933, which led President Hindenburg to

suspend constitutional guarantees of free speech and press. Despite
the free use of violence and intimidation, however, the Nazis gained
only 44 percent of the vote. In a sense it did not matter. The Nazis and
the Nationalist Party convinced the Center Party to pass the Enabling
Act, granting the government full powers for four years. Only the
Social Democrats voted against it. With the power granted it by the
Enabling Act, the Nazi government was able to take control of almost
every sector of German life in the next year. Trade unions, political
parties, virtually all non-Nazi organizations, disappeared or were incorporated into groups dominated by the Nazis. Only the churches
and the army remained capable of any independent activity. Beginning in April 1933, legal discrimination against the Jews was added to
the informal persecution of the past. By 1934 German life had been
redefined according to the viewpoint of the Nazi Party and Hitler.
Even the party itself had been reshaped in the "Night of the Long
Knives" (June 30, 1934), in which the radical wing of the party was
eliminated, including leaders such as Gregor Strasser and Ernst
Roehm, the latter the head of the *Sturmabteilung* or S.A., a paramilitary formation connected with the party. After Hindenburg's
death in August 1934, Hitler became the sole leader of Germany, *Der
Führer*.

The Stalinist Revolution in the Soviet Union

All these events were watched with great nervousness in the one
European country that had not experienced the symptoms of the
Depression, the Soviet Union. It was precisely in the period of the
Depression that the Soviet Union, through incredible hardship and
great sacrifice, established the basis for a highly industrialized economy. By the end of the thirties the Soviet Union had transformed
itself into one of the major industrial powers of the world, and created the means with which to withstand the onslaught of the German
military in World War II.

The achievement of the Soviet Union was without question an impressive one, one that many Europeans, frustrated by their own
country's inability to deal with the Depression, admired and wished
to imitate. Yet the achievement came at astounding cost. Central to
the controversy that continues over the benefits gained versus the
costs incurred is the role of Stalin. By 1928, when the debate on the
Soviet Union's economic future was entering a crucial phase, Stalin
was the single most powerful figure in Russia. Through his various

administrative positions, particularly that of General Secretary of the party, he had built up a large and loyal following, within both the party and the government. In addition, he had emerged in the 1920s as the chief disciple and interpreter of Lenin. Publication of *The Foundations of Leninism* (1924), in which Stalin reviewed and explained Lenin's major ideas in clear, simple language, did much to create the impression in the minds of the people that he was a true follower of Lenin. Finally, to his credit, he had shown a measure of greatness in rising to the demands of the 1920s. Fellow party members and Russians in general had grown accustomed to looking to Stalin for decisive leadership. Where others hesitated, he acted.

Stalin's reputation as a man of action reflected his talents and characteristics, but it also laid the foundation for Russia's tragedy. Stalin was the personification of the fallacy inherent in Machiavelli's ideal of the Prince. One who was ruthless enough to gain power through force and deceit would not necessarily have the wisdom to use it correctly.

Old Bolsheviks, members of the Communist Party before the October Revolution in 1917, called events in the early 1930s "the great change." Western historians have labeled them the "Stalinist revolution." For many in the Soviet Union it was the long-awaited "second revolution" which would complete the first (the October Revolution). Whatever label one might choose, it was a revolution more profound than the revolution of 1917 or, for that matter, the great French Revolution of the eighteenth century.

There were three basic ideas behind the events of the early thirties. Fundamental was the concept of the collectivization of agriculture. This would create, according to the ideas of the planners, possibilities for a more productive agriculture than the kind practiced by individual peasant proprietors. A more productive agriculture would decrease the need for people on the land, which would swell the urban labor force. It would also create a food surplus that could be sold abroad for foreign exchange which, in turn, would be used to purchase machinery or other items not available in Russia, or used for investment capital. The second basic idea, that of economic planning, was implicit. The Soviet Union had limited resources under the best possible circumstances. It was imperative that they be used carefully, and planning was the most likely way to achieve that goal. Most important of the basic ideas, however, and really the end to which the first two were means, was the concept of rapid industrialization. Stalin believed that the Soviet Union had to make herself into a major industrial power within ten years or run the risk of annihilation by hostile capitalist powers. This belief, which Stalin apparently held sincerely, partly explains the often brutal methods employed to achieve the goal.

The Russia that Stalin set to work on in 1929 was still overwhelmingly a peasant Russia. The peasants were considered to be *bezkulturnost* (without culture). They had a culture, of course, but it was not a literate, urban culture. Lenin, and Bukharin after him, had recognized that Russia's fundamental task was an educational one, that of acquainting Russian peasants with twentieth-century ideas and practices. Stalin, however, believed that he could not afford to take the time necessary for such an educational effort. His approach was more direct: beat, imprison, or kill all who resisted collectivization and the other components of the "second revolution."

In Aleksandr Dovzhenko's lyrical film *Earth*, all the peasants are presented as wanting a tractor and the mechanization and collectivization of agriculture that it symbolized. Change was coming to the countryside; even the horses and oxen sensed it. Only the reactionary kulaks, the rich peasants, were against it. Dovzhenko's film, for all its greatness as cinema, was naive propaganda rather than a documentary record of events. In the reality of Russia in the early thirties, it was not easy to decide who was a kulak and who was not. The peasant, living in a harsh and unpredictable world beset by fires, droughts, untimely frosts and other calamities, did not aspire necessarily to equality or justice, but to a position of comfort and respect in his or her village. In the world as God had made it, a peasant wanted to be "top dog." It was this kind of person that Stalin set out to bend to his will.

Early in 1930 Stalin decided that rapid and complete collectivization was the answer not only to economic needs but also to problems of political control. Collectivization, which had been planned to take place gradually, was to be completed by 1933. By March of 1930 more than half the peasant families had been forced into collectives (14 million of 26 million households; 10 million in six weeks). Rapid collectivization brought with it a threatening revolutionary situation and on March 2, 1930, Stalin tried to undo the damage. He claimed in a speech that the figure of 50 percent of the peasants in collectives showed that *"the radical turn of the rural districts towards socialism may already be regarded as guaranteed."* The burden of the speech, however, dealt with the necessity of proceeding more soberly with collectivization. Stalin blamed overzealous subordinates, "dizzy with success," for the excesses of collectivization, conveniently overlooking his central role.

After Stalin's speech, collectivization continued, but not as rapidly. By the end of 1930 about half the peasants were again in collectives. In the process, thousands of peasants had been shot or sent off to inhospitable regions with only an hour or two notice. Many of those who were deported died either on the way or soon after they reached their destination. Officially, these were the kulaks, the rich peasantry, but the process of selection was arbitrary. A kulak might be the peasant with a two-story house instead of a single-story one, or simply that person known in the village as a leader of opinion. The peasants did not always accept collectivization passively. They slaughtered party officials and fought pitched battles with the police. They killed livestock by the millions rather than surrender them to the collectives, and they burned crops, barns, and houses in protest against the new order of things.

In both 1931 and 1932 there were poor harvests and widespread famines. Millions of people died from starvation, malnutrition, mistreatment, and execution. Production rose somewhat, remarkably enough, although the figures for grain were well short of the quota. More indicative of the cost were the figures for livestock. In 1933 there were only half as many horses as in 1928, only one third the number of sheep and goats, and about two thirds the number of pigs. Agriculture had been severely damaged by the process. It had not completely recovered by the time World War II began.

At great cost the peasantry had been organized to provide the resources for industrialization. The first five-year plan (1928-1933) was, like the collectivization process, originally an ambitious but still reasonable proposal. Heavy industry was favored over light industry. Machines to make machines would be a priority. Underdeveloped areas were to be strengthened economically. Sacrifices were unavoidable, but they would be repaid in the creation of a strong, secure socialist state and a higher standard of living. The first five-year plan was ratified in 1929 after the expression of considerable skepticism, especially from Bukharin, Stalin's former ally, who labeled the plan "adventurism" and the "policy of madmen." There are several possible reasons why the plan was ratified: various regional leaders hoped to get something for their area from the plan; many wanted quick, decisive action to deal with what was becoming a crisis for the state and the party; and idealism was also an important factor. Perhaps most important, those who approved the plan saw it as an innovation within the framework of the NEP, a daring venture, but one still predicated on a union between proletariat and peasant.

The rapid acceleration of collectivization early in 1930 and the arbitrary inflation of production quotas made the plan impossible to fulfill. Nevertheless the Russians achieved stunning results, some being driven by dedication and enthusiasm, others by the brutal physical and psychological coercion of the labor camps. Entire cities like Magnitogorsk were created seemingly overnight, complete with major industrial complexes. Gigantic dams were constructed, such as the one on the Dniper River, at the time the largest in the world. The White Sea canal was built by hand at a staggering cost in human terms. Stalin claimed that the plan had achieved 93.6 percent fulfillment nine months *ahead* of schedule. The actual results were spotty (see Table 6.1).

The basis for a modern industrial economy had been created in the period of the first five-year plan. At the same time, the basis for the Stalinist state was formed. By 1933 Stalin was virtually an indispensable figure. His policies could not be seriously questioned without calling into question the right of the Communist Party to rule. Some members of the Central Committee suggested that the second five-year plan could be less rigorous and tensions lessened. Stalin saw it otherwise. To falter now would be to invite an attack by all the enemies of socialism and its great champion, i.e., Stalin. There could be no letup. In fact, the pressure to conform and to sacrifice increased. Those who challenged Stalin in any fashion had to be eliminated. This Stalin set out to do, beginning in 1934, in a series of actions that made Hitler's "Night of the Long Knives" seem benign by comparison.

Politics Polarized

In 1934 not much was known of the suffering of millions of Russians in the processes of collectivization and industrialization. The Soviet Union seemed instead a ray of hope in a world otherwise dreary and uninspiring. By its own efforts* the Soviet Union was creating a new society that promised a decent life for all. In addition, the Soviet Union was speaking out in an unequivocal way against aggression. To be idealistic and hopeful in the thirties, then, meant that one must be at least sympathetic to the Soviet Union and communism. Fellow travelers abounded and many joined the Communist Party in their country,

---

*An important role, never acknowledged, was played by Western technology.

TABLE 6.1

Economic Indices, Russia, 1913-1937*

Year	1913	1921	1927-1928	1932-1933 (first version)	1932-1933 ("optimal version")
Coal (million tons)†	29.0	8.9	35.4	68.0	75.0
Pig iron (million tons)	4.2	.1	3.3	8.0	10.0
Steel (million tons)	4.2	.2	4.0	8.3	10.4
Oil (million tons)	---	---	11.7	19.0	22.0
Electricity (billion kilowatt hours)	1.9	.5	5.1	17.0	22.0
Wool cloth (million meters)	---	---	97.0	192.0	270.0

Year	1932 (actual)	1937 (plan)	1937 (actual)
Coal	64.3	152.5	128.0
Pig iron	6.2	16.0	14.5
Steel	5.9	17.0	17.7
Oil	21.4	46.8	28.5
Electricity	13.4	38.0	36.2
Wool cloth	93.3	226.6	108.3

Year	1916	1922	1928	1930	1932	1934	1940
Grain harvest (million tons)	80.0‡	50.3	73.3	83.5	69.6	67.6	95.6
Cattle (million head)	58.9	45.8	70.5	52.5	40.7	42.4	28.0
Pigs (million head)	20.3	12.0	26.0	13.6	11.6	17.4	27.5

* compiled from Alex Nove, *An Economic History of the U.S.S.R.*, 94, 110, 146, 186, 191, 225, and 277 (first published 1969; reprinted with revisions, 1976)
† figures for 1913 and 1921 exclude lignite; remaining figures are for hard coal
‡ 1913 figure

placed their talents at the disposal of the movement, and tried to over-come their background, which was usually middle-class, by adopt-ing the dress, manners, and life-style of the working class.

The Popular Front, a coalition of political groups on the left, which Communist Parties everywhere began to participate in and to sponsor actively in 1935, presented a direct challenge to the parties on the extreme right, the Fascists. These parties and the nations which they governed, Italy and especially Germany, also appealed to many who were energetic and committed. The middle ground of politics became less and less important. Between the extremes, defenders of democracy and capitalism tried to make a case. This was not easy, for it was perfectly apparent that democracy and capitalism had serious defects. Those in the middle had to defend the system and at the same time suggest ways to reform it.

By the mid-thirties Europeans were taking sides and committing themselves in large numbers, something they had not done in the twenties. The essay became a polemic, the poem or painting a piece of propaganda. Ordinary people expressed commitment as well by marching, listening, and shouting slogans. Europe was coming apart. Postwar recovery was being replaced by something new which, depending on one's point of view, was either frightening or exhilarating. Already some ominous signs had appeared which indicated that aggression would go unpunished and that the will to prevent war was lacking among the democracies. Japan had invaded and conquered Manchuria, nominally a part of China, in 1931. The League of Nations condemned Japan as the aggressor, but did nothing to enforce the verdict. The Disarmament Conference of 1932-1933, so long prepared for, floundered because of French intransigence and the general lack of a spirit of international cooperation produced by the Depression. By 1935 Germany had made clear her intention to rearm. Further revision of Versailles was bound to come.

The ordeal of the Depression weakened the European democracies just at the time when they were faced with a crucial challenge. Nazi Germany, determined to reverse Versailles, presented a series of challenges beginning in 1935 and extending until 1939 and World War II. The Soviet Union, tightly controlling various national communist parties from Moscow, presented a challenge that was different but perceived as no less deadly. The ordeal that followed the Depression was perhaps even more difficult in that it threatened the end of European civilization through war. For those who could remember all too well the calamity of World War I, nothing could have been more frightening.

Suggested Readings

W. Arthur Lewis, *Economic Survey 1919-1939** (1949)

James M. Laux, "The Great Depression in Europe"* (Forums in History, 1974)

John Kenneth Galbraith, *The Great Crash** (3rd ed., 1972)

Charles P. Kindleberger, *The World in Depression, 1929-1939** (1975)

Robert Skidelsky, *Politicians and the Slump* (1967)

Noreen Branson and Margot Heinemann, *Britain in the Nineteen Thirties* (1971)

David Marquand, *Ramsay MacDonald* (1977)

Joel Colton, *Léon Blum: Humanist in Politics** (1974)

Karl Dietrich Bracher, *The German Dictatorship: The Origins, Structure and Effects of National Socialism* (1970)

William Sheridan Allen, *The Nazi Seizure of Power: The Experience of a Single German Town, 1930-1935** (1965)

Hajo Holborn, ed., *Republic to Reich: The Making of the Nazi Revolution* (1972)

Arthur Schweitzer, *Big Business in the Third Reich* (1977)

Alan Bullock, *Hitler: A Study in Tyranny** (rev. ed., 1964)

Joachim Fest, *The Face of the Third Reich** (1977)

Max Gallo, *The Night of the Long Knives* (1972)

Joachim Fest, *Hitler** (1975)

R. W. Davies, *The Socialist Offensive: The Collectivization of Soviet Agriculture, 1929-1930* (1980)

_____, *The Soviet Collective Farm: 1929-1930* (1980)

Moshe Lewin, *Russian Peasants and Soviet Power** (1975)

George Orwell, *The Road to Wigan Pier** (1972)

Christopher Isherwood, *Berlin Stories** (1954)

*indicates paperback edition

7

The Threat of Fascism, 1934-1939

Very quickly after Hitler became Chancellor of Germany in January 1933, fascism became the dominant factor in European politics. The consolidation of power in Germany by the Nazi Party by mid-1934 and the clear indication by March 1935 of their intention unilaterally to revise the Treaty of Versailles led many European observers to fear that Europe might be plunged into war once again. Fascist Italy's conversion from a rival to Nazi Germany in central Europe to a partner in German attempts to reconstruct European politics deepened the sense of foreboding. On the positive side, the Soviet Union seemed deeply committed to peace and willing to cooperate with the Western democracies in an effort to maintain it. She joined the League of Nations in 1934, rapidly becoming the leading proponent of collective security, and sanctioned the formation of Popular Fronts of the parties on the left to fight against fascism within various countries.

The preoccupation with fascism took place against the backdrop of the Depression, which continued with little relief in most countries until the end of the 1930s. Some smaller democracies, such as Sweden, were able to manage a fairly successful recovery, but the only major state that clearly was pulling out of the Depression by the late 1930s was Nazi Germany. Europe also experienced a frenetic cultural life in the 1930s, much of it tied to the political issues of the day in the form of reactions to or in support of fascism.

For some, fascism was simply frightening. It seemed to be forcing Europe closer to war. If nothing else, it showed the extent to which traditional liberalism and conservatism in politics had collapsed. For others—the millions of supporters of fascist and semi-fascist movements, as well as the millions just fascinated by the dynamism of fascism—it offered a way out of the dilemmas besetting the continent in the thirties. Finally, for many Europeans it provided an enemy against which one might campaign. In struggling against fascism, whether it was a point of view, a party, or a nation, one could confirm and renew one's own ideals and traditions. The Depression was a faceless problem; fascism wore a uniform. It was a visible and tangible phenomenon against which one could take concrete, specific measures.

The Nature of Fascism

As a consideration of developments in the late thirties will demonstrate, it is easier to label an idea or group as *fascist* than to say precisely what is meant by the use of the term. It is now apparent that fascism in interwar Europe was a phenomenon closely connected with the events of the times. It did not exist before 1919, although it built on much that had happened in the preceding decades. Essentially, fascism was an extreme expression of a resentment of one or more aspects of life in modern Europe. For some, of course, there was no aspect of modern life that was acceptable. For others, resentment centered on what was regarded as the weak and unsatisfactory system of parliamentary government. The parliamentary system seemed unable to provide strong leadership for the nation. A good deal of the support for Italian Fascism, for example, stemmed from the failure of the postwar Italian governments to gain recognition for Italy's territorial claims at the Paris Peace Conference. And in Weimar Germany, the Nazis made much of their determination to revise the Versailles Treaty and revive the glories of Imperial Germany. In the latter part of the 1930s, many people were impressed by the aggressive nationalism of Nazi Germany and wanted their own government to emulate this. A strong, even virulent nationalism was the one element that fascist movements all over Europe had in common. It was also the one element that held the somewhat disparate groups in a fascist movement together. Parliamentary governments lacked a similar unifying ability.

Many Europeans believed that parliamentary governments were ineffective in dealing with economic matters, too. The middle classes in general were frightened by the economic decline and disorder that they saw around them. They feared for their comfortable life-style and their social status. The lower middle classes—the shopkeepers and white-collar workers—worried that their businesses would be destroyed by the Depression or that they would lose their jobs. In either case, the result would reduce them to the level of the proletariat. They would have to accept not only the burdens of poverty but also the loss of status, of what had formerly set them apart from the working class. Big business and industry, for their part, feared working-class radicalism and wanted a strong, effective government to protect their economic interests.

Fascism fed not only on frustrated nationalism, sharp discontent with traditional parliamentary politics, and gnawing worries about developments in economic life; it also fed both on sentimental yearnings for some golden age of the past and a restless longing for a dynamic and a spiritually superior future. Here it might be best to use the image proposed by the historian Alan Cassels. He views fascism as similar to the Roman god Janus, generally represented as two bearded heads placed back to back so that the god might look both into the past and into the future. Fascism also tended to do both, to look back nostalgically at institutions and ways of doing things which had disappeared or were threatened and, at the same time, to look enthusiastically to the future to a society that did not yet exist or perhaps existed only embryonically within a fascist party. This may explain why both conservatives and radicals could become fascists. Neither was satisfied with the society contemporary to them. Each could see in fascism those elements that it favored. This may also help to explain why fascist parties did so little in domestic matters, once in power. They were paralyzed to an extent by the division between those looking to the past and those looking to the future. And this in turn suggests why many fascist regimes projected their primary energy into foreign affairs.

Even before World War I many Europeans had experienced difficulties in adjusting to the rapid changes taking place in politics, social and economic relations, and in cultural life. These difficulties became significant and led to the triumph of fascism in several states when Europeans had to work out their problems of accommodation with change in the context of a series of sharp, severe crises. The war, followed by inflation, depression, political instability, social unrest, and cultural malaise, sharpened the more general maladjustment and led some to fascism as a way of dealing with changes in the modern world.

There were other characteristics of fascism. Because of its nationalism and emphasis on the mission of the people of a nation, fascism tended to be racist. It was not necessarily anti-Semitic, but it

could be vehemently so. Fascism tended to be aggressive and bellicose. This was the main way in which it expressed its dynamic quality.
It also glorified a single leader and welcomed a rigidly controlled society. General characteristics aside, however, fascism was shaped
mostly by the peculiarities of the country in which it developed. For
this reason, each fascist movement was unique.

There were fascist or semi-fascist movements everywhere in Europe. In general, they may be divided into three categories. The first
comprised those movements which came to power, the Italian and
the German. Secondly, a number of movements were used by authoritarian governments but were prevented from taking power themselves. These included fascist movements in Spain, Hungary, and
Rumania. Finally, some movements presented clear dangers to the
existence of the legitimate governments of particular countries. The
best examples of this third category would be the fascist movements
in France and in Austria.

Nazi Germany: Hitler's Social Revolution

Debate still continues over whether Nazi Germany was a variation
of fascism or whether it was unique. No doubt the debate will never
be resolved to the satisfaction of all, but it seems most appropriate to
consider National Socialism a German version of fascism. Its special
shape and dynamics came from the industrial and military capabilities
of Germany and from the obsessions of Hitler and some of his
associates.

By 1934 Hitler and the Nazi Party effectively controlled Germany.
The process of *Gleichschaltung* (translatable as "coordination") had
produced by then a Germany in which independent institutions had
been either abolished, incorporated into Nazi organizations, or in
some other way made innocuous. Almost every independent source
of power was leveled under the Party-controlled state. Major exceptions were, first, the churches. Attempts to create a German National
Protestant Church were only partially successful and attempts to
control the Catholic Church largely unsuccessful. Another major
exception was, of course, the military. Even these institutions found
their independent positions steadily undermined over the next several
years.

For many Germans, however, not a great deal had changed. If one
was Jewish or a member of a Marxist organization, disturbing signs
were all too evident. For large numbers, however, Nazi excesses might

be overlooked in the hopes that responsibility would settle them down and allow the better elements within the party to rise to the top. Even more important, the rapid decline of unemployment, the apparent economic recovery, and the forceful presence of Germany in international affairs combined to give many the impression that whatever change might be taking place was for the good.

Germany was changing, but not in ways that corresponded to what the most ardent Nazis thought should be taking place. Supposedly, Germany was undergoing a revolution that would transform the country and its people. Views on the nature of the revolution were somewhat contradictory within the party. On the one hand, Germany was to return to a society of peasant farmers and small towns within which the vices of modern life would be eliminated. On the other hand, German society was to take its model from a much more distant past and develop a heroic society based on purity of race and values derived from the traditions of the people. In this society, the *Übermensch*

Der Führer, *Adolf Hitler, arrives at a Nazi Party rally in Bückeberg, 1934. The immense audience is visible in the background. The uniformed men on either side of Hitler's path are members of the* Sturmabteilung *(the Storm Troopers).* (Katherine Young)

(best translated as the "superior man") would dominate—a man of discipline, heroic accomplishment, and capacity for selfless sacrifice.

Neither vision of the revolution described the reality of Germany in the 1930s. Nazi Germany could not overcome the lines of development that existed in modern, industrial nations. Big business continued to grow at the expense of the small, independent businessman. People deserted small towns for the large cities in increasing numbers. Peasants found it more difficult to maintain the small family farm. The Nazis found that they could not counter these developments because a modern economy was necessary if they were to revise the Versailles Treaty and establish Germany as the dominant power on the continent.

The revolution that took place involved few tangible changes in the way people lived. It was a revolution in the minds of people in that they were persuaded, at least in many cases, to believe that things were different. It was mainly a propaganda effort which stressed that a new society was in the making and that, as well, the goals of particular groups were being achieved. For example, while efforts were made to keep the prices of agricultural produce high and some measures were passed to aid farmers, the main thrust of Nazi agricultural policy was to praise farmers as the backbone of the nation and to indulge in mystical talk about the sacred German soil, while ignoring the very real decline in numbers of small family farms. The same pattern prevailed among small businessmen. Scapegoats were made of a few Jewish department-store owners or financiers, but little of lasting importance could be done to offset the pressures that many small businessmen felt. Whatever the regime might say about the importance of the little man in business and commerce, its orientation was toward big business.

If the major social and economic trends operating in the 1930s—increased urbanization and the growth of large units in industry and in commerce—continued without serious interruption, Nazi Germany did nevertheless represent a kind of social revolution. Opportunities were created through which individuals achieved status and income that would have been denied them by the old social structure and by economic conditions in pre-1933 Germany. The Nazi Party was filled with examples of people who had failed conspicuously in Weimar Germany but who had become powerful, important, and wealthy in Hitler's Germany. Perhaps the best example of this type was Heinrich Himmler, a one-time chicken farmer who in the 1930s headed the S.S. The S.S. was the major paramilitary formation in Nazi Germany after the curtailment of the S.A. (the Stormtroopers or "Brown Shirts") in 1934. It became an empire within the empire of Nazi Germany and began to rival the German army by the late 1930s.

Paradoxically, social mobility and careers open on the basis of party loyalty and talent, which led to the creation of new elites that sometimes elbowed out the old and at other times co-existed with them, were balanced by an official egalitarianism. Every "true" German was equal in his or her devotion to the Führer and to Germany's mission. Anyone participating in one of the massive Nazi Party rallies could feel the various distinctions, which had divided Germans from one another for centuries, melt away and the many become one. That this equality was a psychological equality did not make it any less effective.

Whatever the extent of Hitler's social revolution, it could be said that most Germans believed that the advantages outweighed the disadvantages prior to 1939. There was less freedom, certainly. Creativity was at a low ebb, which was painful for those to whom it mattered. Newspapers, movies, and culture in general were either dull or filled with pretentious nonsense. Education and the sciences, long a source of German strength, were wrecked by the dismissal of some of the brightest men in academic life and by the application of absurd theories based on racist and mystical notions. The reorganization of educational institutions and the reformulation of curricula were meant to serve the Nazi movement by stressing racial, national, and political ideas that identified the Third Reich as the high point of world history. Various elite schools were also created to provide future leadership. The efforts by the Nazi movement to use education to bring into being a new and more heroic society did not succeed.

For one large group, the German Jews, Hitler's social revolution was simply a waking nightmare. The Nuremberg Laws of 1935 excluded Jews from many professions and from public life, and placed severe restrictions on them in other ways. These laws were followed by increasingly punitive legislation. Even more frightening was the *Kristallnacht* of November 9, 1938 (the "Crystal Night" referred to the shattered windows of shops and offices of Jews). On this night shops were ransacked and people beaten while the police looked on. Still, it was difficult for many Jews to know what to make of the virulent anti-Semitism of Nazi Germany. While thousands fled to England, France, or the United States, forced to leave behind everything that they had worked for, thousands of others, considering themselves good Germans and the Germans as a whole to be decent people, stayed on.

A crucial question concerns where Germany was headed in this period. Looking back on the march of events, one could easily conclude that Germany was moving to war. In a sense this was true. The restless dynamic of Nazi Germany meant that preparation for war was virtually unavoidable. This is not the same, though, as saying that Germany moved in an organized and coherent fashion toward World War II. First of all, working against any logical progression was Hitler's style of rule, which consisted of reserving for himself those questions he considered interesting—mostly questions involving foreign policy—and the right to make the final decision on any matter. Everything else was turned over to a welter of conflicting bureaucracies, institutions, and personalities. In some areas, the civilian bureaucracies maintained control. Others, like the Foreign Office, became involved in conflict with various Nazi groups, a conflict resolved in this case by the infiltration of one group of Nazis at the expense of another group and, of course, some career foreign service officers. Other areas became battlegrounds for struggles between the lieutenants of Hitler.

The inconsistent style of rule was seconded by an inability to translate rhetoric into reality. The German economy was declared a "war economy" in 1936 and Hermann Goering introduced a grandiose four-year plan that year. Germany was supposed to be ready by the early forties for a decisive struggle with the other European powers. Yet, even if war had been delayed until 1941 or 1942, it is unlikely that Germany would have been adequately prepared. Intentions were too vague and one set of plans tended to cancel out another set. Policy was largely improvisation, sometimes inspired, often ridiculous. What made Germany into a formidable power in the late thirties, apart from the shortsightedness and timidity of most other powers, was the professionalism of the military and the productive capacity of industry.

Fascism in Britain and France

In Britain and France, two powers increasingly disturbed by developments in Nazi Germany, fascism was a less important phenomenon. Although Britain had suffered greatly from unemployment and other effects of the Depression and had experienced a considerable amount of social tension as a result of the alienation of much of the working class, the British Union of Fascists (B.U.F.) under Sir Oswald Mosley was only a minor factor in political life. Reasons for this included the pride many British felt in their country and its empire. There was little play for injured nationalism. Perhaps more important, Britons had long since grown accustomed to a system of parliamentary democracy and industrial capitalism. Rightly or wrongly, many had convinced themselves that the British way was to eschew radical solutions. In part, this view was based on the fact that there was no strong Communist Party to frighten conservatives, only a left-center Labour Party with a small radical left wing. Perhaps a more important point about Britain in the thirties is that it lacked strong leadership. The coalition government, dominated by Stanley Baldwin for most of the decade, simply ignored foreign policy questions and even on domestic matters preferred drift to decisive action.

France was a somewhat different case. It had not suffered the kind of unemployment experienced by Germany or Great Britain, but the Depression had nevertheless come as a great shock when, after some delay, it hit. Furthermore, many in France continued the practice of condemning the Third Republic. Those who had never ceased yearning for the restoration of the monarchy or at least an authoritarian government dominated by the older elites were joined by fascist critics of modernity and even by proponents of parliamentary democracy who found it difficult to continue supporting the system as it was.

Yet France did not become fascist. Again, aggrieved patriotism was not widespread. And if France proved unable to recover in the 1930s from the Depression, its effects were milder than in Germany. Also, the fascist movement in France was in some respects its own worst enemy. It was fragmented into two or three major and several minor parties, plus a number of other groups that were authoritarian rather than fascist as such. Fascism could be accused of being a foreign, specifically a German, import. Finally, France lacked a Hitler. Nevertheless, fascism was a real and frightening presence in French politics. In the late 1930s, the country was deeply divided between radical left and radical right and it would not be an exaggeration to say that the ingredients of a civil war were on hand in the era of Popular Front government in the late 1930s.

Popular Front Government

In both France and Britain there existed an active current of antifascism, expressed most visibly and vividly in literature and the arts, but more importantly, in France at least, in politics. The riots of February 1934, which some observers believed was an attempted coup, convinced many in France that fascism was an internal as well as external menace. Gradually, in the course of the next year, an anti-fascist coalition, the Popular Front, came into existence. This coalition of Socialists, Communists, and Radical Socialists (actually moderate Republicans) was given official sanction by the Communist International (Comintern) in 1935, for an anti-fascist France corresponded with the foreign policy objectives of the Soviet Union. The three parties involved cooperated in the elections of 1936 to achieve a slight majority in the Chamber of Deputies. The Socialist leader, Léon Blum, became the premier of a government composed of Socialists and Radical Socialists and supported by the Communists.

The government was probably doomed to failure from the start. Some have criticized Blum for not taking a more radical tack and ruling with the Socialists alone if necessary. In all fairness, Blum could hardly have succeeded, no matter what he did. First, a large part of the nation, close to a majority, was hostile to a government dominated by socialists and supported by communists. Secondly, the three parties disagreed among themselves in fundamental ways about economic and social questions. Both problems were brought into immediate focus by a sit-down strike of workers in various sectors of French industry. This naively enthusiastic response to the Popular Front electoral victory placed an intolerable strain on the government. Blum was able to negotiate the Matignon agreements in 1936, which established the forty-hour work week, paid vacations, collective bargaining and arbitration procedures; but the cost was the alienation of business and the creation of conditions that made it virtually impossible to extricate France from the grips of the Depression. The Popular Front government continued until its fall in 1937. By then difficult problems in foreign affairs were added to the intractable dilemmas of domestic politics and the Popular Front government gave way beneath the weight.

Europe on the Way to War

A large part of the vitality of the thirties was due to the fact that so many intellectuals, artists, and others took one side or the other in the great ideological and political struggle raging in Europe. The "Auden Generation," for example, which included the poets W. H. Auden and C. Day Lewis, among others, important continental writers such as André Malraux and Ignazio Silone, and artists such as Max Beckmann and Max Ernst, lent their talents in one fashion or another to the defense of democracy and the criticism of fascism. The support offered fascism by intellectuals and artists was less substantial. Scattered examples, such as the playwright Gerhart Hauptmann in Germany or the novelist Louis-Ferdinand Céline in France, come to mind. By and large, however, commitment by artists and intellectuals meant a defense of democracy (and often a defense of the socialist democracy of the Soviet Union) and a condemnation of fascism.

It may be misleading, though, to emphasize those committed to certain values as opposed to other values. In the last half of the 1930s many people, from all walks of life, were simply interested in avoiding the catastrophe of war. This sentiment was perhaps most noticeable in Britain, but was widespread elsewhere in western Europe and even in Italy and Germany where, despite the ritualistic emphasis on nationalistic aggressiveness and preparation for war, popular sentiment favored avoidance of a world war. In part this was due to memories of the senseless carnage of World War I. It was also due to the fears of aerial bombardment which, it was thought, no city could possibly withstand. The black cloud of war seemed to be looming perceptibly larger and closer than it had been earlier in the 1930s.

One of the first steps toward war was Italian aggression against Abyssinia (Ethiopia) in 1935. The Italian Fascist regime, which had reached a high point in terms of accomplishment and popularity in 1929 with the Lateran Treaties (which ended the state of hostility between the Papacy and the Italian state), had begun to stagnate by the mid-thirties. Its domestic policies had done little to change the nature of the economy or society. Its political reforms were mostly empty formulae. In foreign affairs it was rapidly losing ground to a resurgent Germany. An assault on Abyssinia, where Italy had been ignominiously defeated in 1896, was designed to unify the nation and thrust it once more into a position of greatness. Although Italy eventually defeated Abyssinia, she also antagonized Britain and France and destroyed any possibility of the three nations working together to block German moves on the continent.

The lines were being drawn. Italy and Germany, at first rivals because of conflicting interests in Austria and because of Mussolini's feeling that Hitler was becoming too prominent within European fascism, began to see interests in common and to view the other major powers of Europe as threats to those interests. Each had also noted the unwillingness of the other European powers to respond strongly to aggression against the smaller states. Of the two, Nazi Germany was rapidly becoming the more important.

Britain and France sought a common policy against the fascist powers, but without much success. Both had been interested in an alliance with Fascist Italy, but had found this to be impossible after the reaction to Italian aggression in Abyssinia. France also looked to the Soviet Union as an ally; she signed a treaty with that country in 1935 and ratified it in 1936. France was slow, however, to implement the treaty by talks between the military staffs. Facing a Germany that outweighed her in terms of population and industrial capacity, France adopted a defensive military posture. Great quantities of money and materiel were poured into the Maginot Line, a series of blockhouses and tank traps designed to protect the French border from the possibility of German invasion. In line with the defensive emphasis of the military, French foreign policy stressed the necessity of British support. Russia, Poland, and Czechoslovakia were seen as important allies, but Britain was essential. Only Britain was in a position to aid France directly and immediately in the case of a German invasion. By the spring of 1936 the makers of French foreign policy had decided that if Britain did not move in a given situation, France would not move either.

Looking back on events from a vantage point of more than forty years, French policy seems hopelessly timid and shortsighted. Germany could have been stopped in the mid-thirties with little trouble. Of course, France did not perceive this and perhaps could not have been expected to. Nor could she have been expected to predict the tendency within the British government to drift when it came to foreign affairs.

As it happened, Germany built up momentum in the mid-thirties. In quick succession Germany unilaterally suspended reparations payments, walked out of the Disarmament Conference, and withdrew from the League of Nations. In March of 1935, Hitler pulled the first of his "Sunday Surprises," announcing that Germany was going to rearm. The following year, in another "Sunday Surprise," Germany remilitarized the Rhineland. This meant that any French invasion or counterattack would have to cross the Rhine, an important natural defense. The strategic advantage to Germany was considerable. France, awaiting elections in 1936, was under a caretaker government. Some civilian ministers in the government recommended calling Germany's bluff, but the military figures urged caution and the necessity of remaining on the defensive. The consensus was to follow Britain's lead. Britain protested but did nothing to give the protest any weight. Hitler's bluff had succeeded, the first of a string of gambles that appeared to pay off.

The Soviet Union, which had replaced Germany in the League, had all this time been urging strong action against fascist aggression. Time and again, the Soviet Commissar for Foreign Affairs, Maxim Litvinov, had called for collective action through the League. The Soviet Union had also pushed to secure effective agreements with France and with Czechoslovakia. Finally, she had supported Popular Front movements wherever possible, internal political truces, so that the countries affected could devote their full attention to the threat of fascism. The Soviet strategy was put to the test in 1936.

The Spanish Civil War

The Spanish Civil War was, in many respects, the single most important development as Europe stumbled toward war in the 1930s. It was initially a struggle between different groups of the Spanish people. On the one side were the defenders of the Spanish Republic, which had led a troubled existence since Alfonso XIII had been deposed in 1931. These included republican defenders of parliamentary democracy, socialists of various persuasions, communists who supported Stalin and those who supported Trotsky, trade unionists, anarchists, and Catalonian and Basque separatists. The Spanish Popular Front under the republican Manuel Azaña was, even more than the French coalition, a fragmented movement. The Nationalists, for their part, consisted of high-ranking military personnel, church officials, great landowners, other supporters of the old monarchy, and the Spanish fascists organized primarily in José António Primo de Rivera's *Falange*. The Nationalist movement was a good deal more coherent than the Republican movement, even though the *Falange* differed considerably from the more traditionalist monarchists in what they hoped to accomplish. It was the Nationalist side that precipitated outright warfare in 1936, after years of considerable chaos and political bloodshed.

The purely Spanish elements in the Spanish Civil War were quickly overwhelmed by outside forces. The Nationalists were aided by materiel and some men from Italy and Germany. The combination of traditional and fascist forces controlled by General Francisco Franco seemed to be taking on increasingly fascist overtones in the process. For the Republicans, while some assistance came from volunteers, including the International Brigades, the bulk of the aid came from the Soviet Union. Because of the Soviet Union's overwhelming importance, the Spanish Communist Party, aided by agents of the Comintern and the Russian secret police, rapidly became a major factor in politics. The Popular Front shifted steadily leftward, but, at the same time, some groups on the extreme left were eliminated from Spanish politics. The anarchists were suppressed for putting revolution ahead of the defense of the republic while the Trotskyites, the POUM, were destroyed for obvious ideological reasons.

The Spanish Civil War, then, rapidly became a cockpit within which various major powers contended for advantage, each using the Spanish cause for its own purposes. The fascists used the war to refine military technique, to strengthen national pride, and to test the resolve of the democratic powers. The Soviet Union hoped in part to divert the fascist powers from other projects, namely a thrust into eastern Europe, and, more important, to rally the democratic powers to a strong position of anti-fascism.

It was crucially important that Britain and France failed to come to the aid of the Spanish Republicans. Initially, the French Popular Front government had sent help to its sister Popular Front government in Spain. It rapidly became apparent, however, that this might lead to civil war in France itself. Blum then suggested a Non-Intervention Pact in August 1936. It was signed by France, Britain, the Soviet Union, Germany, and Italy. The latter two quickly ignored their pledge and began to aid the Spanish Nationalists. The Soviet Union, although it would have preferred to have maintained the Pact, felt compelled to aid the Republicans. It could not help regarding the British and French failure to act as a failure of nerve and a sign of political blindness, neither of which reassured the Soviet Union about the reliability of Britain and France as allies.

The Spanish Civil War was finally the focus of an ideological struggle between fascism and democracy, a struggle often pictured as one between good and evil. There was, inevitably, a great deal of romanticism involved in people's perceptions of the conflict. Probably the best example of this is Hemingway's *For Whom the Bell Tolls*. A more realistic response, even though surrealistic in style, was Pablo Picasso's *Guernica*, which expressed the anguish of civilian populations in modern war. Also realistic was George Orwell's uncompromising picture of the war in *Homage to Catalonia*, in which he depicted the utterly unheroic existence of those who were doing the fighting, and also exposed the lack of truth in the propaganda of both sides. Orwell's sympathies were clearly with the Spanish Republic, but he could not help thinking that it was the Spanish people who were suffering and paying the price for both sides in the conflict.

1938: The *Anschluss* and Munich

The year 1937 was relatively quiet; 1938 more than made up for it. In 1938 Nazi Germany carried out a concerted effort to incorporate Austria into the new German Reich. This was a move popular with both Germans and Austrians. In Austria the local Nazi party had whipped up considerable enthusiasm for *Anschluss*. The two leading political parties, the ruling Christian Socialists and the Social Democrats, had spent much of their efforts in past years fighting each other. Now that Germany and Italy had formed the Rome-Berlin Axis, there seemed to be little to stop the joining of Germany and Austria. Early in 1938 the Austrian chancellor, Kurt von Schuschnigg, was called to Berchtesgaden in Germany, where Hitler bullied him into agreeing to a series of legal fictions that would allow Germany to swallow Austria. Unexpectedly, Schuschnigg, after his return to Vienna, decided to resist German pressure. Hitler, enraged, arranged for the Austrian Minister of the Interior, a Nazi, to declare a state of emergency and to call for German intervention. German troops quickly took over the country.

Reaction to the *Anschluss* was muted, a startling contrast to the fierce opposition in 1931 to the relatively innocuous proposal of an Austro-German Customs Union. France followed Britain in protesting but doing nothing. There was a widespread feeling that Germany was, in a sense, only righting a wrong of the Versailles Treaty: incorporating the largely German population of a weak and economically unviable state.

Up to this point, even though Hitler had violated the Versailles and Locarno Treaties, it had been possible to justify and to rationalize his actions. Versailles was unjust and deeply flawed; Hitler and the Nazis had not agreed to Locarno. Hitler's next move, an attempt to aggrandize at the expense of Czechoslovakia, presented a different sort of problem, however. There was a legitimate and negotiable issue at stake, the status of the Sudeten Germans. These were ethnic Germans living in the western border areas of Czechoslovakia. They had been treated more fairly than any other ethnic minority in central Europe, but many of them looked to Germany for their future. The problem was how to satisfy their demands, which Germany pressed, without leaving Czechoslovakia exposed and vulnerable. The territory in question formed an important natural defensive barrier and contained important industrial complexes, including the armaments works at Skoda.

North Sea

Baltic Sea

LITHUANIA

MEMEL

KÖNIGSBERG

DANZIG

HOLLAND

HAMBURG

BERLIN

POZNAN

WARSAW

GERMANY

POLAND

LUBLIN

BELG.
LUX.

COLOGNE

LEIPZIG

BRESLAU

RHINELAND

SAAR

CRACOW

FRANCE

CZECHOSLOVAKIA

MUNICH

VIENNA

SWITZ.

AUSTRIA

BUDAPEST

HUNGARY

ITALY

	Germany in 1933		Annexed, 1938
	Gained by plebiscite, 1935		Annexed, 1939
	Remilitarized, 1936		Protectorate established, 1939

Greater Germany in the 1930s. Through a combination of diplomacy and coercion, Nazi Germany took over Austria and destroyed the existence of Czechoslovakia as an independent state in 1938 and 1939. The series of diplomatic crises contrived by Hitler in the late 1930s culminated with a confrontation between Poland and Germany that led to the start of World War II in September 1939.

Both the French and the Russians were vitally interested in maintaining the integrity of Czechoslovakia. Each had a treaty with that country that guaranteed aid in its defense. In addition to military considerations, Czechoslovakia, under the guidance of Tomaś Masaryk and Eduard Beneš, had become a model in eastern Europe of democratic government, fair treatment of minorities, and industrial progress. It was Britain, however, that negotiated with Germany on the

Czech question. Neville Chamberlain had succeeded Stanley Baldwin as prime minister and, to his credit, had begun to take a strong interest in foreign policy matters. It was his belief that the Czech question could be settled by negotiation, that Hitler would sooner or later reach a reasonable agreement. Chamberlain thought that he had secured this agreement, only to have Hitler raise the ante. Further efforts in the summer of 1938 produced no results and it began to look like war. At the last minute Mussolini proposed a conference at Munich, to which he invited Britain, France, Italy, and Germany, but neither the Soviet Union nor Czechoslovakia. At the conference on September 29, Hitler largely had his way. The Sudetenland was transferred to Germany. In districts where Germans formed less than 50 percent of the population, plebiscites were to be held. Germany was to respect the sovereignty of the remainder of Czechoslovakia. Essentially, Czechoslovakia had been sold out. Its continued existence as a sovereign state depended on Hitler's keeping his word.

Hitler's word, of course, was the crux of the matter. Chamberlain arrived back in Britain unsure of how he would be received by the public but believing that he had secured "peace in our time." If the interest of the Czechs had been betrayed, Europe had nevertheless been preserved from the catastrophe of war. Hitler had entered into an agreement of his own free will. A precedent had been set for the peaceful settlement of other outstanding issues. Chamberlain had "appeased" Hitler, but the policy of appeasement had not been one based on cowardice. Chamberlain did not think of his actions as constituting a slow but steady surrender of bits and pieces of Europe to Nazi Germany. Rather, he believed procedure had been established through which difficulties would be resolved and war avoided.

Munich was later defended as a play for time, but this was not the intention of the British or the French. In neither country did the pace of rearmament quicken appreciably. Instead, Munich brought the British and French what Léon Blum called a sense of "cowardly relief" and drove a wedge between the Soviet Union and its would-be allies, Britain and France. But it also involved Hitler in a pledge of his word, the betrayal of which brought many in western Europe, however reluctantly, to the belief that war was inevitable.

The Soviet Union: From the Purges to the Nazi-Soviet Pact

The Soviet Union could not help but draw the conclusion after Munich that Britain and France were not particularly firm in their resolve to fight fascism. A clear pattern seemed to be emerging of indifference to the fate of friends in distant places. What could the Soviet Union, a bitter enemy for most of the years since the October Revolution, expect if Germany turned on her?

For their part, many in Britain and France had begun to wonder about the Soviet Union as an ally. It was not simply a question of whether they could trust a country governed by an ideology so contrary to theirs; there was also the question of how strong the Soviet Union was militarily and economically. Agriculture, dealt a severe blow in the course of the first five-year plan, was recovering very slowly. Industrial production and the infrastructure (roads, canals, railroads, industrial plants, and the like) were increasing rapidly but at enormous cost in human terms. On top of this came the insanity of the purges.

In part, the purges were what they had been in the 1920s and early 1930s, simply efforts to drop from the membership rolls of the Communist Party those who were insincere, careerists, lacking in proper political understanding, and otherwise unfit for the honor of membership in the party. (Part of the effort involved finding out who was a member. Membership records were in a terrible mess in the 1930s.) In the latter part of the 1930s this rather familiar exercise took on unfamiliar contours as Stalin, with the help of the secret police (the NKVD) and those in charge of party personnel sections, sought to eliminate physically those who might challenge his regime. In particular, this involved the Old Bolsheviks, those who had been active in the party before 1917; important elements of the party bureaucracy such as the Central Committee and the party secretaries (heads of party organizations) on various levels; officials in charge of various aspects of the economy; the officer corps in the armed forces; and finally, the secret police themselves.

Conventionally, the purges are dated from the assassination of Sergei Kirov, a close associate of Stalin, in 1934. There is some evidence indicating that Stalin was behind the assassination, but other evidence shows that he was genuinely shocked by the event. In any case, he used it as a way of getting rid of groups that might be sources of opposition. He had to proceed slowly in this because even in the frantic atmosphere of the 1930s in the Soviet Union, it was not easy to persuade people that someone like Zinoviev was linked with Trotsky and Nazi Germany in some plot to overthrow the Soviet state. Nonetheless, a series of show trials in 1936, 1937, and 1938 resulted in the conviction and execution of people like Zinoviev, Kamenev, and

Bukharin. They and others were supposed to have been linked with Trotsky or with agents of Germany or Britain. The charges generally were preposterous and not difficult to disprove, as groups of leftists in the west who examined the evidence were able to do. Still the confessions came with numbing regularity. People confessed not only because they had been beaten down by physical and mental torture, but also because they hoped that their lives and the lives of relatives and friends would be spared. Perhaps some felt that they were in fact "objectively" guilty, that, without intending to, they had somehow harmed the interests of the Soviet Union. Others, as Arthur Koestler suggests in his novel *Darkness at Noon*, might have convinced themselves that it was their final gesture for the Communist movement. Whether they were guilty or not, they might serve some last purpose as scapegoats or examples.

Beyond the show trials and the summary executions in 1937 of a large number of high-ranking Soviet military figures, there were millions who were dealt with administratively, executed without trial or sent off to the slow death of the GULAG, the growing network of prisons and labor camps operated by the NKVD. It is difficult to estimate the number of those who died as a result of the purges, but if those who died as a result of the collectivization process and the ensuing famines are included, the number is over ten million. It is estimated that a million were executed. In the 1930s at least six million died in prison or in labor camps and three million in the process of collectivization and the famine. These figures may actually seriously *underestimate* the loss of life. Certainly they cannot be too high.

The purges can be only partially explained from the standpoint of rational policy. They were, of course, meant first of all to serve political goals. Stalin intended to eliminate anyone—party member, government official, or military leader—who might have served as the focus of an opposition or as a potential replacement for Stalin. It is no accident that the purges largely coincide with the development by Stalin of a cult of personality in which he moved from the position of Lenin's worthy successor to one in which he was fully Lenin's equal. Apparently Stalin came to believe in this period that he alone had the insight and ability necessary to bring about the achievement of a socialist society in the Soviet Union.

The purges were also meant to serve as a distraction and an incentive. The hardships of the plans could be blamed on "wreckers" and Trotskyite conspiracies. People would work even harder and try even more to prove their loyalty out of fear of a midnight visit by the NKVD.

Like the collectivization movement, the purges undoubtedly got out of hand and began to take on a life of their own. Zealous subordinates found it hard to know where to stop. Various individuals, including the future Soviet leader N. S. Khrushchev, climbed over the bodies toward positions of prominence. Possibly Stalin saw that the process was almost out of control and ordered its halt. In any case, in 1938, after the execution of the head of the NKVD, N. I. Yezhov (the purges are also known as the *Yezhovshchina*), the purges ended. Millions languished in the GULAG; the government and party bureaucracies and the military high commands were decimated; and the population of the Soviet Union lived in fear; but the most intensive part of the terror was over.

1939 and the Coming of War

In 1939 Stalin, aware of the Soviet Union's vulnerability, did several things to protect his country's interests. In March 1939 he simultaneously opened the possibility of better relations with Nazi Germany and warned the British and French not to think that the Soviet Union would necessarily pull their "chestnuts out of the fire." Maxim Litvinov, Jewish and married to an Englishwoman, was replaced as Commissar of Foreign Affairs by V. V. Molotov, a move designed also to placate Germany and to warn Britain and France.

As the shift in Soviet policy was becoming apparent, Hitler increased the tension in Europe by smashing Czech sovereignty and establishing a protectorate. This time Hitler had violated an agreement of his own making. At nearly the same time, Hitler put pressure on Poland, this time focusing on the German city of Danzig, which had been made a "free" city by Versailles, and on the Polish Corridor. Somewhat quixotically, Britain and France rushed to guarantee Polish independence. It did not make much sense to support authoritarian Poland after having betrayed democratic Czechoslovakia, but political or military sense was not the point. Rather, the goal was to express the inescapable conclusion that Hitler could not be trusted, that he was not simply another German statesman, that he had to be stopped.

Having gone this far, the British and French seemed unable to take the last step. Part of the difficulty lay with Poland. Although it feared Germany, Poland shrank from allowing Russian troops on its soil. Yet without this, the Soviet Union could do little to aid Poland. Britain and France made their own contributions to the tragi-comedy of the

Unhappy Czechs line the streets of Prague to watch the German army enter the city. The Germans, by occupying Czechoslovakia in March 1939, violated the agreement reached at Munich the year before. **(Wide World Photos)**

summer of 1939. They sent their negotiators to the Soviet Union quite literally on a slow boat and the negotiators, relatively low-ranking, lacked full powers.

In the meantime, Russia and Germany had been moving rapidly toward a major political agreement. In August the German foreign minister, Joachim von Ribbentrop, pressed to be allowed to come to Moscow for conversations. In the last week of August, just when Hitler thought that he might have to postpone the invasion of Poland, Stalin suddenly called Ribbentrop to Moscow and quickly agreed to a Non-Aggression Pact, with a secret protocol dividing Poland and setting out spheres of influence in eastern Europe. In one of those little ironies of history, the British negotiator was winning a tennis tournament at the German Embassy at almost the same time that the Germans and Russians were executing a diplomatic revolution.

The Nazi-Soviet Pact left Hitler free for his little war with Poland. He seems to have expected an easy victory and then for the British and French, unable to do anything, to back off. With Poland in hand, he could then look around for another angle to work. It did not happen that way, of course. The invasion of Poland by Germany on September 1, 1939, touched off a war that lasted six years and left not only Europe but the entire world wondering what civilization had come to.

Suggested Readings

Alan Cassels, *Fascism** (1975)

Eugen Weber, *The Varieties of Fascism** (1964)

Stanley Payne, "Fascism and National Socialism" (The Forum Series, 1975)

Karl-Dietrich Bracher, *The German Dictatorship* (1970)

Henry Ashby Turner, Jr., ed., *Nazism and the Third Reich** (1973)

Daniel Horn, "Adolf Hitler and the Third Reich" (The Forum Series, 1976)

Allan Bullock, *Hitler: A Study in Tyranny** (rev. ed., 1964)

David Schoenbaum, *Hitler's Social Revolution** (1980)

Alan D. Beyerchen, *Scientists under Hitler* (1977)

Edward N. Peterson, *The Limits of Hitler's Power* (1969)

Joachim C. Fest, *Hitler** (1975)

Ivone Kirkpatrick, *Mussolini: A Study in Power* (1964)

Ignazio Silone, *Bread and Wine** (1962)

Joel Colton, *Léon Blum: Humanist in Politics** (1974)

Gabriel Jackson, *The Spanish Republic and the Civil War, 1931-1939** (1965)

Edward E. Malefakis, *Agrarian Reform and Peasant Revolution in Spain: Origins of the Civil War* (1970)

Hugh Thomas, *The Spanish Civil War** (rev. ed., 1965)

Ernest Hemingway, *For Whom the Bell Tolls** (1940)

George Orwell, *Homage to Catalonia** (1969)

Robert Conquest, *The Great Terror: Stalin's Purge of the Thirties* (1968)

_____, *Kolyma: The Arctic Death Camps** (1979)

Vera Dunham, *In Stalin's Time: Middle Class Values in Soviet Fiction** (1976)

Roy Medvedev, *Let History Judge: The Origins and Consequences of Stalinism** (1973)

Nadezhda Mandelstam, *Hope against Hope** (1976)

Arthur Koestler, *Darkness at Noon** (1970)

Adam B. Ulam, *Expansion and Coexistence: The History of Soviet Foreign Policy, 1917-1967** (2nd ed., 1974)

Gordon Craig and Felix Gilbert, eds., *The Diplomats, 1919-1939**, 2 vols. (1963)

Jurgen Gehl, *Austria, Germany and the Anschluss* (1963)

A. J. P. Taylor, *Origins of the Second World War** (1978)

Christopher Thorne, *The Approach of War, 1938-1939** (1969)

Martin Gilbert and Richard Gott, *The Appeasers* (1963)

Telford Taylor, *Munich: The Price of Peace** (1980)

Anthony Adamthwaite, *France and the Coming of the Second World War, 1936-1939* (1977)

Anna M. Ciencala, *Poland and the Western Powers, 1938-1939* (1968)

*indicates paperback edition

8

War, Peace, Cold War, 1939-1949

The ten years of war and diplomacy that began with the invasion of Poland in September 1939 almost completely changed Europe's position vis-á-vis the remainder of the world. From apparent dominance, Europe shrank in the decade to near impotence before the two great powers, the Soviet Union and the United States. Actually, European civilization had been hollowed out by World War I and the two decades that followed it. World War II only confirmed what some had already perceived as the major lesson of World War I: the easy dominance of the rest of the world by Europe had ended.

The momentous string of events that completed the end of European hegemony began with the rapid conquest of Poland by Nazi Germany. The German army made brilliant use of the strategy of *Blitzkrieg* (lightning war). This involved the use of mechanized spearheads of troops, tanks massed in groups, and close tactical support by fighters and dive-bombers. It was a strategy that demanded a rapid and decisive victory. Germany was not prepared for a protracted struggle in 1939. The easy victories of that year and the next led her to believe that she need not prepare. This fundamental misunderstanding of the nature of modern warfare proved fatal over the next few years.

By mid-September, Poland lay prostrate, divided between Germany and the Soviet Union. Under the cover of the secret protocol to the Nazi-Soviet Pact, the Russians had taken the eastern part of Poland as the Germans were smashing resistance in the western part.

A strange interlude followed the flurry of activity in September, the "Phony War." Hitler was undecided about his next move. He had apparently expected Britain and France to accept his offer of peace. The British and the French did not take the offer seriously, but, unprepared for real war, they did not know where to turn either. Only the Soviet Union seemed to know where the next tasks lay. It demanded small bits of territory from Finland to enhance the defenses of Leningrad. The Finns refused and a winter war began which Finland conducted skillfully and victoriously at first. Skill and valor were not enough, however, to offset the massive resources of the Soviet Union. After beating the Finns, the Russians helped themselves to the territories they had originally wanted. They also pressured the Baltic states—Lithuania, Latvia, and Estonia—to accept the status of satellites of the Soviet Union.

Germany returned to the offensive in April 1940, taking over Denmark and Norway in response to a rather muddled Anglo-French effort to seize the initiative in Scandinavia. In May a massive German effort was launched against the Netherlands, Belgium, and France. The Netherlands and Belgium were quickly beaten. The events of May 14 indicated that this war would be even more senselessly brutal than World War I. That day Rotterdam's center was flattened by German bombers, and 40,000 defenseless civilians died.

The Summer of 1940

France crumbled with unexpected quickness after German forces cut through the Franco-British forces to the channel. An allied counterthrust failed, but the allies managed to turn defeat into a kind of victory by evacuating tens of thousands of soldiers at Dunkirk. The remaining allied forces were shattered. By mid-June the French cabinet voted to ask Germany for armistice terms. The armistice was signed on June 22 in the same railroad car in which the Germans had signed the armistice ending World War I.

The fall of France was mainly due to military mistakes. French generals, preparing for the last war instead of the one to come, had emphasized defense, the symbol of which was the Maginot Line. They had largely ignored innovative suggestions from people like Colonel Charles de Gaulle, whose ideas about tank warfare the Germans had closely noted. It may be that some deeply rooted causes existed, too: the dislike which many French felt for the Third Republic, the lack of a clear-cut national purpose, and the paucity of leaders of imagination and daring. Still, while the defeat was "strange," as described by the historian and Resistance hero Marc Bloch, it did not result from treason, but rather from bad judgment and failure of nerve.

In the summer of 1940 only Britain remained to carry on the struggle against Nazi Germany. (Fascist Italy joined Germany in the war against France at the last moment; it was to prove time and again a burden rather than an asset.) Britain was now led by the veteran politician Winston Churchill, Chamberlain having resigned after the Scandinavian debacle. Churchill became the man to match the hour. More than any other single individual, he has been associated with World War II and generally with its finest moments. By both his oratory and his pragmatic leadership, Churchill kept Britain going through the war.

The hour could not have been darker that summer. Hitler engaged in planning for an invasion of Britain while Marshal Hermann Goering, commander of the Luftwaffe, sent his planes to prepare the way. The British responded by evacuating urban areas, organizing air raid defense systems, and, of course, by sending up squadrons of Spitfires and Hurricanes. By fall they had forced Goering to call a halt to his attempts to bomb England into submission.

Several factors help to explain British success. Perhaps the most important factor was the nature of the Luftwaffe and the way in which it was commanded. It was designed more for tactical support of offensives than for bombing runs. The German bombers were slow and the Luftwaffe found it difficult to maintain adequate fighter protection. Even more damaging was the fact that Goering, improvising without a clear plan of attack, changed targets from the air defenses in the south to the planes of the Royal Air Force (RAF) to the terror bombing of London. Had the Luftwaffe concentrated on destroying the RAF on the ground, they might have won. The British, for their part, had just recently put into production new, improved versions of Hurricanes and Spitfires that gave them an advantage in one-on-one combat. British scientists had contributed, too, with their work on radar which made it generally possible for the RAF to have a crucial few minutes warning. Victory in the Battle of Britain was enormously important psychologically for Britain. Victory in the war still seemed almost impossibly out of reach, but at least defeat had been averted for the near future.

Operation Barbarossa

Germany, primarily because of her defeat in the Battle of Britain, decided against attempting an invasion of Britain. Possibly Hitler thought that the British would eventually accept peace terms. Probably he and his advisers realized that the odds against success were unacceptable. In any case, he had already been thinking about invading the Soviet Union. With no good possibility of defeating England soon, Hitler turned east. Operation Barbarossa was set for late spring, 1941. Looking back on the decision, it may seem odd that Germany would dare to take on a country of such vast resources and manpower. Ideologically, of course, the decision accorded with some of Hitler's pronouncements in *Mein Kampf*. And, Germany had traditionally gone east to expand. This was where Hitler intended to find *Lebensraum*, space for a rapidly growing Germany. In addition, the Slavs were second only to the Jews as objects of Hitler's hatred. They were "subhuman," fit only to serve as slaves in the Third Reich. Practical considerations also weighed heavily. The Soviet Union seemed still disorganized by the purges and the five-year plans. It would only be stronger as time went on. It was already beginning to take action and make claims that conflicted with Germany's interests in central and eastern Europe.

Before the invasion, Germany made a few efforts to secure her flanks. Hitler traveled to Hendaye to talk with Franco about the alliance of Spain with the Axis. Spain, for all the favors that the Nationalists owed the Axis, declined. Germany was indifferent to efforts by leaders in Marshal Phillippe Pétain's government in Vichy, France, to discuss where France might fit into the "New Order." (Germany occupied northern and western France, including the Atlantic and Channel coastlines; a nominally independent French government, sitting in the resort town of Vichy, had responsibility for government in the somewhat smaller southern and eastern portion of France.) Germany could already take what it wanted from the occupied part of France. If it needed more, it could put pressure on the unoccupied part, Vichy. There was no need yet to make Vichy a regular part of the New Order. Germany was more interested in bringing states in central Europe into its orbit, such as Hungary and Rumania. It also found it necessary to bail out its ally Italy in Greece. This last task caused a slight but significant delay of the invasion of Russia.

The invasion, which began in June 1941, was even more successful than the German strategists had hoped. The Russian military, which had been kept from making adequate preparations for a possible invasion by Stalin's fearful insistence on adhering fully to the terms of the Nazi-Soviet Pact, was caught off guard. Whole armies collapsed and were cut off. Attempts to retreat and regroup turned into routs. Stalin fell completely apart and sank into a deep depression. He was not heard from for weeks. Within a short time, Leningrad was besieged, German troops were advancing toward Moscow, and most of the rich croplands and important industrial complexes of the Ukraine had been taken.

Yet the Soviet Union did not surrender. She had lost millions of soldiers, but she followed traditions of old, giving ground and slowly bringing to bear her enormous resources. Stalin returned to leadership and called on the patriotism of the masses. The Russian Orthodox Church was pressed into service. Able young leaders appeared in the military, government, and party.

Not only the resilience of the Russian people but even the weather had a hand in slowing the German advance. Winter came early in 1941 and the Germans were totally unprepared for winter warfare. As before, they had counted on quick victory. They had come close to getting it, but had failed largely because Hitler insisted that the military attempt three major campaigns simultaneously: against Leningrad in the north, Moscow in the center, and the Ukraine in the south. Errors of logistics and strategy were compounded by errors of tactics. Rather than regroup and establish winter quarters, Hitler demanded that the army push on until in some cases major units were cut off and lost. By the end of 1941, the Soviet Union had only a precarious lease on life, but it had stopped the German army short of victory.

The fatal flaw in Nazi strategy had begun to appear. War-making, like politics, had been a matter of improvisation and intense but short-term efforts. Neither the German economy nor society had been mobilized for the kind of prolonged warfare that World War II came to demand. Germany had learned nothing from its victories. Other nations, Britain and the Soviet Union, had been forced by disastrous defeats to accept the fact that only an extensive, long-term effort could possibly bring them victory. Their potential was in some ways less than Germany's but they utilized it more effectively.

In the last month of 1941, as the Germans prepared for a hard winter, the United States was catapulted into war by the Japanese attack on Pearl Harbor. American aid to the British and Russians, who had themselves immediately allied in the wake of the German

invasion of the Soviet Union, was limited at first mainly to supplies
and money, but the knowledge that the resources of the United States
were being thrown into the conflict had a tremendous impact on the
morale of her European allies.

Stalingrad and D-Day

In 1942 two important questions were asked. The first concerned
whether the Russians could hold Stalingrad, a city on the Volga
River which was important for reasons of strategy and prestige. The
other question had to do with the establishment of a second front by
Britain and the United States.

Hitler insisted that the German army capture Stalingrad at any
cost. The Russians began to believe that they might lose the war if
they lost the city. Not only was it named for their leader, but it was
also a gateway to the area beyond the Volga. It would be difficult to
make another stand short of the Ural mountains.

The fighting was carried on block by block and then house by
house. In the latter part of 1942 the Russians launched a pincers
movement that cut off a large German force. The Germans were
unable to re-establish contact with the cut-off troops. Finally, in
February 1943, even though Hitler had given orders not to surrender,
about one hundred thousand troops did, one third the original number
of invaders.

The Russian victory at Stalingrad was the turning point of the war
in Europe. In the campaigns of 1943 the Soviet Union began steadily
pushing German troops back on all fronts. By 1944 they had relieved
the siege of Leningrad and were nearing various capitals in eastern
Europe.

During this time the Russians had pressed for a second front in
Europe to ease some of the burden they were shouldering. The
United States, however, was preoccupied by the war against Japan in
Asia. Britain spent most of 1942 dealing with General Erwin Rommel,
the "Desert Fox," in Libya and Egypt. The best that the allies could
do in the way of a second front in 1942 was the occupation of French
North Africa. It was as much a diplomatic as a military maneuver in
that the area was nominally controlled by Vichy France. The allies
risked the possibility that Germany would sweep the Vichy regime
aside or force it to join Germany as an active combatant in retaliation
for the invasion.

The Soviet Union was not satisfied with the occupation of French
North Africa. Nor was it satisfied the following year with the Anglo-

American invasion of Sicily and the Italian mainland. The invasion took Italy out of the war when the Fascist Grand Council deposed Mussolini. Considerable numbers of German troops were committed to the defense of Italy. These troops and the mountainous terrain meant that the campaign up the peninsula was difficult and bloody. For the Soviet Union it was not the diversion that they sought.

Only in June 1944, on D-Day, did the Soviet Union get something like what it had wanted all along. The landings on the beaches of Normandy by American, British, and Free French forces were as much a feat of logistics as anything else. Simply to amass and coordinate the equipment and men needed was achievement enough. Then to wait for the right combination of weather and tides, and to prevent the German intelligence services from discerning the nature of preparations, constituted an even more formidable task. The war still had almost a year to run at this point, but Germany was now caught between the vise formed by the two main armies of its opponents.

Home Fronts

Germany lost the war because it did not make a commitment to an all-out effort until it was too late. Throughout 1941 this kind of commitment seemed unnecessary. Quick victories made it possible to re-equip the German military without placing much strain on the civilian economy. Occupied countries had the tops of their economies skimmed off for the German war effort. When the Soviet Union did not collapse in 1942, however, it became apparent that something had to be done to coordinate the economy for military purposes. Goering made efforts in this direction, as did army personnel. The major effort, however, was that made by Albert Speer, who reorganized the German economy to the extent possible given the existence of a virtual state within a state in Himmler's S.S. The S.S. used vital resources for its own purposes, purposes that often had little to do with the war effort. Nevertheless, production of munitions and weapons tripled over the next two years under Speer, even when allied air raids began punishing German cities at will. Germany had not begun soon enough, however. She quickly began running out of raw materials and manpower, and in 1945 production declined rapidly.

Germany could never have matched the enormous productive capacity of the United States in any case, but she failed even to make the best of what she had. Britain, on the other hand, worked to organize her resources and to transform a peacetime economy into one fully mobilized for war. Using experience from World War I, Churchill reorganized the War Cabinet and within it turned over direction of the economy to a small ministerial group called the Lord President's Committee. From 1940 on, Britons suffered materially from the war, but this was borne by most with good grace in the realization that it was necessary and in the expectation that the postwar period would usher in a new social order, equitable if not egalitarian.

The Soviet Union had the advantage of a tightly-controlled command economy from the beginning. Even before the war, it had been engaged in shifting industry to the east. At the outbreak of war, entire plants were dismantled, relocated, and put back into production in a matter of weeks. Until 1943 Germany controlled large amounts of Russian farmland and significant parts of industry. As the German army retreated, it destroyed as much as possible. Still, the Soviet Union, with American aid and a population completely mobilized for the war effort, built up productive capacity. The standard of living for the individual Russian dipped even below the previous lows reached in the days of the Civil War or the early 1930s, but the war effort was sustained.

Behind the successful war effort stood the enormous resources of the United States, its productive capacity freed from the Depression by the demands of war. The war cost the United States a great deal in both men and money, but it also made it the richest and most powerful country in the world.

Collaboration and Resistance

Germany exploited occupied Europe in order to ease the burden of war on its people. Countries paid enormous amounts in "occupation costs," a disguised tribute. Various groups were brought to Germany to serve as forced laborers, including more than a million Poles and a large number of the five million Russian prisoners. Later in the war laborers were drawn from the Low Countries and from France.

At no point did the Third Reich attempt to use to advantage the possibilities for constructing a "New Order" in Europe. Those who wanted to collaborate with Germany were forced to do so under extremely disadvantageous conditions. Some groups, the Ukrainian nationalists for example, who were eager to help in the destruction of the Soviet regime, were treated so badly that they had no choice but to resist the Nazis.

In occupied Europe there were resistance movements as well as efforts at collaboration. It was difficult at times to draw clear distinctions between the two. For example, where did the state functionary draw the line between doing his duty, which might include services vital to the welfare of the people in his country, and aiding the German war effort? This was the essential dilemma of those who governed Vichy France. It was later argued by Pierre Laval, premier during much of the existence of Vichy, that his policies were necessary in order to keep the German occupation at a distance. It was better for Vichy to supervise the recruiting of workers for labor in the German war industry than to turn this task over to the Germans themselves. Similarly, Laval argued that it was important for the French police to function as fully as possible, even if this meant cooperating in the process of tracking down Jews or in the efforts to deal with the Resistance movement.

Not many of those involved in Vichy could be accurately labeled as fascists. Most were conservatives who practiced collaboration because it seemed unavoidable. At first, between June 1940 and April 1942, members of the Vichy government believed that they were carrying out a "National Revolution" which would replace the shopworn values and institutions of the Third Republic with something far better. Nazi Germany, however, allowed little scope for movements of regeneration. By 1943, Pétain, Laval, and the rest of Vichy found it possible to do only what Germany allowed or required them to do. What had possibly been a sensible policy in the shock of defeat in 1940 had become by 1943 and 1944, through a series of almost imperceptible changes, no longer justifiable.

Elsewhere in occupied Europe there was even less possibility than in Vichy of convincing oneself that one was engaged in working out a national regeneration within the context of the German occupation. The pressure to conform, to supply food, workers for the factories, and Jews for the death camps, was too great. Here and there efforts were made to save the young men and the Jewish population of a country. One of the best known efforts was that made to save the Frank family in Amsterdam. It failed, but the diary left behind by Anne Frank has inspired millions in the years since its publication. Some countries did a better job of protecting their populations than others. Denmark was extraordinarily successful in hiding its Jewish population. Somewhat ironically, the record of Fascist Italy was also quite good in this respect.

The organized resistance movements in Europe have often been romanticized and exaggerated. There is a poignant scene in Marcel Orphul's documentary on Vichy, "The Sorrow and the Pity," in which a man talks about being a part of the resistance: he had kept a gun hidden under a woodpile throughout the war. This was, of course, dangerous in that he might have been shot had the gun been dis- covered, but it meant, in reality, that his role in the Resistance had been played out only in his mind, and probably after the fact at that. This was the case for many who, once the war had ended, repressed any instance of collaboration and blew up all out of proportion any- thing that might be interpreted as resistance. For those who played an active part, there was always the question of whether it did any good. Again, there was a moral ambiguity involved. Did it accomplish anything and was it "right" in any sense of the word to ambush and kill a few German soldiers returning to their camp from the cinema, especially when reprisals might result in the deaths of dozens of innocent people?

Much that was of crucial importance was accomplished by the resistance movements, of course. They furnished intelligence, helped downed pilots and escaped prisoners of war, and, in some cases, severely hampered the German war effort. The most successful re- sistance movement in the war was that led by the Yugoslav partisan, Tito. In a three-cornered struggle with the conservative Yugoslav Chetniks and the Germans, Tito's partisans were able to defeat the other two and to liberate Yugoslavia largely without outside aid. This furnished the basis for some crucial developments in eastern Europe after the war.

Whatever the evaluation of the effectiveness of resistance move- ments during the war, there is no question that they left important legacies to the postwar world. Communists dominated or played important roles in most movements because of their previous expe- rience with underground work. Even the noncommunists among resistance workers tended to reject the old order, which they held responsible for the problems of the 1930s and the war itself, and to look to different ways of organizing society, politics, and the econ- omy. Various resistance "charters" such as the Charter of the National Council of Resistance in France provided guidelines for postwar reconstruction programs.

The tendency to romanticize resistance has been especially notice- able in Germany. A great deal has been made of the circles, composed largely of military officers and aristocrats, which eventually were led to attempt the assassination of Hitler. By 1943 there was a growing realization within these circles that Hitler's plans and directives were leading Germany to disaster. There was also a growing uneasiness about the activities of the S.S. and the Gestapo. The efforts to assas- sinate Hitler and stage a coup were delayed in part by the reluctance of some to break the oath of loyalty sworn to Hitler as the supreme commander and by fears for the integrity of Germany after the coup. Most of those involved in the plot, because of their social background and political orientation, did not envision Germany as changing much. They certainly did not want to open the way to a victory by the Allied Powers.

Various attempts on Hitler's life failed. The effort of July 20, 1944 nearly worked, leaving Hitler wounded but alive. Since the plotters thought he had been killed, they put the machinery of the coup into action. Goebbels, in Berlin, refused to believe the reports of Hitler's death and kept the coup contained until information could be obtained that confirmed that Hitler was in fact still alive. The failure of the plot resulted in the virtual destruction of the German resistance movement.

The Holocaust

While some Germans had been occupied with the need to assassinate Hitler and take over the government, other Germans had been active in planning a program of genocide. One of the major points in the Nazi program was anti-Semitism. In the 1930s this had been expressed mostly in measures designed to shut German Jews out of public life and, where possible, to force them to emigrate. After the war began, millions of additional Jews were brought under the control of Nazi Germany. At first, continued thought was given to emigration. Then efforts were made to create large ghettos into which Jews from across Europe would be packed. The S.S., experimenting with various ideas about racial purity, tried diverse methods of killing large numbers of people, Jews and others, in Russia. Although thousands were murdered in one fashion or another in the first years of the war, no organized, coordinated efforts were made until after the Wannsee Conference in January 1942. At this conference in a suburb of Berlin, leading officials of the Third Reich approved a plan presented by Reinhard Heydrich, an official in the S.S., for the assembly-line destruction of the Jewish race by gassing. Six killing centers were established in Poland, the largest at Auschwitz and Treblinka. Trains came from all over Europe to Auschwitz, which was also attached to an industrial complex. From the trains people walked down a road to the main gate where they were separated into those headed for the gas chambers and those headed for the labor camp. The operation was run with a grotesque efficiency, a terrible parody of a rationalized industrial enterprise. The group taken to the gas chambers was told

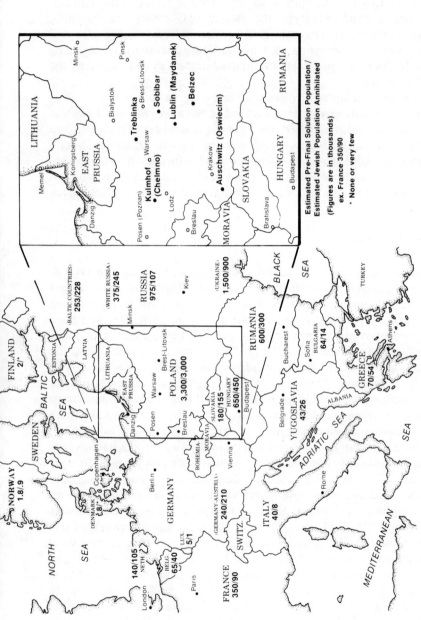

The "Final Solution." During World War II, the Nazi government in Germany made a deliberate effort to annihilate the Jewish population of Europe. The inset shows the location of the Nazi "Death Camps," where Jews, gypsies, and others whom the Nazis considered undesirable were murdered with industrial efficiency.

Map labels (main map):

NORWAY 1.8/.9
FINLAND 2/*
SWEDEN
NORTH SEA
BALTIC SEA
DENMARK
Copenhagen
.8/.1
(BALTIC COUNTRIES)
253/228
ESTONIA
LATVIA
(WHITE RUSSIA) 375/245
RUSSIA 975/107
Minsk
LITHUANIA
EAST PRUSSIA
Danzig
NETH. 140/105
BELG. 65/40
LUX. 5/1
London
Paris
GERMANY
Berlin
Posen
Warsaw
Brest-Litovsk
POLAND 3.300/3.000
Breslau
BOHEMIA
MORAVIA 180/155
SWITZ.
(GERMANY-AUSTRIA) 240/210
Vienna
Budapest
SLOVAKIA
HUNGARY 650/450
Kiev
(UKRAINE) 1.500/900
RUMANIA 600/300
Bucharest
BLACK SEA
FRANCE 350/90
ITALY 40/8
Rome
YUGOSLAVIA 43/26
Belgrade
ADRIATIC SEA
ALBANIA
BULGARIA 64/14
Sofia
GREECE 70/54
Athens
TURKEY
MEDITERRANEAN SEA

Map labels (inset):

Minsk
Pinsk
LITHUANIA
Konigsberg
Memel
Danzig
EAST PRUSSIA
Bialystok
Brest-Litovsk
Treblinka
Warsaw
Sobibar
Lublin (Maydanek)
Belzec
Posen (Poznan)
Kulmhof (Chelmno)
Lodz
Krakow
Auschwitz (Oswiecim)
Breslau
MORAVIA
SLOVAKIA
Bratislava
HUNGARY
Budapest
RUMANIA

Estimated Pre-Final Solution Population/
Estimated Jewish Population Annihilated

(Figures are in thousands)
ex. France 350/90

* None or very few

that it would first go to the showers, then receive new clothing and further instructions. The gas chambers were constructed to resemble showers, but it did not take long to understand what was happening. Death came quickly, but in the moments beforehand people experienced panic and intense agony. Evidence of this still exists in the grooves and marks clawed into the concrete ceiling and walls of the chambers.

Efforts were made to run the killing centers as productive enterprises. Anything of value was collected and stored—mounds of human hair, warehouses full of shoes, handbags, and dresses. The economic irrationality was all too apparent. In the midst of a war effort beginning to go badly for Germany, vital resources were being squandered for the purposes of slaughter. The moral dilemma for those involved in the process was acute. Some ignored it, comforting themselves with the idea that the victims of the death camps were not fully human. Others insisted that they were only following orders. A few might do what they could to help individuals, but felt powerless to do anything on a large scale. Protest or failure to act would not help; it could only lead to their own death. Even for those who were inmates of concentration camps and the killing centers, moral dilemmas existed. Some survived by losing every shred of humanity and by taking part in crimes against their fellow prisoners. Much has also been made of the inmates' passivity, of their failute to do anything to protest or prevent their deaths. It would be fairer, however, to point out that the Holocaust, like other extreme experiences which people have endured, brought out both the best and the worst in people. There was resistance, protest, sacrifice, and selflessness, just as there was passivity, wishful thinking, opportunism, and selfishness. People responded in a great diversity of ways, as they always do. It was the scale of the Holocaust and the cold-bloodedness with which it was carried out that set it apart. Six million Jews were killed, approximately two thirds the prewar Jewish population. Most of those killed had come from Poland (3 million) and the Soviet Union (1.5 million), but sizable groups had also come from Hungary, Rumania, and Germany (see Map p. 170).

Yalta and Potsdam

The Holocaust now seems like a central element in any consideration of the nature and impact of World War II, but in the minds of those working in 1944 and 1945 to establish the bases of the postwar world, it was a relatively unimportant factor, even when there was some conception of the dimensions of the event. Uppermost in the minds of the leaders of the Allied Powers was the war in the Pacific. By the fall of 1944 it was apparent that the German Reich was doomed. Planners thought that the war in the Pacific might easily continue another year or more, resulting in a million casualties for the allies. A second crucial consideration involved political arrangements for European countries that had been either belligerents or occupied territories. In many cases it seemed impossible to return to the boundaries of 1938 or 1939, and out of the question to allow some regimes to continue in power unaltered.

All the above concerns were voiced by the representatives of the Soviet Union, the United States, and Britain when they gathered at Yalta in February 1945. Prior to the Yalta meeting, the foreign ministers of the three nations had met in October 1943 in Moscow, to talk in general terms about forcing Germany to accept unconditional surrender and about their determination to cooperate after the war in a United Nations organization. The leaders of the three states, Churchill, Stalin, and Roosevelt, had then met the following month in Teheran, Iran (then occupied by Soviet troops). Although many topics were discussed, the major decision taken at Teheran was the firm promise of a second front in France in 1944.

The meeting at Yalta has often been viewed as either a failure of American diplomacy or a triumph of Russian duplicity. It should be viewed as neither, but rather as an agreement that made sense in the context of the times, yet also one that was badly flawed by misunderstandings. In part the agreements were shaped by the desire to involve the Soviet Union more fully in the war in the Pacific. This represented a considerable concession on the part of the Soviet Union in that it had borne the brunt of allied efforts in the war in Europe. The major problem, however, concerned eastern Europe and Russian interests there. Beginning with the Nazi-Soviet Pact, the Soviet Union had worked consistently to make sure that the states along her western borders were sympathetic to her interests and non-threatening to her security. A major focus of concern was Poland. The Soviet Union anticipated that the postwar government of Poland, while not necessarily communist, would be friendly toward the Soviet Union and willing to accede to its wishes, including incorporation by the Soviet Union of territory that had been disputed by the two states between the wars. The Soviet Union believed that it had a natural right to act in its interests and was encouraged in this belief first by the Anglo-American occupation of Italy, in which policies based on American and British institutions and values were set up, and secondly, by the "percentages deal" in October 1944 between Churchill and Stalin. In this deal most of central and southeastern Europe was divided into areas in which the Soviet Union or Britain would have predominant influence. Problems came later when the Soviet view, pragmatic and hard–nosed, began to clash with the American view, also pragmatic but somewhat colored by ideals drawn from documents such as the *Atlantic Charter*, which had been issued by President Franklin D. Roosevelt and Churchill in 1941. Part of the difficulty was due to the way phrases such as "free elections" and "democratic governments" were interpreted. To the Soviet Union, an election was not free nor a government democratic if the result was a state hostile to its interests.

A final major issue concerned plans for Germany after the war. Proposals to destroy German industrial capacity were not accepted, but it was agreed that reparations could be extracted from Germany, from both current production and facilities. It was further agreed that the country and its major city, Berlin, were to be divided into four sectors, each to be run by one of the occupying powers (including France) but all to cooperate economically. The seeds of a number of disputes were contained in the discussions on the fate of Germany.

Between Yalta and the next meeting of the allied leaders at Potsdam the war in Europe ended. By February 1945 the Russians were within fifty miles of Berlin. In March the Americans crossed the Rhine, the last major obstacle to the conquest of Germany. In the latter part of April, American and Russian troops met on the Elbe River. On April 30 Hitler committed suicide in his bunker in Berlin. It was left up to the German military commanders to surrender early in May to the allied forces.

At Potsdam in July 1945, the Allies dealt with an entirely different set of circumstances. First, the war was nearing its close. It had, of course, already ended in Europe. Its end in the Pacific now seemed only a matter of weeks. A second change had to do with leadership. Stalin continued to speak for the Soviet Union, but Harry Truman, inexperienced but astute, had replaced Roosevelt when the latter died shortly after Yalta. The British did not know until the conference was underway who their representative would be. The elections brought a stunning defeat to Churchill and the Conservatives and victory to Clement Atlee and the Labour Party. Finally, by the time the Allies assembled at Potsdam, a number of serious differences of opinion had begun to surface, particularly the composition of the Polish govern-

Inmates of the Nazi concentration camp at Buchenwald just after the American army had liberated the camp. This photograph is by one of the most famous photographers of the war, Margaret Bourke White. (Wide World Photos)

ment and the administration of Germany. Again, it was largely a question of misunderstandings. The Soviet Union would not tolerate a Polish government unreceptive to her ideas about the reordering of eastern Europe. She saw nothing wrong with installing a government that she had sponsored and largely excluding a government put forth by Britain. It was, the Soviet Union believed, similar to what the United States was doing in Italy and Britain in Greece. Problems were beginning to appear in the administration of Germany as well. The Soviet Union was starting a policy of wholesale confiscation of material and facilities in her zone and the other zones. The United States feared that this would lead to the economic collapse of Germany and necessitate greatly expanded American aid.

Truman's approach to these problems was altogether different from Roosevelt's. He took a much more aggressive stance. Whereas Roosevelt had sometimes been as suspicious of British imperialism as of Russian communism, Truman mainly distrusted the Russians. There is a question as to whether Truman's blunt approach shaded into out-and-out bullying based on the American monopoly of the atomic bomb. Truman timed the announcement that the United States possessed the bomb for maximum effect, but there is no evidence that he sought to use atomic blackmail. It would not have worked in any case. Stalin took the announcement in his stride and seemed to have been unperturbed by the implications of the American atomic monopoly.

Since the details of the treaties with Germany and her allies were yet to be worked out in the period after Potsdam, it would not be correct to say that either Potsdam or Yalta created conditions in which an allied falling-out was inevitable. What the meeting did was to strain the wartime alliance, already tried by the questions of a second front and by rumors of secret negotiations by each of the allies with the Germans. A volatile situation was created which, bit by bit, led to a series of crises in 1947 and 1948 and to the beginnings of the Cold War.

The Crisis Years of 1947 and 1948

In 1946 there was as yet no cold war. The wartime alliance still functioned through such means as the meetings of the allies' foreign ministers. Some hopeful beginnings had been made in establishing a new system of world politics in the creation of the United Nations in 1945. Still, incidents that fanned the flames of suspicion continued: the United States rather abruptly cut off lend-lease aid to the Soviet Union; it "lost" an application from the Soviet Union for a five-billion-dollar loan; it criticized Soviet activities in eastern Europe. The Soviet Union, for its part, created distrust by the active role that the Red Army played in the politics of Hungary, Rumania, and other states. Its presence in northern Iran appeared to be a prelude to a communist coup that would capture that state's vast oil reserve for the Soviet Union. Churchill spoke of the "iron curtain," the veil of secrecy that hid the Soviet Union from the West and kept Western influence from the Soviet Union.

The first year of the Cold War was 1947, the year in which World War II was replaced by a tense situation that threatened to lead directly to World War III, which many viewed as being the same as the end of civilization. The immediate origins of the Cold War lay in the situation in Turkey and Greece. Turkey had been pressured by the Soviet Union and there appeared to be some danger that outside forces would attempt to take over the country. In Greece, where the British had worked to reinstate the monarchy despite its lack of popularity, a civil war was tearing the country apart. Britain no longer had the resources by 1947 to continue propping up the Greek monarchy. Victory by the communist movement in Greece appeared imminent. The Truman Doctrine was addressed to both situations. Speaking to Congress in March 1947, Truman proclaimed American willingness to help any government threatened by invasion from without or subversion from within. Though the Soviet Union was not specifically mentioned, the Truman Doctrine was widely regarded as an expression of hostility to Russia and to the communist movement in general. It was, in effect, the initial event of the Cold War.

Three months after Truman's speech, General George C. Marshall, at that time Secretary of State, announced in a Harvard commencement address America's willingness to provide vast sums of money for the reconstruction of Europe. Almost immediately, the Marshall Plan came to be viewed as an economic instrument of Cold War policy. The original intention had been to include all European countries. The Soviet Union, Poland, and Czechoslovakia sent representatives to the initial meeting held to discuss the workings of the plan. The Soviet Union quickly became convinced that it was simply a means whereby the United States could gain control of the European economies and later dictate their policies as well. She withdrew from further participation and pressured states on her borders to boycott the plan.

By the end of 1947 the major elements of the Cold War were falling into place. In September the Communist Information Bureau (Cominform) was formed, headquartered at first in Belgrade. This was viewed as a direct successor to the Comintern and as evidence that a monolithic communist movement, controlled by Moscow and dedicated to the subversion of democratic governments everywhere, existed. Even more serious, the communist parties in France and Italy were expelled from the respective coalitions that had governed each country right after the war, and the communists led party members and trade union militants out in general strikes in 1947 and 1948.

The wreckage that was Berlin at the end of World War II. In the left center of the photograph are the ruins of the Reichstag building. (Wide World Photos)

This seemed an even clearer indication of Russian efforts to encourage revolution.

The Two Germanies

During all this time the Allied Powers found themselves growing farther apart in their ideas about the administration of occupied Germany. The Soviet Union had set out to strip its zone of raw materials and factories. It also exercised its rights to take reparations in kind from the other zones. At first, the French also followed a policy of extracting reparations from their zone. They began to see, however, as the British and Americans already had, that it was not to their advantage to destroy the German economy if this meant that later they would have to send food, goods, and money back into Germany to prevent social unrest and instability. The American zone was closed in 1946 to Russian efforts to extract reparations and the British and Americans began to move toward consolidation of their zones. In each zone an effort was made to carry out a program of de-Nazification, demilitarization, and democratization, but the programs were only partially successful. The zones were effectively demilitarized, but the process of de-Nazification moved slowly. Many of the higher-ranking Nazis escaped trial because of the often cumbersome process, which was aimed at combing through the entire population. Efforts were made as well to find responsible Germans, untainted by association with the Nazis, for positions of leadership. One such person was Konrad Adenauer, former Lord Mayor of Cologne, then already seventy-seven years old. Elections on the local level were held. While the Russians followed many of the same policies as the other allies, they viewed British and American efforts with some suspicion. These seemed to be aimed at putting Germany back together again without first effectively destroying the threat of National Socialism.

In 1946 the British and Americans agreed to the economic fusion of their zones into an entity known as "Bizonia." France and the Soviet Union were invited to join, but did not. The next year, the Council of Foreign Ministers of the Big Four met twice unsuccessfully and by 1948 disagreement over the quadripartite administration of Germany reached the flashpoint. Two distinct zones were being created. "Bizonia" served as the nucleus of one; the Soviet Union worked to change its zone into a separate economic and political unit. After the three western powers announced the introduction of currency reforms, a necessary prelude to economic recovery and the functioning of the zones as an economic unit, the Soviet Union closed down rail and road traffic between Berlin and the west. The Berlin blockade, and the Berlin airlift that countered it, continued over the next thirteen months as the most visible sign of increasing Cold War tension.

In the next several months, the division between east Germany, organized as the German Democratic Republic (DDR), and west Germany, the Federal Republic of Germany (BRD), was set. West Germany began to move from the status of former enemy to that of potential ally to the western powers.

The Cold War Launched

By 1949 the postwar world had taken on ominous outlines. In addition to the quarrel over Germany and its division into two distinct states, there was the phenomenon of rapidly tightening Soviet control of eastern Europe. This was symbolized most vividly by the Czech coup in February 1948, when the Czech foreign minister, Jan

Masaryk, son of the founder of the Republic, died in a mysterious fall from his office window and the democratic government was replaced by one dominated by the communists. Czechoslovakia had been up to that time a sign of hope that a democratic, freely-elected government might be able to coexist with the Soviet Union. Elsewhere the picture was even bleaker. The Chinese Communists took control of the mainland from the Chinese Nationalists. The French were fighting a losing war in Indochina with the Viet Minh, a nationalist coalition heavily influenced by the communists. And in Korea, the communist state of North Korea prepared to launch an invasion of the American-sponsored South Korean state the following year.

The American response to all this was the formation of the North Atlantic Treaty Organization (NATO) in 1949 and a search for additional allies in other parts of the world. The United States viewed the Soviet Union as the center of a vast, monolithic communist movement bent on subversion of democratic governments everywhere. Europe remained the center of concern, but the United States began to see conspiracies and dangers in every part of the world. American policy also began to shift from the idea of containment—confining communism to areas already under its influence—to the idea of rollback, a crusade to free nations from communist systems of government.

The Soviet Union, however, believed itself to be weak and vulnerable. In the late 1940s it was desperate to gain security. Its tightening grip on eastern Europe was one effort. Its policies toward its zone in Germany, which betrayed an almost irrational fear of German potential, was another. It viewed the United States as an immensely wealthy, powerful, and hypocritical nation, denying the Soviet Union what was important to its security but reserving for itself the right to act as it saw fit. The Soviet Union, paradoxically, feared revolution, too. Anything that disturbed the status quo was dangerous. This was a major reason for its quarrel with Yugoslavia, which had tried to make the Cominform into a truly revolutionary organization. The other was Tito's independence in terms of doctrine and policy, an independence that Stalin could not tolerate.

Europe was divided by 1949 into two hostile camps. The Soviet Union controlled eastern Europe. It had incorporated once again the three Baltic states, Estonia, Lithuania, and Latvia. It had also taken considerable territory from Poland (which was compensated by territory taken from Germany) and Rumania. Under its control were several satellite states: the German Democratic Republic, Poland,

Czechoslovakia, Hungary, Rumania, and Bulgaria. The United States influenced western Europe, especially through the economic aid that it provided through the Marshall Plan. It never attempted, however, to dictate policy and to dominate affairs as the Soviet Union was doing. Between the camps were three nations. Finland sought to avoid offending the Soviet Union and escaped the imposition of satellite status. Austria was still occupied by the four powers. Yugoslavia was beginning the difficult task of balancing between east and west and thereby following its own course.

Outside Europe, in addition to the struggle between the two antagonistic blocs, Europeans faced the necessity of dealing with colonial liberation movements. By 1949 the British had already taken the first major step in dismantling the empire on which the sun never set by granting India and Pakistan independence; the Dutch had been forced to grant independence to Indonesia; and the French were losing ground in the war in Indochina. In every colonial area in Africa and Asia liberation movements were being formed or expanded, and pressures put on the European colonial powers to give way peacefully or face rebellion.

The European colonial powers found it difficult in the aftermath of World War II to recognize and deal constructively with the desires of the various colonial populations for greater self-government or for independence. The French, for example, clashed with Algerian nationalists in May 1945, with the result that over one thousand Algerians were killed. Most European countries sought to regain or to maintain control over their colonies in order to utilize their resources in the reconstruction of the mother country. Then, too, for those countries defeated and humiliated in World War II, re-establishment of the empire was a matter of national pride and honor.

The loss of some colonial possessions and the difficulties involved in holding on to others, along with the realization that the major directions of world events were being charted outside Europe, in the Soviet Union and the United States, combined to make the struggle to deal with the chaos of postwar Europe even more difficult. Europeans, however, were determined not simply to recover from the effects of war but also to build a future free of the defects of the past. Recovery alone was a formidable task. The war had caused enormous physical destruction. Unlike World War I, destruction was not confined to the front lines or to the paths taken by advancing and retreating armies. It included most of the major cities of Europe. Warsaw, Berlin, Vienna, Rotterdam were in ruins. Many other cities were badly damaged. Roads, railroads, and bridges were destroyed throughout Europe. At least thirty million people had died; more than ten million former prisoners of war, forced laborers, displaced persons, and former inmates of concentration camps were without homes. Food, fuel, and raw materials for factories were lacking.

The governments of the various European states, in the first years after the war nearly always broad coalition governments including communists, socialists, and democrats, were faced with enormous economic and social problems which the political issues of the cold war and anti-colonialism greatly exacerbated. As it turned out, Europe had the resources necessary for its recovery (although American help certainly made the process easier). It could also hope to provide an alternative to paths marked out by the United States and the Soviet Union. It would in any case play an important role in the postwar world. However, the long, continuous expansion of power and influence within the world was over. The imperial dynamism that had characterized Europe since the sixteenth century and reached an apogee around 1900 no longer existed. A new era was beginning, one filled with new challenges and opportunities for European civilization.

Suggested Readings

John C. Cairns, "Consequences of World War II in Europe" (The Forum Series, 1977)

Gordon Wright, *The Ordeal of Total War, 1939-1945** (1968)

Winston S. Churchill, *The Second World War*, 6 vols. (1948-1953)

Alan S. Milward, *War, Economy, and Society, 1939-1945** (1977)

Leila J. Rupp, *Mobilizing Women for War, 1939-1945* (1978)

Marc Bloch, *Strange Defeat** (1968)

Percy Ernst Schramm, *Hitler: The Man and the Military Leader** (1971)

Alan S. Milward, *The German Economy at War* (1965)

Albert Seaton, *The Russo-German War* (1971)

Alexander Dallin, *German Rule in Russia, 1941-1945* (1957)

Alexander Werth, *Russia at War, 1941-1945* (1964)

John A. Armstrong, ed., *Soviet Partisans in World War II* (1964)

Robert O. Paxton, *Vichy France: Old Guard and New Order, 1940-1944** (1975)

Charles de Gaulle, *The Complete War Memoirs of Charles de Gaulle** (1967)

Henri Michel, *The Shadow War: The European Resistance, 1939-1945* (1972)

John F. Sweets, *The Politics of Resistance in France, 1940-1944* (1976)

Peter Hoffman, *The History of the German Resistance, 1933-1945* (1977)

James D. Wilkinson, *The Intellectual Resistance in Europe* (1981)

Lucy S. Dawidowicz, *The War against the Jews: 1933-1945** (1976)

Eugen Kogon, *The Theory and Practice of Hell* (1950)

Raul Hilberg, *The Destruction of the European Jews* (1961)

Jerzy Kosinski, *The Painted Bird** (1972)

N. B. Feis, *Churchill, Roosevelt, and Stalin: The War They Waged and the Peace They Sought*, 2nd ed.* (1967)

_____, *Between War and Peace: The Potsdam Conference* (1960)

Diane Shaver Clemens, *Yalta** (1972)

Bradley F. Smith, *Reaching Judgement at Nuremberg** (1979)

Lloyd C. Gardner, *Architects of Illusion** (1972)

John L. Gaddis, *The United States and the Origins of the Cold War, 1941-1947** (1972)

Daniel Yergin, *Shattered Peace: The Origins of the Cold War and the National Security State** (1978)

Lynn E. Davis, *The Cold War Begins* (1974)

Vojtech Mastny, *Russia's Road to the Cold War: Diplomacy, Warfare, and Communism, 1941-1945** (1980)

John W. Wheeler-Bennett and Anthony Nicholls, *The Semblance of Peace:The Political Settlement after the Second World War** (1974)

*indicates paperback edition

Overview: 1949-1979

Europe after World War II was gradually shorn of most of its colonies. It also ceased to carry the economic and political weight that it once had. The two great postwar powers, the Soviet Union and the United States, divided the world—and Europe—between them, with those countries on the Soviet Union's side of the Iron Curtain adopting a distinctive political ideology and economic system. In the late forties, given all that had taken place in the immediate aftermath of the war, there were some grounds for pessimism and despair. It became apparent, however, by the fifties and certainly by the sixties that Europe had more than just recovered from the ravages of war. It had struck out in new directions, directions of importance to people everywhere.

Europe, both east and west, continued the processes of industrialization and urbanization. In eastern Europe the process was at first almost a carbon copy of earlier Soviet experiences, but after Stalin's death some national variations on common themes were allowed. In western Europe, a number of approaches were tried involving varying degrees of state intervention and planning. Cooperation and coordination among the economies of countries, especially in the case of the European Common Market, became a factor of major importance. Standards of living rose appreciably, more so in western than in eastern Europe. By the 1960s, some European countries enjoyed a higher standard of living than the United States. Comprehensive welfare systems, which took care of most major social needs, were constructed in nearly every European state. The details of the arrangements differed from state to state, but nearly all made efforts to protect their citizens from the worst effects of misfortune.

A more affluent society and a welfare system designed to meet most of the difficulties of life were two developments that helped to change the makeup of European society. It became less class-conscious and more democratic. If class division was no longer as obvious, however, European societies still tended to be made up of elites and non-elites, with both groups perpetuating themselves with the help of a restrictive educational system. Ironically, the more blatant examples of elitism and special privilege were to be found in the theoretically egalitarian societies of eastern Europe and the Soviet Union.

By the mid-sixties Europeans had gone through most of the important political, economic, and social changes of the postwar period. The Cold War framework in which all this had taken place was itself now being transformed by the softening of alliance systems on the one hand and by the appearance of a détente between the Soviet Union and the United States on the other. Europeans could no longer expect to play their old roles in global politics, but in the circumstances that prevailed in the sixties, they were able to take the lead in various other areas. Continuing experiments provide a range of possible political and economic arrangements, from state-directed socialism (such as in the Soviet Union and its satellites) to a mixture of state control and direction by private enterprise (as in Sweden or France) to a system largely dependent on private initiative but carefully supervised by the state (as in West Germany). Much thought has been given also to social policy, whether directed toward the aged, the handicapped, the artist or writer, or some other group. Perhaps because of special ties with former colonies, many Europeans have been especially concerned with North-South relations, with relations between the affluent, industrialized countries of the north and the poor, usually underdeveloped countries of the south. Europeans have also been concerned with human rights issues.

Various economic shocks in the seventies, particularly the rapid increase in the price of petroleum products, have led some observers to talk about the decline of Europe politically, economically, and culturally. Pessimistic assessments cannot, of course, be easily dismissed, yet in surveying the thirty-five years since the war, the main impression would have to be that of a Europe that continues to be important in the life of the world.

Because European life takes place now largely in an urban and industrial environment, it seems in many respects to resemble American life rather closely. It should be emphasized, however, that while Europeans enjoy many aspects of American culture, Europe has not been Americanized. European culture continues to be distinctive and to offer alternative ways of constructing political and economic systems and developing social policy. Understanding the distinction is as important in grasping the nature of contemporary Europe as realizing Europe has "caught up" with the United States as an advanced industrial society.

Europeans will continue to play a part in both East-West relations and in the halting dialogue between North and South. In the process of Europe's brilliant recovery from the effects of World War II, it has carved out for itself a new position of crucial importance in world affairs.

9

Postwar Reconstruction, 1949-1957

Europe in the late forties was nothing like Europe in the twenties. There could be no pretending that life would again be like it was before the war. For one thing, the international context, both the Cold War and the effort at decolonization, made it unlikely that the pieces could be put back together as they had been. Perhaps even more important, many Europeans did not want to return to the Europe that had been. In the difficult years of World War II, many people had thought of how Europe could be different and better if national antagonisms were removed, if class hatreds were eliminated, if cooperation replaced conflict.

In the period from the mid-forties to the mid-fifties, Europe changed enormously. Politics became far more democratic than before (although the People's Democracies in eastern Europe offered only limited scope for political participation and emphasized conformity). Comprehensive welfare systems appeared in most states. Industry dominated nearly all the economies. In western Europe that industry was increasingly aimed at the consumer and based on new techniques.

In the first decade after World War II, the life-styles of Europeans underwent startling changes. The changes were more extreme in eastern Europe, where societies formerly composed mostly of peasants and ruled by the upper classes became societies of workers, peasants, and a new, ruling class of bureaucrats and communist party functionaries. In the west, prosperity and affluence, which spread to nearly all sectors of society, helped to create a way of life that had not existed before. Europe did not regain its former predominance in world affairs but, in triumphing over the effects of the recent past, European civilization gained a new lease on life and a different but important relationship with the world.

The Impact of War

The obstacles to the successful reconstruction of Europe were formidable. Between twenty-five and thirty million people had been killed in the war; slightly more than half were soldiers, the rest civilians. Millions survived with disabilities of one kind or another. Millions more fled from their homelands before the advancing armies or were forced to migrate after the war in massive shifts of population. (See Map p. 187.) The largest group of the latter were the approximately ten million Germans forced to move west from the Sudetenland and from what had been East Prussia.

Material losses were also enormous. In 1945 dollars, the losses ran between two and three trillion. This included damage to farmland, destruction of cattle and other livestock, devastation of villages, towns, and cities, bridges, railroads, and highways. Europeans struggled with inflation, soaring war debts, and badly damaged economies. Not just Germany, but every country that had been involved in the war faced the need to rebuild its economy and to repair the social fabric. Some countries had suffered more than others, of course. Denmark was, comparatively speaking, unmarked by the war. The Netherlands, by way of contrast, suffered a great deal, particularly in the "Hunger Winter" of 1944-1945. Germany looked as if it would never recover. There was much pessimism everywhere, whatever the level of damage; some believed that Europe had been hopelessly weakened.

This assessment was reinforced not only by the emergence of two enormously powerful countries on either flank, the United States and the Soviet Union, but also by the loss of colonial empire. The Dutch lost their empire in the immediate aftermath of the war, the British bowed to pressure and expectation and withdrew, mostly in good order, while the French fought a bitter delaying action that nearly tore the nation apart in the late 1950s. The Belgians and the Portuguese clung to their empires until the 1960s in the first instance and the 1970s in the second, but at great cost.

Finally, the spiritual cost of war and its aftermath had been great. It was not just that Europe in World War II had fallen back into barbarism after decades of apparent progress, but that the barbarism

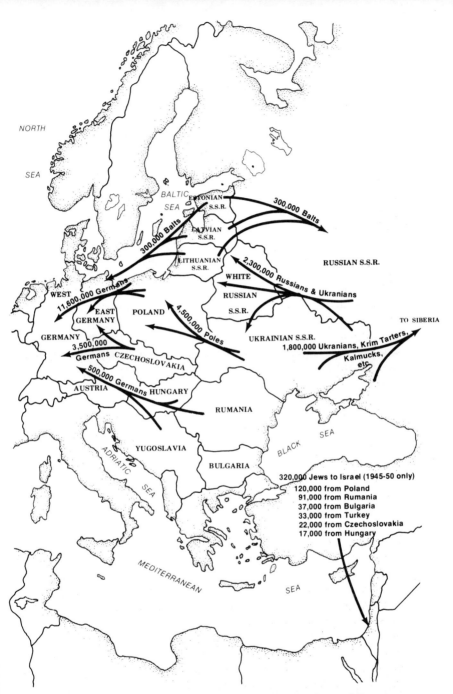

Postwar deportation and resettlement. After World War II, millions of Europeans fled their homelands or were deported. A large number of Germans were expelled from Czechoslovakia, Poland, and other areas in east Europe. In the Soviet Union, many were accused of collaboration with the enemy and were sent east into Siberia. Not noted on the map are the many thousands of former prisoners of war, guerrillas, and other members of the Soviet military arrested after the war and sent to forced labor camps in Siberia.

practiced was so cruel and on such a large scale. The "Final Solution," and the atrocities associated with it, were the major example of barbarism in the war, but the firebombing of Dresden in 1945 and the atom-bombing of Hiroshima and Nagasaki that same year were also barbarous acts. Any claim to cultural or moral superiority by Europeans seemed to have been made hollow by the events of the war. A spiritual malaise accompanied military impotence and economic poverty.

Yet, despite the bleakness of prospects in 1945, Europe recovered rapidly in the late forties and fifties. Part of the reason for this recovery was the impact of the war itself. Catastrophe was so widespread that there was little choice for most Europeans: either they turned away from the war and went forward or they would cease to exist. Part of the legacy of the war was positive, also. The British, for example, had agreed during the war that their country would not go back to prewar conditions. In France, documents existed from the Resistance Movement that spelled out some steps to be taken for a better future. Hope ran high in the Soviet Union that, after decades of suffering for which World War II had been only a culmination, the socialist society would now become a reality. Nearly everywhere, there was determination not to make the same mistakes that had plagued the two decades after World War I.

The Cold War and Reconstruction

The Cold War affected reconstruction in two rather contradictory ways. By creating an atmosphere of distrust and tension in which strong military forces seemed important, it caused resources to be diverted from the reconstruction of the civilian economy. This was particularly noticeable in eastern Europe where the Soviet Union shaped the economic development of various satellite nations in such a way as to enhance her military strength. The same was true, however, when the United States put pressure on its allies to contribute to collective security under the North Atlantic Treaty Organization (NATO) and in the early fifties worked to secure the rearmament of West Germany as a means of offsetting Soviet military power in Europe.

If the United States sometimes diverted resources from reconstruction to rearmament, it made up for it by pouring more than twenty billion dollars in aid into west European economies under the Marshall Plan. Here the Cold War and reconstruction needs worked reciprocally on one another. Europeans could increase the amount of aid made available to them by playing on the American fears of social unrest. Italian officials, for example, frequently asserted that larger amounts of aid were necessary in order for them to purchase sufficient food supplies or to expedite industrial recovery. Otherwise, they claimed, they would face strikes or widespread protests, particularly from the lower classes. In the context of the Cold War, unrest was viewed as increasing the opportunity for subversion and revolution—for a communist takeover. Although American officials sometimes recognized that their fears were being manipulated, they often took reports of the imminent collapse of a government at face value. The Soviet Union was far less likely to be manipulated in such a way since its control was either direct or thinly veiled and based on a readiness to use its military.

Reconstruction and Domestic Politics

Reconstruction took place with unexpected rapidity because the damage caused by the war had been somewhat exaggerated and sometimes had a "positive" effect as well. The destruction of a factory could have a "positive" effect, for example, if that factory were replaced by a more efficient plant which gave that industry a competitive edge. In addition to these factors, the economies of the belligerent nations had expanded greatly during the war so that they were often still larger than prewar economies even after damages had been deducted. A productive capacity—wartime industrial damage proving surprisingly superficial—that was largely intact and could be modernized where it had been damaged, together with a great shortage of goods of all kinds, created the basis for a rapid recovery. What was missing was the capital to finance economic growth and a means of directing that growth.

The United States provided the capital required for recovery through the Marshall Plan and other smaller programs. Until 1947 the United States made available nearly 15.5 billion dollars in aid, about 7 billion of that in gifts. Between 1947 and 1952, it gave Europe 23 billion dollars in Marshall Plan aid under the European Recovery Program. After that, European recovery was financed largely by Europeans through the expansion of exports.

The Marshall Plan, administered through the Office of European Economic Cooperation (OEEC), was based on national plans which the OEEC helped to coordinate. The national plans gave Americans some assurances as to how their money would be spent and also encouraged participants to use their resources in a constructive manner.

Other factors involved in the recovery and expansion of the European economies in the decade after World War II included an increase in world trade, in which Europe shared, and the development of European trade itself. Various demographic factors were also important. A rising birthrate (which was surprising given postwar conditions but which perhaps reflected an instinctive reaction to the suffering and destruction of the war), the influx of refugees, and, somewhat later, the arrival of large numbers of foreign workers added to the capacity to produce and consume. Heavy consumer demand, especially in areas of housing and automobiles, was important in maintaining a long-term expansion of the economy.

Part of the impetus behind long-term expansion was provided by a new kind of capitalism characterized by a large degree of state intervention and by such devices as planning and nationalization. Government control of banks and budgets made it possible to determine the rate of growth of an economy and, to a large extent, the direction of that growth. In other words, governments extended their activities beyond those areas having to do with the welfare of large segments of the population—unemployment, retirement, working conditions, public health, and housing, to the workings of the economy itself. In their efforts to make the economy function in the most effective and equitable way possible, they followed beginnings made in each of the two World Wars and patterns set by the Scandinavian states between the wars. These various factors enabled most European countries not only to recover but also to develop at a fairly rapid rate through the first decade after the war and into the early 1960s.

Reconstruction in the West: Britain

Three developments characterized Britain in the first decade after the war. Basic was the slow recovery of the economy and its failure to share fully in the rapid growth of the fifties. Britain was initially plagued by a huge war debt and by commitments in areas such as India, Palestine, Greece, and Malaysia. Even after those problems had been largely eliminated, Britain faced a severe balance of payments problem. An aging industrial plant, a labor force more concerned with benefits than productivity, and poor management policies, which included a disinclination to modernize facilities or push for innovations in products, combined to make Britain less competitive on the world market. The loss of markets and investments during the war increased the diffiulty of balancing imports by exports. Despite economic difficulties, Britain resisted long-term economic planning and restricted interference in the private sector. Nationalization was regarded as a rescue operation more than as a tool for restructuring or directing the economy.

A second development was the establishment of a welfare state. Based on two acts passed in 1946, the National Insurance and the National Health Services Acts, the Labour Party erected a comprehensive social security system and a socialized medical care system. Criticism was heavy, but both measures quickly became integral parts of British life. Even during Labour's long absence from power between 1951 and 1964, no serious attempts were made to dismantle the systems.

Finally, because of economic diffiulties, Britain spent most of the postwar period in a "retreat from empire." Only in 1956, when the Egyptian government nationalized the Suez Canal, did Britain attempt to reassert its old position in world affairs. Opposition from the United States and the United Nations forced Britain and its allies, France and Israel, to back down.

The Labour Party presided over the initial period of recovery and the development of the welfare state. After it had carried out most of its program and had become badly divided between left and right wings, it was defeated in elections in 1951 by the Conservatives. The Conservatives took advantage of the modest economic prosperity of the fifties and the gradual easing of international tensions to stay in office under Churchill until his retirement in 1955; then Anthony Eden, who resigned in 1956 after the Suez Canal crisis; and, finally, Harold Macmillan ("Supermac"), the most able in the series. By the end of the fifties Britain had recovered from the war. Much changed in terms of social policy, it enjoyed a precarious prosperity at the end of this decade. Its economy was still vulnerable, however, in that it continued to depend heavily on exports and yet, because of the various factors already discussed, remained relatively uncompetitive.

Reconstruction in the West: France

France, more than any other nation in western Europe, followed the general pattern of economic recovery outlined earlier. Wartime destruction and social dislocation demanded strong economic measures. Social and economic programs based on discussions in the

Resistance movements and on the experiences of the Popular Front also had an impact. Some industries were nationalized. Emphasis was also placed on economic planning. A four-year plan under the direction of Jean Monnet was put into effect in 1948. The initial efforts were designed to channel investment into such basic areas of the economy as coal, electricity, steel, and farm machinery. Later four-year plans were directed toward consumer goods, housing, and farm production.

For France to have an economy with a large public sector, planned and guided from above, was a radical departure from past policy. It was one that was resisted by small business and by many French farmers. Still, in the course of the 1950s and early 1960s, a "silent revolution" took place that made France industrially and technologically competitive with other nations. In the process, large numbers of people moved into urban areas and agriculture was thoroughly modernized. Despite a tenacious rearguard action by the small businessman and the farmer, the French economy changed drastically in little more than a decade after World War II. Accompanying the silent revolution in the economy was the construction of a welfare state in France. Although not as comprehensive as the British system, it was a far greater break with the past. With the exception of efforts during the Popular Front in the 1930s, the French government had done virtually nothing in the way of welfare reform before the 1940s and 1950s. The French welfare system provided not only health, maternity, and old-age benefits but also family allowances paid to families with two or more children. The aim of the welfare state in France and elsewhere was to provide the population with benefits in such important areas as health services, education, and family life, which would improve the quality of people's lives and at the same time protect them from catastrophes such as long-term illness, accidents on the job, or unemployment.

Accomplishments in the social and economic sphere made it possible for Frenchmen to ignore for a time the conspicuous political failure of the Fourth Republic. The initial efforts of the provisional government, established by General Charles de Gaulle in 1944, were directed to the making of a constitution. Elections in October 1945 resulted in three parties sharing power. Two, the Communists and the Socialists, favored a strong national assembly with the power to choose and remove the premier. The third, the Popular Republican Movement (MRP), a Christian Democratic movement similar to those appearing simultaneously in Italy and Germany, favored De Gaulle's solution of a strong executive.

De Gaulle resigned leadership of the government in January 1946, when he saw that his idea of a strong executive was not being accepted. His views and the efforts of the MRP led to a defeat in May of the first draft constitution, which did not provide for executive power. The June elections returned the MRP as the largest party, and in November a revised constitution was accepted that strengthened the executive somewhat. In part, victory resulted from the Socialists' fears that the Communist version of a strong legislature might too easily lead to a one-party dictatorship.

In the middle of 1947 the coalition governing France fell victim to Cold War tensions. France was forced to take sides in the developing antagonism. Shortly after the announcement of the Truman Doctrine, the Communist Party stopped supporting the governmental efforts to regain Indochina. In April the Communist Party felt compelled to support a strike in the government-owned Renault automobile plant. After the premier won a vote of confidence, he demanded that the Communists resign from the government. Tripartism ended.

The end of coalition government based on three major parties created the situation of "immobilism" in politics that became the hallmark of the Fourth Republic. Coalitions had to be constructed from several different parties. With little agreement on policy, coalitions could survive by doing little or risk collapse in an attempt at a major effort. Fortunately the economy and domestic matters in general presented few serious problems and these could be left largely to the bureaucrats to manage.

Colonial questions provided the major dilemmas of the 1950s, resulting in frequent changes of government. An important effort by Premier Pierre Mendès-France in 1954 ended French involvement in Indochina. That same year, however, the Algerian crisis began. The crisis emerged with efforts by the Moslem inhabitants of Algeria to gain independence for that colony. Their efforts were resisted not only by the French army, still angered by defeat in Indochina, but also by the *colons*, the European settlers in Algeria. The Algerian crisis grew over the next four years to such proportions that it blew the Fourth Republic apart.

France successfully reconstructed its economy after the war and, in the 1950s, developed rapidly. The Fourth Republic, however, bore an uncanny resemblance to the Third. Political adjustments were clearly necessary but no one, except perhaps De Gaulle, anticipated the actual magnitude of the changes that were to take place in 1958.

Reconstruction in the West: Italy

Italian politics restricted the scope for social and economic reform in the first decade after the war. Following Mussolini's ouster in 1943, the Committee for National Liberation, a coalition of anti-fascist parties operating in the liberated south, pressed for a republic. It was agreed to hold a referendum on the question after the war. In the German-occupied north, a more radical coalition of resistance organizations, the Committee of National Liberation for Northern Italy (CLNAI), urged a variety of reforms, but refrained from any attempt to seize power directly. The allies, as they moved north, systematically destroyed the bases of the strength of the CLNAI, making the Christian Democratic Party (DC) the major political force in Italy.

In 1946 and 1947 the DC governed in coalition with the Communists and the Socialists. The coalition accepted the results of the referendum of June 1946, ending the monarchy, but broke up the following year because of increasing Cold War tensions and disagreements over social change.

In the 1948 elections, the United States made it clear that the wrong kind of government from its point of view would lead to a cut off in aid. The elections gave the DC a working majority, and over the next decade it governed in coalitions, mainly with the Social Democratic Party, a splinter from the old Socialist Party which was distinguished from the latter chiefly by its opposition to cooperation with the Communists. Alcide de Gasperi was the major figure in the DC, one of several postwar politicians who were important influences not only in their own country but also in European affairs in general. The coalition restored Italy to economic and social stability by the late forties, largely with the help of Marshall Plan aid, but it was unable to take the initiative in the fifties as the coalitions grew increasingly weaker. A curious situation prevailed. Voters in each successive election supported the left in larger numbers, weakening the center-right coalition. At the same time, the left was moderating. The Communists, led by Palmiro Togliatti, moved to the right under the influence of moderate trade unionists and in reaction to the Soviet Union's suppression of the Hungarian Revolution in 1956. The Socialists, led by Pietro Nenni, moved away from the Communists and openly sought a coalition with the DC.

Frenetic political activity produced little social reform in the first fifteen years after the war. Land reform in the south in 1949-1950 fell far short of the need. A concerted effort to develop the south came only after a high level of prosperity had been reached in the industrialized, urbanized north. Overall economic growth, however, propelled Italy toward full industrialization for the first time. By the 1950s Italy enjoyed a rapid rate of growth and became a major supplier in Europe of automobiles, refrigerators, office machinery, and other goods. Part of its success was due to the concentration of capital and the reduction of competition made possible by large enterprises such as the government-controlled holding company, the Institute for Industrial Reconstruction; the government energy concern; and FIAT, the giant automobile manufacturer. The first two, holdovers from the Fascist regime, were government-owned but administered by private enterprise. The other major element in Italian economic success was cheap labor, in large part drawn from the underdeveloped south.

Like France, Italy went through the 1950s enjoying an expanding economy and a decrease in international tension. Unlike France, it had strong political leadership, from the DC and De Gasperi. Unresolved problems remained, however.

Reconstruction in the West: West Germany

The Federal Republic of Germany was a creation of Cold War antagonism. As such, it almost by definition excluded the left from politics. The Communists were formally banned in 1956. The Social Democrats found acceptance only after they dropped their Marxist trappings and became a party of reform. Little interest in radical social and economic change existed. Reconstruction, the "economic miracle" of Germany's rapid rise to the status of a major industrial power, was accomplished by private enterprise, aided by state supervision and limited intervention.

The dominant figure in postwar German politics was Konrad Adenauer, the leader of the Christian Democratic Party (CDU). Adenauer was popular with his fellow Germans and highly acceptable to the United States. The elections in 1949 gave a majority to the CDU in coalition with the Free Democratic Party. Adenauer ruled over the next decade in a paternalistic fashion, excluding parliament from political questions whenever possible. His style of government, featuring a strong executive and a restricted democracy, has been called "chancellor democracy." It was accepted in the fifties, despite the fact that it verged on the authoritarian, primarily because of Germany's economic success but also because of her delicate situation in international affairs. Adenauer seemed particularly qualified to deal with the latter.

Under Adenauer's lieutenant, Ludwig Erhard, Germany sought economic recovery and expansion rather than social equality or even an elaborate welfare state. Good business management, including efforts by industry to channel investments and control prices, government intervention where necessary, and a long period of labor peace, enabled German business to become competitive in the world market. An expanding economy led eventually in the 1960s to high wages and a comprehensive welfare system for the workers. Some degree of sacrifice was imperative, given the state of the German economy in the postwar period, but Erhard's "socialmarket" policy placed an undue burden on the workers.

In most ways, the German economy was a laissez-faire economy. There was, however, enough government intervention, cooperation within industry, and influence by large banks to moderate and direct the workings of the economy. Long-range planning of the French type was not practiced, but, in effect, a great deal of short-range planning took place. What had made German industry successful before the war—concentration of capital and other resources, economies of scale, reduction of competition—worked to make it successful after the war. In turn, this success made most political questions appear to be insignificant. The one question that would not go away, however, was that of reunification. Kept alive by the millions of Germans displaced from their homes after the war, it was an insoluble dilemma in the 1950s. No European state, least of all the Soviet Union, wanted a reunited Germany. Only as the German refugees were integrated into the new West German society, contributing vital skills and labor, did the tension diminish over this issue.

The Smaller States After the War

The several Scandinavian states started at different points in the postwar era, but followed roughly similar paths under the leadership of Social Democratic or Labor Parties toward a comprehensive welfare state. Finland, which had lost a war to the Soviet Union and maintained a precarious autonomy only by carefully considering potential Russian reactions to its activities, had the most difficult situation. Sweden, which had remained virtually untouched by the war, undoubtedly had the most favorable position. Norway and Denmark, both occupied by Germany during the war, were somewhere between the first two.

The Netherlands and Belgium each faced divisive religious-political problems. The Belgian problem was the more intractable in that the split between the Flemish- and French-speaking Belgians involved geographic, ethnic, and cultural differences as well. This problem was made more difficult by the slow growth of the economy in the fifties, the consequences of which were felt more severely in the French-speaking south. Conversely, in the Netherlands, where religious divisions were mirrored in the areas of education, culture, and social relationships, rapid economic growth helped to smooth over differences. Rotterdam, badly damaged during the war, became the leading seaport in Europe and the Netherlands was soon the leader in shipping. Along with commercial growth, industrial production doubled between 1954 and 1964.

Austria had a unique position in postwar Europe, one for which the easing of Cold War tensions was essential. In 1955 the four-power occupation of Austria ended in exchange for a pledge of permanent neutrality. In politics, the two parties whose struggles with one another in the thirties had prepared the way for the Nazis—the Social Democrats and the Christian Socialists—governed together in a red and black coalition. Political stability was seconded by economic growth.

The Iberian peninsula changed little in the late 1940s and the 1950s. Because of the necessities of the Cold War, both Spain and Portugal were brought back into the community of nations. Otherwise, Francisco Franco in Spain and Antonio de Oliveira Salazar in Portugal continued to govern as before the war.

Reconstruction in the East: The Soviet Union

Victory for the Soviet Union had been costly. More than half the casualties in World War II were suffered by Russians, about fifteen million people. Twenty-five million were homeless. Great stretches of European Russia had been devastated by the fighting. Despite the enormity of human and material losses, many Russians believed that a new era had begun. Life would become better than it had been; past sacrifices would be rewarded.

Instead, the Soviet Union returned to the Stalinist practices of the thirties. The fourth five-year plan, introduced in 1946, stressed heavy industry and armaments. Andrei Zhdanov carried out Stalin's directives in cultural and educational matters, emphasizing ideological conformity and socialist realism. The NKVD, headed by Lavrenti Beria, rounded up thousands who might in any way be suspected of disloyalty, including artillery captain and later novelist

Aleksandr Solzhenitsyn. Military heroes such as Georgi Zhukov were assigned to relatively minor posts.

By 1950 the Soviet Union had reached prewar levels in industry and agriculture through the utilization of its own resources, reparations from some nations, and one-sided economic agreements with several east European states. Although the Soviet Union was a major industrial power in basic categories such as coal and steel production, and was closing the gap between itself and the United States in some areas, it lacked the technological range of a truly modern industrialized society. Much that it produced in the 1950s was inferior in quality or outmoded in design. There were serious shortages from the consumer's point of view, too. Agriculture, despite the strenuous efforts of a rising young politician, Nikita S. Khrushchev, was still inefficient and insufficiently productive.

Even more ominous for Russians in late 1952 and early 1953 were signs of an impending purge on the scale of that of the 1930s. One indication was the "Doctors' Plot," allegedly a plot by several prominent physicians to murder important party and governmental officials under the guise of medical care. Fortunately, Stalin died in March 1953, before any new repressive plans could mature.

Although a major panic was feared, the succession took place quietly. Georgi Malenkov was named premier. The party secretariat, Stalin's old source of power, was reorganized. The Office of General Secretary was abolished, but Khrushchev was named first on the list of secretaries. Collective leadership was stressed. Beria apparently challenged this or was thought ready to do so. He was removed as head of the NKVD in June 1953 and unceremoniously shot. The NKVD was reorganized to curtail its independence, then renamed the KGB.

In February 1955 Malenkov resigned his post. His "New Course," emphasizing consumer goods, had run counter to the other leaders' fears about military security. In the "guns vs. butter" argument, the guns won. Bulganin replaced Malenkov. He, Khrushchev, and Molotov became the major figures in Soviet politics.

At the Twentieth Party Congress in 1956 Khrushchev made a so-called secret speech in which he criticized Stalin's cult of personality and detailed many of Stalin's arbitrary actions. De-Stalinization, for which Khrushchev's speech was only the beginning, was meant to accomplish several goals. By blaming Stalin for many past wrongs, the present leadership deflected much criticism of the existing situation. Criticizing Stalin was also a way to improve Soviet relations with those western communist movements that had resented Stalin's autocratic behavior toward them. Finally, distancing the present regime from Stalin's tactics made the relaxation of Cold War tensions more likely.

The following year, in June, Khrushchev was nearly deposed by the Stalinist faction of the party. However, with the backing of the military, particularly Zhukov, Khrushchev took his case to the Central Committee of the party and won. He became the leading figure in the party and government although not all-powerful.

As Khrushchev was settling the question of power in the Soviet Union, he was also forced to deal with a complex situation in eastern Europe. Originally the Soviet Union had intended to use eastern Europe first as a buffer area and then as an aid to Soviet reconstruction and development. In the late 1940s the eastern European states became carbon copies of the Soviet Union, with the exception of Yugoslavia. According to a well-known theory put forth by the British historian Hugh Seton-Watson, eastern Europe underwent a three-stage process. First, coalition governments were organized. Then, non-communist groups were persecuted while the communists gained sensitive posts such as the ministry of the interior. Finally, the coalition was destroyed by the elimination of the non-communists and the state adopted the characteristic features of the Soviet regime. This somewhat deterministic view must be modified by the recognition that Cold War tensions contributed by forcing Stalin to move from stage one to stage two and then to stage three. His goals remained the same; the means to achieve them were adjusted according to circumstances, circumstances that seemed to require absolute control as a guarantee of the desired protection from the West.

Reconstruction in the East: Poland

Next to Germany, Poland was the country in eastern Europe that most concerned the Soviet Union. In addition to disputed territory that Stalin was determined to keep after the war, there was the problem of the Polish government-in-exile in London, a government that appeared hostile to Soviet interests. Stalin created his own Polish government-in-exile, the "Lublin Poles," and installed them in power. In the course of liberating Poland, he also seems to have deliberately allowed the Germans to annihilate the Polish Home Army forces in Warsaw. Polish underground forces elsewhere were brought under the control of or eliminated by the Soviet army.

The allies at Yalta pressured the Soviet Union to allow some members of the London government-in-exile to join the "Lublin Poles" in a coalition. The Russians accepted this, but made sure that the Peasant Party, the major force within the old government, did poorly in the 1947 elections. Blunders by its leader, Stanislaw Mikolajczyk, did not help. In 1948 the Russians forced the other independent political force, the Polish Socialist Workers' Party, to merge with the Communist Party into the Polish United Workers' Party. Quickly after this Poland began copying the institutions of the Soviet Union: economic planning with emphasis on heavy industry, collectivization of agriculture, ideological conformity, and one-party dictatorship. Those who stressed a national approach to communism, such as Wladyslaw Gomulka, were arrested, tried, and sometimes executed.

Despite indications of restiveness in other countries, the situation in Poland was quiet until after Stalin's death and Khrushchev's hints that things might be different. At the end of June 1956, riots began in Poznan protesting the low standard of living of the working class. The Polish United Workers' Party was divided between Stalinists and those who wanted to improve the lot of the workers. The example of Yugoslavia's independence was influential. The workers' revolt and the refusal by the police and army to put it down led to the end of collectivization and to promises of reforms for the workers. Gomulka returned to power.

Gomulka and his supporters retained power mainly by convincing the Soviet Union that Poland would remain in the Soviet bloc and that the United Workers' Party would continue to control Poland. Aside from concessions in agriculture and a de-emphasis of heavy industry, little changed in Poland. Gomulka restricted the revolution to areas acceptable to the Russians. He avoided the mistakes made by the Hungarians who, in October and November 1956, became involved in a revolution that seemed open-ended.

Reconstruction in the East: Hungary

Hungary became a People's Republic in 1949 after a slow, rather cautious passage from coalition government to one-party dictatorship. It followed the Stalinist path of economic development to the point of economic collapse in 1953. Four months after Stalin's death, the moderate communist Imre Nagy was appointed premier. His policy mirrored that of Malenkov's "New Course" and included diversion of resources to light industry and an end to forced collectivization. The change in economic policy and the example of Yugoslavia's independent course fostered a re-evaluation of Hungarian communism by some intellectuals. In 1955, however, in the wake of Malenkov's fall from power in the Soviet Union, his protégé, Nagy, was ousted from the premiership. The following year, the government ran into trouble when Khrushchev's speech on Stalin revealed previously unknown facts about events in Hungary in the early fifties. Open opposition was encouraged by Gomulka's successful efforts in Poland. In October 1956 the government made a fundamental error in calling in the Soviet Army to deal with Hungarian demonstrators. Throughout Hungary councils were formed demanding free elections, the withdrawal of Soviet troops, and an end to the security police.

At first it appeared that the Hungarians had won the day. On October 28 Nagy established a new government and Soviet troops began to leave. Nagy set up a coalition government and, on October 31, declared Hungary's neutrality. In the face of such a challenge, the Soviet Union had little choice but to crush the revolution by force. In November Nagy's government was smashed and a new one established under Janos Kádár. The repercussions of the revolution were far-reaching. Along with other factors, the revolution led to a questioning of Khrushchev's leadership and to the 1957 attempt to oust him. It forced the Soviet Union to revise its relationship with other communist movements in the direction of polycentrism. Finally, it impressed western communist leaders unfavorably and led to greater independence of action.

Yugoslavia and Revisionism

Rumania and Bulgaria followed patterns roughly similar to those which Hungary and Poland had followed before 1956. Czechoslovakia was a different case in that President Eduard Beneš sought to avoid problems with the Soviet Union while Klement Gottwald, the communist party leader, believed that the communists could dominate Czechoslovakia by indirection. The situation changed rapidly in 1947 when the Cold War began. Czechoslovakia, as would again prove to be the case in 1968, was too crucial to Soviet security interests to allow any chance that it might fall under the control of an unfriendly government. In 1948 Stalin pressured Gottwald to establish a one-party state, which he did. East Germany was also a special case in that the Soviet Union supervised its affairs with extreme care and imposed on it extremely one-sided trade and economic arrangements. Protests in 1953 against the harshness of the system were brutally

Rioters in East Berlin throw stones at Red Army tanks in June 1953.
The riots in East Berlin and elsewhere in East Germany were protests
against the Stalinist regime of Walter Ulbricht. (Wide World Photos)

suppressed by Soviet troops. The East German communist leader,
Walter Ulbricht, remained a dedicated supporter of Soviet policies.

   Throughout the 1950s the Soviet Union remained in a position to
dominate the affairs of all the east European countries except Yugoslavia. In the course of the first decade after the war, the Soviet Union
not only shaped the political systems of the east European states but
also their social and economic systems. The major change here was
the emphasis on industrialization and urbanization in what had been,
Czechoslovakia aside, countries with large peasant populations and
small industrial bases before the war. Heavy industry was favored
over industry geared more toward the consumer. In Bulgaria and
Rumania industrialization was not given as much attention as in
nations such as East Germany and Czechoslovakia, but in each
nation the pattern was similar: centralized planning, rapid economic
growth, and the development of heavy industry were the main
features.

The one state in eastern Europe that the Soviet Union could not control was Yugoslavia. The parting of the ways between the two came within a few years after the war. The Yugoslav communists, who had liberated their country from the Germans, refused to follow Stalin blindly. In particular, they wanted to support worldwide revolution and, at the same time, to follow their own social and economic policies. Stalin, jealous of Tito, wished to discredit him and gain control of the Yugoslav party. Efforts to do this failed. Stalin then had the Cominform expel Yugoslavia in 1948. An economic embargo was placed on Yugoslavia by the Soviet bloc, but Yugoslavia got around this by opening up trade with the west and by procuring aid from the United States.

In its ideological war with the Soviet Union, Yugoslavia moved to reduce the power of the central bureaucracy, increase worker participation in factory management, and operate the economy according to supply and demand and profitability of an enterprise. Tito also changed from supporting world revolution to favoring the idea of coexistence with the west and non-alignment in politics. Yugoslavia became in the 1950s a bridge between communist and capitalist systems and a good example of pragmatic adaptation of ideology to existing conditions.

On the Way to a United Europe

Movement toward European unity took place along three parallel paths, two of which ended to all intents and purposes in the early 1950s. One path was that of political union. In May 1948 a Congress of Europe was held. Among the participants were leading European- ists such as Churchill, De Gasperi, Robert Schuman of France, and Paul-Henri Spaak of Belgium. The congress proposed the political and economic unification of Europe, and to that end the Council of Europe was established. The Council's efforts were weakened by the fact that the eastern European states would have nothing to do with it. In addition, Britain, which joined reluctantly, made sure that the Consultative Assembly of the Council could only recommend. A Committee of Ministers, the foreign ministers of the member states, had the power of decision and, as might be expected, guarded the sovereignty of their respective nation states. The attempt at political integration had been too ambitious. The Council became a mori- bund institution.

A second effort at integration, this involving military forces, was also stillborn. In 1950 the French proposed to create a European army from small national contingents. This would circumvent the problem of German rearmament and, simultaneously, add to the defensive capabilities of western Europe at a time when the United States was diverted by the Korean War. Before the European Defense Community (EDC) could be organized, events passed it by. Stalin's death, the end of the Korean War, and the easing of Cold War tensions removed some of the more pressing reasons for the EDC. The French had second thoughts about such a drastic turn toward supranationalism. The British finished off the plan by declining to participate. After this, a German military force was created and made part of NATO, which remained a collection of armies rather than an integrated military force.

The third plan grew out of cooperation under the European Recovery Program (the Marshall Plan) in the OEEC. Two Frenchmen, Commissioner of Planning Jean Monnet and Foreign Minister Robert Schuman, proposed, in what became known as the Schuman Plan, a pooling of coal and steel resources in Europe. The plan was put into operation in 1952 with France, Germany, Italy, and the Benelux countries (Belgium, the Netherlands, and Luxembourg) cooperating in establishing the European Coal and Steel Community (ECSC). Britain, worried about its ties to the Commonwealth and aware of a special relationship with the United States, did not join.

The ECSC was an indisputable success. What drove its members toward further economic integration, however, was not simply the potential economic advantage but also a painful awareness of their vulnerability and weakness as individual states. In 1956 this point had been made clear by the French and British failure to regain control of the Suez Canal as contrasted with the Soviet Union's relatively easy crushing of the Hungarian Revolution. Negotiations, initiated by the Benelux countries, were already underway on the subject of a customs union. The events of 1956 convinced the French of the importance of creating a large European market with no internal customs barriers. In 1957 the Treaty of Rome established the European Economic Community (EEC) or Common Market. The EEC was to work toward the elimination of customs barriers among its member states and toward common tariffs for the rest of the world.

While the six member nations of the EEC began working toward an integrated economy, the British sponsored a seven-nation European Free Trade Association (EFTA). Britain, Sweden, Denmark, Norway, Portugal, Switzerland, and Austria worked to eliminate trade barriers among the members of EFTA, but not to integrate the economies of those nations. In eastern Europe, the Council for

Mutual Economic Assistance (Comecon), in existence since 1949, took on new life. Formerly little more than a cover for Soviet exploitation of the eastern Europe economies, Comecon became directed more toward mutually advantageous economic relations in the wake of growing restiveness and independence in eastern Europe and the example of the EEC.

The genuine and widespread interest in European unity in the postwar period had given way rather quickly to more typical concerns for national interests. In part this was due to the overly optimistic belief of a generation of European leaders that obstacles to unity formed by historical experience, language, and customs could be easily swept away. The attempt to move directly and swiftly toward political unity floundered on the realities of national and international politics. Nonetheless, some important steps toward unity on social and economic policies had been taken and a process created by which much more could be achieved. It was one of the most significant developments of the period, one that helped to characterize the new Europe that was emerging from the ruins of the old.

By 1957 Europe had managed to recover from the war and had broken new ground. Throughout Europe, the economic picture had changed. Industry had become the major factor in almost every European economy, even in eastern and southern Europe. The nature of industry itself was changing, too. Especially in northwestern Europe, the emphasis in industry was on the production of consumer goods, the development of new products, and the use of new machines and techniques. Standards of living had surpassed prewar levels in most countries. Societies were becoming more homogeneous, even in western Europe where there were no ideological pressures working toward egalitarianism. The working class, at least in western Europe, had considerably more power than it had commanded before the war. Both society in general and the governments were more sympathetic to the needs and aspirations of workers and less apprehensive about what they might do.

In politics, both east and west, the concern of government for social and economic issues led to the creation of the welfare state in some nations and its extension in others. Greater government intervention in economic matters meant not only increased regulation but also government-owned sectors of the economy in most states. Of course, in eastern Europe the government sector all but squeezed out the private sector.

The political spectrum itself had changed. The prewar type of liberal or conservative party had largely disappeared (although the

Conservative Party in Britain remained a major factor). The two major developments were the emergence of Christian Democratic parties, which dominated the first two decades of politics in Italy and Germany, and reform-minded, nonrevolutionary Socialist parties in a number of states. In a sense, the Christian Democratic parties, while attracting members with widely differing interests, replaced the old conservative parties. The Socialists, definitely more moderate than they had been before the war, replaced the liberals (but, of course, were far more enthusiastic about government intervention). Politics were far less polarized than in the period between the wars. Even the large number of votes given to the Communist parties in Italy and France and the occasional appearance of right-wing protest movements did not alter the essential moderation of west European politics.

The political system in eastern Europe was drastically different from the prewar era, with communist states subservient to Moscow (with the exception of Yugoslavia) in place of the mostly authoritarian right-wing governments that had existed in the 1930s. In the west, parliamentary democracies existed in all states but Spain and Portugal, which had 1930s' style authoritarian governments.

There was less nationalism visible in Europe in the decade after World War II than in the years immediately preceding. In part this was a reaction to the war itself. Nationalism was also submerged to an extent in the east-west conflict. Many Europeans were interested in an international approach to questions and in the possibility of European unity. There was more substance to efforts in the west to establish unity, but even there the progress that was made depended clearly on the economic advantages that could be gained and not on idealism.

Europe had not yet made itself into a third great power. In fact, it was losing rather than gaining power in world affairs, as its steadily eroding colonial authority demonstrated. But it had found its own way. European civilization had done more than survive. It had undergone something close to a renaissance and by the end of the 1950s had become a guide and example for both the United States and the Soviet Union.

Suggested Readings

Walter Laqueur, *Europe since Hitler* (1972)
Maurice Crouzet, *The European Renaissance since 1945** (1971)
Francis Boyd, *British Politics in Transition, 1945-63* (1964)
Samuel H. Beer, *British Politics in the Collectivist Age* (1965)
Phillip Williams, *French Politicians and Elections, 1951-1968** (1970)
Stanley Hoffman, ed., *France: Change and Tradition* (1963)
Edward Mead Earle, ed., *Modern France: Problems of the Third and Fourth Republic* (1964)
Norman Kogan, *A Political History of Post-War Italy* (1966)
Alfred Grosser, *Germany in Our Time* (1971)
Richard Hiscocks, *The Adenauer Era* (1976)
Ralf Dahrendorf, *Society and Democracy in Germany** (1979)
William B. Bader, *Austria between East and West, 1945-1955* (1966)
D. A. Rustow, *The Politics of Compromise: A Study of Parties and Cabinet Government in Sweden* (1955)
Arend Lijphart, *The Politics of Accommodation: Pluralism and Democracy in the Netherlands** (1976)
Stanley G. Payne, *Franco's Spain* (1967)
Hugh Thomas, *The Suez Affair* (1970)
M. M. Postan, *An Economic History of Western Europe, 1945-1964** (1966)
Jean Monnet, *Memoirs* (1978)
Hans Schmitt, *European Union: From Hitler to De Gaulle** (1969)
F. Roy Willis, *France, Germany, and the New Europe, 1945-1967* (rev. ed. 1968)
Wolfgang Leonhard, *The Kremlin since Stalin* (1975)
Adam Ulam, *Stalin* (1973)
Edward Crankshaw, *Khrushchev: A Career** (1971)
Zbigniew Brzezinski, *The Soviet Bloc: Unity and Conflict** (rev. ed. 1967)
Joseph Rothschild, *Communist Eastern Europe* (1964)

Hugh Seton-Watson, *The East European Revolution* (rev. ed. 1957)
Milovan Djilas, *Conversations with Stalin** (1963)
Vladimir Dedijer, *Tito* (1972)
Morton Kaplan, *The Communist Coup in Czechoslovakia* (1960)
Hans Roos, *A History of Modern Poland* (1966)
Paul E. Zinner, *Revolution in Hungary* (1962)
H. Stuart Hughes, *The Sea Change: The Migration of Social Thought, 1930-1965** (1977)

*indicates paperback edition

10

A New Europe, 1957-1967

The period from 1957 to 1967, which lies between such calamitous events as the Suez Canal crisis and the Hungarian Revolution in 1956 and the Events of May in France and the Czechoslovakian crisis of 1968, was Europe's quietest decade since before World War I. There were shocks, of course; France on the edge of civil war in 1958, the Berlin Wall in 1961, and large-scale American involvement in Vietnam after 1965 are only some of the more memorable crises of the period. Yet the positive signs are more numerous. The Cold War seemed to be winding down. Economic prosperity was widespread. Intellectually, Europeans moved away from the cosmic despair that so many had felt the first decade after the war. It seemed to many a pleasant and easy time. It was also a time in which, as it turned out, a new Europe was being constructed.

The International Context

International relations, particularly relations between the Soviet Union and the United States, continued to form a framework for events. In the late 1950s relations between the two major powers improved considerably. Progress, symbolized by the visits of then Vice-President Richard M. Nixon to Moscow and of Khrushchev to the Iowa cornfields, was interrupted in the early 1960s by various events. The construction of the Berlin Wall in August 1961, plus other efforts to seal the border between East and West Germany, increased tension and distrust. The Cuban missile crisis in late October the following year threatened briefly the possibility of thermonuclear war.

Khrushchev had originally gambled that he could obtain a strategic edge by installing missiles in Cuba. President John F. Kennedy also gambled that Khrushchev would not risk war for the slight edge that this maneuver would give him. Kennedy's bluff worked.

After the Cuban missile crisis, and quite likely because both sides perceived that the risks involved in continual confrontation were too great, relations again improved. One example of this was the Nuclear Test Ban Treaty, which became effective in October 1963.

Within the context of decreasing tension, the two great blocs began loosening. As early as 1965 Europeans began to criticize American policy in Vietnam. The primary factor, however, in the loosening of the North Atlantic Treaty Organization's bonds was France, the major spokesman for a European-centered foreign policy free from American dominance. De Gaulle withdrew France from active military collaboration with NATO and forced the allies to move NATO headquarters to Brussels. France remained in NATO, but retained total control over its armed forces. NATO remained important, of course, in that it was still recognized that an American presence in Europe was vital.

Deteriorating relations with China, which began in 1956 and became public in 1960, were a serious problem for the Soviet Union. China emerged in the 1960s as a major element in the world communist movement. Because of its long common borders with the Soviet Union, China also represented a distinct threat to Soviet security. The Soviet Union had little trouble with the Warsaw Treaty Organization (WTO) in this period. Unlike NATO, the WTO was not a voluntary association of sovereign states. The Soviet Union had some difficulty, though, especially in the case of Rumania, in dominating all aspects of the foreign policies of the east European nations.

Decolonization

Another major part of the international picture was related to the decolonization movement, a movement that took place in two large waves. Most of Asia gained independence in the first wave, the years immediately following the war. Nationalist movements, sometimes heavily influenced or dominated by communists, had existed in the area before World War II, but it was the war that created conditions which made the conquest of power a distinct possibility in several instances. Where the Japanese had smashed colonial regimes in the process of conquest, a power vacuum was created into which nationalists could move after the war. In 1949 the Dutch were forced to recognize the independence of Indonesia. The latter had originally declared independence in 1945, taking advantage of the destruction of the Dutch colonial regime by the Japanese. The Dutch returned after the war in an effort to regain control. They lacked the military forces to subdue the rebels completely and found themselves under considerable pressure from the United States, which throughout most of the late 1940s followed Roosevelt's policy of anti-imperialism. With the loss of Indonesia, the Dutch lost all but a few fragments of what had been one of the major empires of the world and a significant factor to the Dutch economy.

The Vietnamese, like the Indonesians, took advantage of the destruction of their colonial government during the war. In 1945 they, too, declared their independence. Under the leadership of Ho Chi Minh, the Viet-Minh, a broadly-based nationalist movement heavily influenced by a large component of communist cadre, took control of the north after the Japanese surrender. British forces prevented the Viet-Minh from seizing control in the south. An uneasy truce between Ho's forces in the north and the French in the south was reached in 1946 only to break down in December of that year after a French attack on the Viet-Minh. Over the next several years the Viet-Minh, at first employing tactics similar to those used by Mao Zedong in China and later moving more to conventional warfare, stalemated French efforts. Finally, a French attempt to defeat the Viet-Minh decisively led to a major French defeat at Dien Bien Phu in 1954 and an agreement at the Geneva Conference that year to divide Vietnam and abolish the French colonial regime. Full independence was not achieved, however, until 1974.

The major exception to this pattern was India. India and Pakistan, the latter a nation carved out of the former in an effort to deal with growing hostility between Muslims and Hindus, gained their independence in 1947. The British, finally realizing their growing lack of control over the situation in the period after World War II, abruptly created the two states by the passage of the India Independence Bill in July 1947. Ceylon (now Sri Lanka) and Burma gained their independence shortly afterwards.

Other important developments that owed much to prewar and wartime events took place in Africa and the Near East. The French had had no time to recover from their humiliating defeat in southeast Asia before their rule in northwest Africa was challenged. In 1954 the National Liberation Front (FLN) began a revolution in Algeria that steadily grew more brutal and bitter. In 1956 Tunisia and Morocco were granted independence, but a similar move for Algeria was out of the question for French politicians. They had to contend with the desires of one million Europeans who lived in Algeria, controlled its economy and government, and considered it a part of France, and with the French army which could not bear the idea of yet another defeat. By 1958 it appeared likely that France would be driven to civil war over the issue of Algeria.

Elsewhere in Africa and the Near East changes were taking place of considerable consequence for all of Europe. Briefly, these changes consisted of the establishment of Israel as a Jewish state, which, in turn, created a situation of continuing hostility between Israel and the surrounding Arab states, and led to the appearance of radical regimes in many of those states. The two developments were closely connected to the Arab-Israeli war of 1948-1949 which developed from the efforts to establish Israel. Israel's success in defeating the Arab attempt to destroy it led to military revolts in Egypt, Syria, and Jordan. The British and the French lost most of their influence in the area. Neither the United States nor the Soviet Union was particularly successful in replacing the British and the French as leaders in the region.

The second wave of decolonization came in the late fifties and early sixties, largely as the result of postwar efforts by nationalist and radical leaders. In most cases, independence was granted voluntarily by the colonial power. In 1960 the former French colonies in Africa, which had earlier been given autonomy within the French community of nations, were granted full independence. The Algerian revolt was resolved by a separate agreement in 1962. The French dream of assimilation, of transforming the inhabitants of colonial areas into Frenchmen, ended. Britain, reacting to its experience in India, had already begun moving in the fifties toward independence for its various African colonies. The transition was reasonably smooth in most cases, with Africans gradually replacing Europeans in governmental administration. The major exceptions were Kenya, where the Mau Mau terrorist movement in the early fifties increased tension dramatically for a time, and Rhodesia, where a white minority government declared its independence unilaterally in 1965. Belgian colonies were also granted independence in the early sixties, but with much less preparation. By the mid-sixties all of Africa had achieved independence except southern Africa, where white minority governments ruled in South Africa and Rhodesia and where Portugal maintained colonies in Angola and Mozambique.

Many new African states retained ties to Britain or to France. They did not always follow the political traditions of the former colonial rulers, however. Again, as in the Near East, when the European states lost their preeminent positions, the United States, the Soviet Union, and also the People's Republic of China maneuvered for influence. None was particularly successful.

Despite the bitterness felt by many of those Europeans whose lives had been based on one colonial system or another, Europeans in general, once over the trauma of decolonization, found the loss of colonies offset by the loss of responsibilities that the colonies had entailed and by the appearance of new possibilities. In some cases, new relationships with former colonies proved more beneficial than the old ties. Some countries, such as the Netherlands, once heavily dependent on colonial wealth, enjoyed sufficient economic development at home to offset the loss of colonies. For others, such as France, the loss was more psychological and political than economic. In any case, the emergence of literally dozens of new nations in the 1950s and 1960s created completely new conditions for international relations. European nations, like other industrialized and modern states, had to contend with the claims of the "Third World" that they be given not only political independence but also a share of the wealth generated by modern industry. Nevertheless, by the early 1960s western Europe was largely free from the problems associated with the efforts to maintain colonial empires in the postwar era. It had begun to enjoy as well the diminution of tension in the relations between the two dominant powers, the Soviet Union and the United States. Eastern Europe, too, benefited from this development.

A Consumer Economy

Many Europeans scarcely missed the former colonies in their preoccupation with the rapid expansion of the European economies. In western Europe, the extent of prosperity and its widespread distribution were the most striking phenomena of the postwar period. There were, of course, considerable differences between the more industrialized and affluent north, especially the Scandinavian countries, the Benelux countries, and Germany, and the south, particularly Spain and Portugal. Even within a country there might be considerable differences, as was the case in Italy, for example, where the north contained most of the industry and employment opportunities. Overall, however, Europe was prosperous to an extent never before realized in its history.

One way of measuring the development of a wealthy, consumer economy is to examine the composition of the work force. A work force in which the agricultural sector declines while the industrial sector remains largely stable and the service sector grows is considered to be moving in the direction of a modern economy, in twentieth-century terms. In the 1950s, taking France, West Germany, and Italy as examples, the industrial sector and the service sector both increased in size while the agricultural sector declined. In the 1960s the decline of the agricultural sector continued, resulting in a figure of less than 10 percent of the West German work force engaged in agriculture and related activities. In that same period the industrial sector declined slightly in France, grew slightly in West Germany, and somewhat more in Italy, while the service sector grew substantially in each state. Each economy was becoming increasingly modern.

As the nature of the economy changed, the work force gained larger amounts of disposable income, that is, more money to spend on food, clothing, and other goods after paying fixed expenses such as rent and taxes. While per capita disposable income in the United States increased 117% between 1960 and 1973, it increased 258% in France, 312% in Germany, and 323% in Denmark. Disposable income increased more rapidly in nearly every west European country than it did in the United States, although only Denmark, Germany, Switzerland and Sweden were close to (or in the case of Sweden, above) the total figure for per capita disposable income in the United States. France and Belgium remained substantially below the total figure despite rapid increases; Britain and Italy were considerably below. Portugal and Spain in 1973 were still considerably below the American figure for 1960. Nevertheless, the important point is that the amount of money which the average individual in Europe might spend after satisfying basic obligations had increased enormously in the 1960s. It is also important to note here that the old patterns of national affluence were shifting in Europe. Britain, the wealthiest country in Europe at the beginning of the century, continued to lag behind most west European nations. The beginnings of this trend go back to the interwar period. The French and especially the Italians moved dramatically in the opposite direction, constructing much stronger and more affluent economies than they had had before World War II.

An examination of the range of consumer goods available and the increasing levels of consumption provides a graphic illustration of how much more disposable income Europeans had by that decade. Not just refrigerators and washing machines, but automobiles as well came to be items that Europeans might expect to own in the sixties. The rapid increase in ownership of automobiles indicates one way in which the economy and people's habits were changing. By 1969 two of every ten people in Britain, Sweden, West Germany, and France owned an automobile. The United States was still considerably ahead with a figure of four in ten, but the gap had been narrowed.

TABLE 10.1

Automobiles in 1957 and in 1965

	1957	1965
France	3,476,000	7,842,000
Germany (West)	2,456,288	8,103,600
Italy	1,051,004 (1956)	5,468,981
The Netherlands	375,676	1,272,898
Sweden	796,000	1,793,000

Sources: *The Europa Year Book 1959* (London, 1959) and *The Europa Year Book 1967,* volume I (London, 1967).

Television, a shaper as well as symbol of a consumer society, provides an even better index of change.

TABLE 10.2

Televisions in 1957 and in 1965

	1957	1965
France	683,000	6,489,000
Germany	798,586	11,379,000
Italy	367,000	6,044,542
The Netherlands	239,000	2,113,000
Sweden	75,817	2,110,584

Sources: *The Europa Year Book 1959* (London, 1959) and *The Europa Year Book 1967*, volume I (London, 1967).

Along with the acquisition of goods came considerable changes in life-styles and attitudes. The American-style supermarket began to spread in the late 1960s, competing with the small neighborhood butcher, green grocer, baker, and retail grocer. The number of people who ran routes through neighborhoods selling milk, bread, coal or sundries began to decline. Once- or twice-weekly markets became smaller and less important in some areas and disappeared in others. It would be easy to exaggerate the extent of the changes, yet the trends were clear by the late 1960s. The France that Laurence Wylie found in 1951 and described in *Village in the Vaucluse*, a France of peasants living on small farms and in isolated villages, was undergoing rapid change and a profound reorientation. What Wylie found to be true of France was found by others to be true of other areas as well, with allowances for national or regional variations.

Social Changes: Farmers

Changes were perhaps most visible among the farming population. The number of farmers shrank in the fifties and sixties, yet production per capita and overall levels of production increased. This was due to what some have seen as an "agricultural revolution." Primarily, it involved greater use of machinery and more attention to scientific techniques in areas such as breeding of livestock, selection of seed, use of fertilizers, and utilization of the land—in general, capital-intensive rather than labor-intensive farming methods. The results of these changes, augmented by policies favorable to agriculture in the EEC and elsewhere, have been a decline in the number of marginal, self-sufficient farmers and a growing level of prosperity among those who approached their work in many cases as if they were running a factory. While this approach sometimes robbed farm life of some intangible benefits which many prized, such as a feeling of kinship with nature, it did contribute to a closing of the gap between life-styles in the city and in the country. The great improvement in transportation and communication facilities also brought the farmer closer to life in the mainstream. The village that Wylie visited in 1951 had been cut off from life in Paris and even the departmental center. On return visits in the 1960s, Wylie found the villagers more involved in a complex pattern of economic and social exchange with other areas and living in ways increasingly similar to Frenchmen in urban areas.

Social Changes: Workers

The working classes were also changing, although not at the same rate in each country. In Sweden and West Germany, for example, the process of "embourgeoisement" was far advanced. This meant simply that Swedish and German workers differed less and less from members of the middle classes in terms of housing, clothing, leisure activities and the like. On the other hand, in Britain the distinctions between working-class and middle-class styles of life remained prominent. Practically everywhere in western Europe, however, the working class had sufficient income to participate in the consumer economy. Advertising and the mass media created a life-style that both workers and the middle classes desired. A common, mass culture was being created.

Workers inside and outside the trade union structure largely accepted industrial capitalism, though not without reservations and criticism. Their interests were directed increasingly toward gaining an equitable share of the national income, better working conditions, more fringe benefits, and an expansion of the welfare state—in short, economic security. This generally cooperative attitude was most fully developed in Sweden and Germany. In Britain, expectations were similar, but relations between workers and employers more antagonistic. In France and Italy, unions became more reformist in the 1960s, but were less effective in improving the workers' situation than unions in Britain, Germany, and Sweden. Working-class satisfaction with its situation was based in part on the role played in the economy by the "guestworkers," immigrant workers from Yugoslavia, Greece, Turkey, Spain, and Portugal, who took the lowest paying and least desirable jobs. These groups, especially important in Germany, Switzerland, and the Netherlands, and present in large numbers in Sweden and France, gave European economies a certain flexibility. In good times, they were available to work cheaply. In bad times, they could be shipped home to cut unemployment. The indigenous working classes, like other elements of the population, did not worry much in the 1960s about this "sub-proletariat."

Social Changes: The Middle Classes

The middle classes by the sixties could be divided into two large groups. On the one hand, a large number of white-collar employees working as clerks, technicians, sales personnel, lower-ranking professionals (such as teachers and nurses), and supervisory and lower-level managerial personnel made up the lower and middle segments. On the other hand, a relatively small number of higher-ranking professionals (lawyers, doctors, university professors), upper-level bureaucrats and managers, and technocrats made up the upper segment. It was the upper segment that controlled a disproportionate share of wealth, political power, and status in European society. It constituted in some ways a new elite, drawn in part from older elites and in part from the traditional middle classes. The aristocracy as such had largely disappeared. In Britain and France the new elite was essentially a continuation of the old establishment. Elsewhere, the new elite was more open to new members. Education, especially a specialized or technical education, was increasingly a necessity. Family ties still played a role, although a declining one. The new elite, like the older upper class, could be generally characterized not only by educational attainment and social background but also by an attachment, genuine or not, to high culture and by distinctive patterns in housing and leisure-time activity. The role of the very rich differed from country to country; it was extremely important in Germany and Italy, but only minimal in Sweden. The difference had to do with taxation and other income distribution policies. The middle classes in general might be characterized as more conservative in their approach to politics, economic matters, and culture than the working class. Class differences remained strong in Europe, despite the apparent democratization of life.

Economic and Social Change: The East Bloc

Rapid and thorough economic and social changes characterized eastern Europe in the postwar period. Most economies in that area had been agrarian before the war. The major exceptions were Czechoslovakia and the Soviet Union. The latter, even taking into consideration the effects of the first three five-year plans, was still largely agrarian in its economic orientation in 1945. Following the war and the development of a system of states modeled closely on the Soviet Union, collectivization of agriculture, rapid industrialization, and social leveling were introduced. In Rumania, Albania, and Bulgaria, there was less emphasis on industrialization than in the other states. East Germany was also something of a special case in that its economy was so thoroughly subordinated to the needs of the Soviet economy. While the establishment of these policies worked out differently in each country, according to its particular circumstances, there were broadly similar patterns. In theory each society became more or less egalitarian in terms of pay scales, living and working conditions, and rights and privileges. The composition of the various societies changed drastically. Aristocracies, as they had existed before World War II, were no more. Working classes and urban populations made up a much larger percentage of the total population than previously, although the percentage of rural population, except in East Germany, was high compared to percentages in most western European countries.

What the Yugoslav Marxist and writer Milovan Djilas called the "new class" emerged in eastern Europe by the late fifties. The "new class" in each society was made up of communist party functionaries, government bureaucrats, industrial managers, army officers, and leading figures from the world of culture, entertainment, and sport. These people, somewhat analagous to the new elite in western Europe, often had privileges unavailable to the general population, privileges that money alone could not buy such as travel abroad or access to special resorts. The extent to which the "new class" led a different kind of life from the masses and the codification of their position and privileges set them apart from the more informal system of elites in the west.

In each state the economy was state-directed and controlled, with emphasis on industrialization. Comprehensive welfare systems linked society and economy. The patterns did not apply completely to any country, of course. Yugoslavia was the most divergent with such policies as worker co-management in the factory, the use of profit and loss and supply and demand indicators in the economy, peasant ownership of the land, and the decentralization of decision making. Rumania refused to be simply a granary and supplier of raw materials for the East Bloc and began an industrialization program. Other countries varied in more minor ways.

By the early sixties each state had acquired distinctive economic and social frameworks and had reached the point where evaluations could be made. The Soviet Union, the model and dominant influence, was by the early sixties experiencing severe difficulties which Khrushchev's policies only exacerbated. Soviet industry had never performed as well as the planners had hoped. Growth rates began to tail off by the late fifties. A major part of the problem was the extreme centralization of decision making. The economy had become too complex for this approach to be effective. Khrushchev instituted extensive decentralization, a policy that failed largely because the sudden shift from one extreme to another created a great deal of confusion. Added to this were Khrushchev's efforts to increase agricultural production through spectacular but badly planned efforts such as the Virgin Lands program, which brought into cultivation land that had long been pasture land because of limited rainfall. After initial success, the program floundered because of soil erosion problems and the lack of sufficient moisture. The conjunction of domestic policy disasters and foreign policy failures created a situation in which Khrushchev's fall from power became both possible and necessary.

The collective leadership that replaced Khrushchev, Leonid Brezhnev and Alexei Kosygin, returned to more conventional policies to stabilize the economy, and from that base began in the late 1960s to institute reforms that would meet the problems which still existed within the Soviet economy. Those problems were the inability of agriculture, except in the best of years, to produce enough to feed the population; the inability of industry to produce a range and quantity, not to mention quality, of consumer goods that would meet the demands of the population; and, finally, the growing technological gap between the Soviet Union and the West.

These problems had, of course, an important impact on society. Although the position of the Soviet consumer had begun to improve by the sixties, with refrigerators and television sets becoming items that people might be able to purchase, the contrast with the consumer economy of western Europe was startling. Soviet consumer goods tended to be scarce, expensive, and of poor quality. Housing in the cities was difficult to find even twenty years after the war, and was cramped and poorly constructed when available. It was customary to wait in long lines to get almost anything; one estimate is that Soviet women spent as much as two hours a day waiting in lines. Standards of living had improved from the period before the war, but not as rapidly as many had hoped and not very much in comparison to the West.

Some had it better in the Soviet Union. The "new class" of party officials, high-level bureaucrats, military personnel, technocrats, scientists, ballet and movie stars, world-class athletes, and some literary and intellectual luminaries had not only higher incomes but a range of privileges unavailable to the ordinary citizen. The *dacha* (a small cottage in the countryside) for weekends or vacations, special stores with a wider selection than ordinary stores, special clinics for medical treatment without crowds and long waits, official cars for private use, and an "old boy" network that opened up educational and career opportunities to the sons and daughters of the prominent, were among the privileges of the Soviet "new class."

For the Soviet Union, then, the sixties were a time of considerable tension as some contradictions of the economy and society posed problems that required answers. This may explain, in part, both a greater willingness to cooperate with the West but also a continuing reluctance to let experiments in satellite countries on its western borders go very far.

Among these countries, Poland, Czechoslovakia, East Germany, and Yugoslavia were more successful than the Soviet Union in meeting consumer demands, if not nearly as successful as countries in western Europe. East Germany, despite the restrictions imposed by the Soviet Union over the years, was successful in making itself into a major industrial power by the late 1960s. Czech performance, on the other hand, was disappointing considering the industrial base available after World War II. Poland, which had de-collectivized agriculture, enjoyed greater agricultural productivity despite the existence of numerous small and theoretically inefficient farms. Complaints about the existence of a "new class" surfaced in eastern Europe as well. As in the Soviet Union, standards of living were, for the average person, considerably higher than they had been before the war. Each society was beginning to establish distinctive approaches to economics and politics that were appropriate to prevailing conditions rather than a slavish imitation of the Soviet Union.

De Gaulle

Most countries in Europe enjoyed a considerable degree of political stability from the late fifties to the mid-sixties, undoubtedly due to a large extent to the existence of widespread affluence. Much of what was interesting and significant in politics was the work of one man, Charles de Gaulle, who returned from self-imposed political exile to shape the Fifth French Republic and to mold in major ways the development of institutions outside France such as the European Economic Community (EEC) and the North Atlantic Treaty Organization (NATO). De Gaulle returned to active politics in May 1958. He was the only person acceptable as a national leader to all groups after the collapse of the Fourth Republic. The republic had collapsed after a coalition of *colons* (Europeans resident in Algeria) and army officers seized power in Algiers, the capital of Algeria. The coalition was prepared to attack the mainland. (It had already seized Corsica.) It intended to bring to power a regime that would keep Algeria French. The coalition saw in De Gaulle a leader who would do that and at the same time unite France. Probably De Gaulle intended at the time to keep Algeria attached to France. In the next few years, however, he saw the impossibility of this and created a position of power in the new government sufficient to allow him to overrule the *colons* and the military. Accords were signed in 1962 giving Algeria independence. Sporadic protests were mounted against this, but De Gaulle was able to deal with them easily.

The process of extricating France from Algeria was a complicated one, but the major factor that made it possible was the restructuring of the government carried through by De Gaulle and his associates in 1958 and 1959. This resulted in the Fifth French Republic within which the president occupied a position of considerable power. Whatever range of constitutional powers were available to De Gaulle, he added to them by activities which no politician without his force of personality and moral stature could have gotten away with.

By the early 1960s, De Gaulle had achieved one important aim: the reestablishment of unity within France. In the remainder of the decade, he worked to make France once again a great power, the leader in a Europe free of American dominance. One method was to make France an independent nuclear power. A great deal of money was invested in this, despite the protests of some who wanted more invested in social programs. A second method involved the attempts to weaken NATO, at least the dominant American position within NATO. There were other methods also, such as De Gaulle's attempts to create special relationships with Third World nations and his talks with other political mavericks such as Nicolae Ceausescu of Rumania. One of his major efforts, a good example of both motives and goals, was directed toward the reshaping of the EEC.

First, De Gaulle blocked British membership in the EEC, ostensibly because of the insurmountable differences between the British economic situation and that of the member nations of the EEC. It was readily apparent, however, that De Gaulle also objected to Britain's Atlantic orientation, fearing that American influence would follow the British into the EEC, and to the idea of sharing leadership in the EEC with the British. De Gaulle also worked to slow the tendency for the EEC to develop into a supranational organization, which led to repeated clashes with the head of the Commission of the EEC, Walter Hallstein. The crisis in 1965 that threatened to destroy the EEC was resolved the following year with an agreement that made it clear that national sovereignty was still the operating principle in the EEC and the Council of Foreign Ministers the locus of power. Thanks to De Gaulle's efforts, supranationalism remained dormant within the EEC. It continued to function well as a stimulus for the economies of its member nations, but it did not develop as many of its founders had hoped and as many observers had predicted in the early 1960s.

While De Gaulle was increasingly preoccupied by foreign affairs in the middle 1960s, domestic problems continued to develop. One of the most serious concerned the contrast between the sophistication of French technology and science and the backwardness of some aspects of life in France, two examples being telephone systems and housing. Secondly, society was, if no longer a class society, one of strata. The different strata were determined by educational achievement to a large extent, but the way to a proper education in most cases involved money, family background, and connections. An indication of domestic dissatisfaction was the 1965 presidential elections in which François Mitterand, leader of the left coalition of socialists and communists, forced De Gaulle into a runoff. Although De Gaulle won and continued to govern virtually unchecked, developments were taking place that would lead to another crisis of state and society almost ten years exactly from the 1958 crisis.

The only other figure of similar stature to De Gaulle in the sixties, Konrad Adenauer, retired as chancellor of West Germany in circumstances that did no credit to his crucial achievements in the fifties. Adenauer had promised to turn over the chancellorship to Ludwig Erhard, his finance minister, in 1959 and to accept the ceremonial office of the presidency. He decided against this when he realized how limited his power would be. The *Der Spiegel* affair (*Der Spiegel* is a German newsmagazine somewhat similar to *Time*), in which the defense minister arbitrarily arrested some of the magazine's staff and Adenauer failed to step in and decisively defend constitutional processes, led to his promise to resign in 1963.

Ludwig Erhard proved to be a lackluster chancellor. His failure to deal with economic problems left the Christian Democrats little choice but to agree to a coalition with the Social Democrats. In the several years before the coalition, the Social Democrats had become a broadly-based party of reform under the leadership of Willy Brandt. After three years of coalition government, the Social Democrats gained power on their own.

By the mid-sixties a definite political trend had emerged in western Europe. Parties of the right and center, long dominant in the affairs of their nation, found it increasingly difficult to maintain power. Parties on the left, especially the Socialists and Social Democrats but also the Communists, gained in elections and in several cases became part of the government. In Italy, for example, the Christian Democrats established an "opening to the left" in 1963, which resulted in a coalition with the Socialists. The major figure behind this move in the Christian Democratic party was Aldo Moro. His efforts were aided by papal acceptance of the welfare state as expressed in the papal bull *Mater et Magistra* (Mother and Teacher) issued by Pope John XXIII in 1961. Throughout western Europe, Socialists were accepted as potential or actual participants in government. There was also less suspicion of the Communists who, on the local and regional levels in France and Italy, demonstrated an ability to function effectively in

politics. Socialists and Communists alike emphasized their prag-
matism, their ability to operate in a pluralistic society, and their in-
corruptibility.

Throughout Europe, from the Soviet Union westward, new leaders
had emerged to replace those prominent in the immediate postwar
era. De Gaulle was the major exception to this, but even he had appeared on the scene essentially as the leader of a group of new men to
replace those leaders worn out by the frequent cabinet shuffles of the
Fourth Republic. This new leadership found a set of problems different from those faced by the politicians of the era of reconstruction.
From the mid-sixties on, rates of economic growth were slowing, inflation was rising, discontent seemed a part of the new consumer economy. In most of western Europe, but particularly in Germany, Italy,
and France, groups appeared to challenge the political consensus
and the prevailing economic wisdom.

Intellectual Currents

From the pessimism and despair of the immediate postwar period,
European thought had moved in slow and complex fashion through
existentialism where, despite the efforts of people such as the essayist
and novelist Albert Camus, the emphasis was on the passive acceptance of the insignificance of human action in the face of the blind,
powerful workings of the universe; and from there on to radical cri-
tiques of democratic society calling for massive change through revolution. The change from pessimism and passivity to political and social
activism was in part simply the product of improved conditions that
gave Europeans a reason to believe that they could affect the developments of events. As Cold War tensions eased and the two opposing
blocs loosened, Europeans began to sense once again that they controlled their own destiny. In part, the change was grounded in more
concrete developments. In the late 1950s many Europeans became
involved in ban-the-bomb movements. Others became disillusioned by what they had learned about various efforts to defeat liberation movements in the colonies. Particularly in Algeria, there had
been methods used and attitudes assumed that were strongly reminiscent of the worst of Nazi Germany. Closer to home, some won-
dered why, in a society where the level of material comfort was so
high, they should feel so dissatisfied.

This kind of critical attitude toward society was still relatively rare
in the early and even the mid-sixties. The Vietnamese struggle against
the United States helped to form and to spread it, but it was neverthe-

less confined largely to students, intellectuals, a few workers, and others who considered themselves to be on the margins of society.

Another small minority was involved in the affairs of high culture. Here the modernist movement, which had conquered the art world in the interwar period, continued its advance after the war. The center of the art world, however, was now New York and most prominent practitioners, whether Americans or Europeans, worked in the United States. The modernist approach was also prominent in the theater, in plays such as Samuel Beckett's *Waiting for Godot* or Eugene Ionesco's *The Chairs*, and in film, in the efforts of Alain Renais and Michelangelo Antonioni, among others. In addition, there was the "new novel," as practiced particularly in France. However, the theater, film, and the novel generally continued to follow more conventional patterns. The British playwright John Osborne and the German novelist Heinrich Böll were largely conventional in technique. Others, such as the German novelist Günter Grass, shaded toward a modernist approach in their works but not to the extent that plot and the representational qualities of the work disappeared. High culture remained sharply divided between those who experimented largely without regard for the audience and those who remained for the most part within the conventions that had been shaped by the end of the nineteenth century. Music was particularly bedeviled by this. Experiments with aleatory (chance) music and electronic compositions found sparse audiences. Much larger audiences flocked to hear the great classics of the eighteenth and nineteenth centuries. Only in art was the victory of modernism clear-cut and complete among all the constituencies—artists, critics, and the art public.

Popular Culture

Europeans, like Americans, were interested in the late 1950s and 1960s not as much in social and political activism or high culture as in diversion and entertainment. Commercialized popular culture in the form of popular music, television, movies, spectator sports, fashion, and cheap literature and journalism of all sorts almost completely eliminated what had remained of the older popular culture that had been associated with the working classes and the peasantry. A growing affluence and a shortened work week were the keys to the spread of popular culture. Other factors also contributed, such as improved communications and transportation networks which brought parts of a single country and various different countries closer together.

Aspects of American culture, especially those connected with American mass or popular culture, began to permeate Europe. Coca Cola was a pioneer in this. By the 1960s it was Levi jeans and rhythm and blues. On the whole, people were more cosmopolitan and literate (although falling far short of standards set by the minority of truly cosmopolitan, literate Europeans). Europeans, especially the French, worried about American culture corrupting European values and institutions. Ironically, it was Britain, a shadow of its former self politically and economically, that took the lead in music and fashion, the two staples of a burgeoning youth cult. (The youth, as never before, had money and time at their disposal; also, they had a sense of the necessity of creating their own culture since that of their elders did not seem to apply particularly well to rapidly changing conditions.) The Beatles, with their soft, romantic, ironic, tuneful music, symbolized much of the culture of the times. Coming from the working class of Liverpool, they also represented the way in which popular culture had moved from roots that were largely lower class to capture the allegiance of large numbers of all classes.

The spread of a popular culture much like that prevailing in the United States was only one indication that Europe had changed in fundamental ways. Other indications were the development of a consumer economy and the increasing importance of the service sector in that economy. The social structure was also changing. Class distinctions were no longer as rigid. Elites still existed and were largely self-perpetuating, but they were now formed differently and were more open. The new role of government as partner in the economy and as guarantor of social well-being was now accepted. Finally, Europe seemed more comfortable with its new international role, now that it had divested itself of most of its colonies and had seen that both the Soviet Union and the United States had their areas of vulnerability.

A new Europe had emerged in the second decade after the war. It had not solved all the problems that had plagued the old Europe and it had created some of its own. But it had put in place institutions and processes that turned out to be surprisingly durable in the difficult years of the late sixties and early seventies. And it continued on into the seventies to provide an alternative to both the American and the Soviet styles of life.

Suggested Readings

Anthony Sampson, *Anatomy of Europe* (1968)

Stanley Rothman, *European Society and Politics: Britain, France and Germany** (1976)

Stephen Graubard, ed., *A New Europe?* (1964)

Herbert Marcuse, *One-Dimensional Man** (1964)

Michael Crozier, *The Bureaucratic Phenomenon** (1967)

Milovan Djilas, *The New Class** (rev. ed., 1974)

_____, *The Unperfect Society: Beyond the New Class** (1970)

Arthur Marwich, *Class: Image and Reality in Britain, France, and America since 1930* (1980)

Roland N. Stromberg, *After Everything: Western Intellectual History since 1945** (1975)

Laurence Wylie, *Village in the Vaucluse** (third ed., 1974)

Ronald Blythe, *Aikenfield: Portrait of an English Village** (1980)

Stephen Holt, *The Common Market: The Conflict of Theory and Practice* (1967)

Richard Mayne, *The Recovery of Europe, 1945-1973* (rev. ed., 1973)

Anthony Sampson, *The New Anatomy of Britain** (1973)

Charles S. Maier and Dan S. White, eds., *The 13th of May: The Advent of De Gaulle's Republic** (1968)

John Ardagh, *The New French Revolution* (1969)

Alexander Dallin and Thomas B. Larson, eds., *Soviet Politics since Khrushchev* (1968)

Stanley Rothman and George Breslauer, *Soviet Politics and Society** (1978)

David Lane, *Politics and Society in the U.S.S.R.** (sec. ed., 1978)

Abraham Rothberg, *The Heirs of Stalin: Dissidence and the Soviet Regime, 1953-1970* (1972)

Rudolf L. Tohes, ed., *Dissent in the USSR: Politics, Ideology, and People** (1975)

Stephen Fischer-Galati, ed., *Eastern Europe in the '60s* (1963)
James F. Brown, *The New Eastern Europe* (1966)
Robert L. Wolff, *The Balkans in Our Time** (rev. ed., 1978)
Jean Edward Smith, *Germany beyond the Wall* (1967)
Alec Nove, *The Soviet Economy* (second ed., 1969)
Michael Kaser, *Comecon: Integration Problems of the Planned Economies* (second ed., 1967)
_____, *Economic Development in Eastern Europe* (1969)

*indicates paperback edition available

11

Europe and the World, 1968-1975

By the end of the 1960s, Europeans had enjoyed an unprecedented era of nearly two decades of political stability and economic prosperity. The events of the years between 1968, a year of political turmoil in western and in eastern Europe, and 1975, the year when the extraordinary economic difficulties caused by the rise in oil prices in 1973 and the recession in 1974 began to ease somewhat, called into question the easy progress of the postwar period. The social and the economic premises of the consumer economy were challenged. Domestic politics seemed a great deal more difficult than in previous years, particularly in eastern Europe. Relations between eastern and western Europe changed dramatically. Less dramatic but still significant were the new connections between Europe and the two world powers, the Soviet Union and the United States.

Most of the political and economic crises of the late 1960s and early 1970s were resolved in pragmatic fashion, much to the disappointment of some who had hoped for more visionary solutions. Perhaps more important, Europe emerged from these years of political upheaval and economic difficulty as a more independent force in world affairs than it had been. It was still not possible to think of Europe as a third force able to match either the Soviet Union or the United States, but European states individually and collectively had begun to play an important role in such activities as the north-south dialogue between developed and developing countries, and the search for suitable policies dealing with social issues connected with urban life, protection of the environment, and old age, among others.

Western European military strength and diplomatic activity lagged behind economic development, but some western Europeans questioned whether the United States could continue to shoulder the major part of the burden of defense and called for an expanded role for Europe. Eastern Europe, much stronger militarily in relation to its economic base than western Europe but more closely tied to its protector, the Soviet Union, nevertheless showed some cautious signs of greater independence. Although no fundamental changes occurred, many relationships between Europe and the greater and lesser powers underwent modification as Europe increasingly moved out from under the shadows of the two postwar giants.

Europe and the United States

Europe's relations with the United States reached a postwar low in the late sixties and early seventies. The major problem was the American involvement in Vietnam, which by 1968 had taken on massive proportions. American emphasis on European relations inevitably declined. Beyond this, numerous European states, even some NATO allies of the United States, condemned American actions. Another serious problem was related to the possibility that Europe might become a battleground in the event of war between the Soviet Union and the United States. Europeans feared that the United States might not use nuclear weapons in the event of an invasion of western Europe by the forces of the Warsaw Treaty Organization (WTO). This could prevent a nuclear exchange between the United States and the Soviet Union, but it would not prevent the ruin of much of western Europe, given the superiority of the WTO to NATO in terms of conventional weaponry.

American commitments to European defense and especially to the Vietnam conflict were partially responsible for a growing balance-of-payments deficit in the United States. This, together with Europe's growing productive power, lent a special twist to diplomatic-political relations between the two areas. If Europeans questioned the reliability of America's "nuclear umbrella," Americans constantly urged Europeans to pay more for their own defense. Although there was considerable comment at the time about the "American Challenge," as a French commentator termed it, Europe was, in fact, developing a strong economic position relative to the United States. The period saw a loosening of western Europe's ties with the United States and a shift in the economic balance in Europe's favor, but, at the same time, continued European dependence on American military power.

Europe and the Soviet Union

Relations between the Soviet Union and eastern Europe remained as they had been since the mid-fifties. It was only an illusion that there was any loosening here. When Czechoslovakia exceeded the narrow limits of what the Soviet Union would tolerate in eastern Europe, the Soviet Union reasserted its primacy in the area by crushing the Czech reform efforts (see below). Rumania, more limited in its aspirations, succeeded in achieving a modest measure of independence. With the exceptions of Yugoslavia and Albania, other eastern European countries followed Soviet leads fairly closely.

Relations between the Soviet Union and western Europe improved considerably, despite dismay at the Soviet repression of the Czech experiment in 1968. Improved relations were based in part on the Soviet-American détente and the relaxation in tension that it produced. They were based also on the West German initiative provided by Willy Brandt's *Ostpolitik* (east policy). Brandt, the Social Democratic chancellor of West Germany, launched an effort at the end of the sixties to recognize the facts of postwar life: the division of Germany and the loss of German territory to Poland and Czechoslovakia. In so doing, he hoped to reassure the Soviet Union and to reduce barriers between eastern and western Europe in general, and West Germany and East Germany in particular.

Despite the obvious concern of the Soviet Union with European affairs, a concern made clear by its actions against Czechoslovakia, both the Soviet Union and the United States were preoccupied by non-European matters. While the United States struggled in Vietnam, the Soviet Union faced deteriorating relations with China. Both nations pursued strong interests in the Near East. Europe was no longer the focus of great power concern.

Europe and Other Areas

Because the great powers were engaged elsewhere, Europe, both east and west, enjoyed a more independent position in foreign affairs in the early 1970s. The development of détente and Europe's strong economic position contributed to this situation. European countries got along surprisingly well with Third World nations, even with their former colonies. In the case of the former colonies, European states sometimes achieved greater influence and more advantageous arrangements than under the old colonial system. The French, for example, maintained good relations in the 1970s with old colonies in sub-Saharan Africa. The Dutch continued to play an important role in Surinam (in South America) after its independence. The major exception here was Portugal, which only in 1974 began to negotiate seriously to extricate itself from a series of colonial wars. This aside, European relations with African and other Third World nations generally improved. Germany joined France in providing substantial aid and technical advice to various African states and also Turkey, Pakistan and several Latin American nations. Many Europeans held that their continent was taking the lead in developing constructive ties with the underdeveloped areas.

Europeans, like nearly everyone else, were surprised by the response of several oil-producing states in the Middle East to the Arab-Israeli war of 1973. Europe found itself the target, along with the United States, of an oil embargo and later an extraordinary price increase. Although the European economies made the adjustment to greatly increased energy costs, it became clear that they were more vulnerable than they had realized. Not only did they depend on resources the supply and price of which they could not control, but they also could not control or anticipate what the various oil-producing nations would do with the large amounts of capital that Europe was providing in exchange for oil.

These major questions aside, foreign policy matters largely went well for the European states in the early 1970s. Certainly compared with several internal political challenges, foreign affairs took on a favorable light during much of the period under review.

Radicalism and Rebellion in 1968: Western Europe

Internal developments were less clearly favorable than the diplomatic environment. Toward the end of the sixties, several western European states seemed to be virtually besieged by radicals questioning not only the political frameworks of the various states but also social institutions and economic arrangements. In general, radicals accused governments in western Europe of ruling in an authoritarian style at home and aiding "imperialism" and counterrevolution abroad. Social and economic institutions were seen as consciously contrived to perpetuate political and economic power in the hands of small ruling cliques while keeping the masses both ignorant of the true situation through control and manipulation of the media and satisfied through the production and distribution of inexpensive consumer goods. The most radical groups saw themselves as part of a worldwide revolutionary movement answering the call of the famous Cuban revolutionary Che Guevara for "One, Two, Three . . . Many Vietnams!" Few identified with established socialist or communist parties in Europe. Some called themselves Maoists or joined organizations of student radicals. Many protesters had rather limited aims, dealing mostly with the reform of what they saw as undemocratic and elitist educational systems designed to reinforce the inequities of the larger political and socioeconomic systems. The organized radical movement, much smaller than the number of protesters but also largely composed of students and young intellectuals, varied from country to country in terms of its impact on the existing system. France was affected more than any other European country by radicalism in 1968. Germany and Italy each confronted large-scale movements but escaped a major crisis. Britain and the Netherlands had important movements which, however, had limited impact on the course of events in each country.

Events in Germany were as dramatic as those in France, and in the United States as well, but they failed to have a major impact on state and society. The German radicals were organized in the German Socialist Student Federation (SDS). The first major protest was directed against the Shah of Iran during his visit to West Berlin in 1967. The publications empire of Axel Springer became the next focus of SDS attacks. Efforts to disrupt the distribution of Springer publications, which had been editorially hostile to the student radicals, were intensified after one of the SDS leaders, Rudi Dutschke, was shot in April 1968 and seriously wounded. Despite the dramatic nature of events in Germany in the spring of 1968, the government was not seriously challenged. The German SDS lacked the circumstances that prevailed in France in May, where brutal police repression of student demonstrators led to confrontations between the forces of law and order and those of freedom and anarchy which, especially in Paris, brought much public sympathy to the radical student movement. In Germany, student radicals remained isolated from the general public, which was largely satisfied with existing arrangements and unsympathetic to the radical demands.

France in May

The French movement, although based on several years of agitation prior to 1968, was largely a spontaneous reaction to a specific event, the arrest of a number of students demonstrating against the United States' involvement in Vietnam. On March 22, 1968, a meeting to protest the arrests was held outside Paris at the University of Nanterre. It led to the formation of a radical movement called the March 22 Movement. Various events followed leading up to "Anti-Imperialist Day" on May 2. That day the members of the March 22

French students clash with police in Paris during the confrontation between students and the government in May 1968. (Wide World Photos)

Movement, locked out of Nanterre, went instead to the Sorbonne, a part of the University of Paris. The next day police came into the Sorbonne and arrested hundreds of students, violating long-standing traditions of academic freedom. This in turn led to repeated demonstrations and confrontations in the Latin Quarter in Paris, climaxing on the night of May 10, the "Night of the Barricades," when events were described minute-by-minute on the radio. On May 13 more than a million people demonstrated in Paris against the government. The day after that workers seized the Sud-Aviation plant, and soon nearly ten million workers were on strike.

Toward the end of May the government, which had not dealt effectively with events throughout that month, took the initiative by dissolving the National Assembly and setting a date for elections. De Gaulle appealed for "civic action" against a "totalitarian plot." Many Frenchmen began to worry about the possibility of anarchy. Numerous people were simply tired of the confusion and the disruptions caused by the demonstrations and strikes. The student radicals themselves were not in agreement on aims and goals. The workers generally wanted only moderate changes connected with their jobs, including a substantial pay hike. The public, initially sympathetic in many cases, drew back from the idea of a genuine revolution.

France was closer to revolution in 1968 than any other European country but, as it turned out, was not as close as it appeared. Government inactivity coupled with some blunders had resulted in a situation in which the overthrow of the government seemed possible. The government, however, was still viable. It had capable leadership in President de Gaulle and Premier Georges Pompidou and a monopoly of the military and police forces. The social and economic strains that it labored under were not as severe as they appeared to be. In summary, the strength of the establishment was still overwhelming.

Contrasting with the strength of establishment was the lack of organization on the part of the radicals. They were also hampered by the lack of a precise target—the ''system'' was the enemy. There was no agreement among the radicals as to a definition of the system and certainly no agreement on a program to combat or replace the system, whether it be the French university system, the Gaullist government or modern industrial society. Without a clear-cut program and a leadership recognized by all groups, the radicals tended

Daniel Cohn-Bendit, the best-known of the European student radical leaders of the 1960s. Cohn-Bendit, a German enrolled in the French University system, played a major role in the confrontation between the students and the government in May 1968. (Sven Simon/Katherine Young)

to think in terms of tactics—short-run, limited responses to government initiatives—rather than in terms of strategy. In addition, the radicals were more isolated than it appeared. They did not understand the aspirations of those who temporarily allied with them, both the workers and the general public.

The major immediate results of the radical movement were changes in the educational systems of France, Germany, and Italy which created possibilities for revised curricula, less elitist student bodies, and less authoritarian structures of university administration. Politics were affected in that many turned back to moderate or conservative parties. The parties on the left felt compelled to strike a moderate pose in order to distance themselves from the radicals. The Communists, however, who had done nothing in France to aid the radical movement, found themselves distrusted once again by moderate forces and under heavy criticism from many radicals. The larger changes that radicals had hoped for, reorientation of the goals of society and the economy and a new relationship between the people and the government, did not come about. The year 1968 was the high point of postwar radicalism in Europe. The radicals had made an impact, but the sweeping and comprehensive changes that they envisioned were not acceptable to most Europeans. Most people found life reasonably enjoyable as it was, and worried more about the economy slowing or other problems which would prevent them from achieving those goals that they had come to see as realistic possibilities.

The Prague Spring

Just as the radical reform movement in western Europe peaked, reformers in Czechoslovakia attempted to carry out far-reaching changes in the political and economic systems of their country. Events in the early sixties prepared the way for the extraordinary developments of the spring and summer of 1968. Communist party leadership, especially that of Antonin Novotny, first secretary of the party, increasingly came under criticism in the early sixties. Questions were raised about the political trials held between 1949 and 1954. Slovak communists were especially active in pressing for party reform and a change in leaders. Novotny's attempts to deal with the situation were hampered by economic difficulties. Czechs, who at the end of the fifties enjoyed the highest standard of living among the satellite countries, had to cope with over-investment in heavy industry in the early sixties and with a stagnating economy later in the decade.

*Soviet troops entering Prague almost thirty years after the invasion of Czecho-
slovakia by Germany. When the Soviet Union and several other members of the
Warsaw Treaty Organization feared that Dubcek's reforms had gone too far, they
authorized a military occupation of Czechoslovakia.* (Wide World Photos)

In January 1968, Novotny was replaced as first secretary of the
party by Alexander Dubček, a Slovak and leader of the reform im-
pulse. Dubček moved first to liberalize the economy by decentralizing
it, increasing emphasis on consumer goods and on investments in
Slovakia, and establishing more trade with the West. He also lifted
censorship and opened up cultural and intellectual life. An "Action
Program" was presented in April which called for, among other
items, continued loyalty to the Soviet Union.

The reform movement began to get out of hand in the late spring.
The growth of clubs and discussion groups threatened the monopoly
of political power by the Communist party. The Russians, East
Germans, and Poles began to grow apprehensive about developments. Two meetings were held in the summer of 1968, the first with
the Soviet Union on July 31, the second a few days later with repre-
sentatives of the member nations of the WTO. The invasion of
Czechoslovakia came on August 20. Efforts just short of armed
resistance were made by the Czechs to block the invasion. Demonstrations followed, including some acts of self-immolation. The

Soviet Union was not able to engineer the installation of a more orthodox regime until the spring of 1969 when it forced Dubček's resignation and his replacement by Gustav Husák. Dubček's supporters were thrown out of office. Many went into exile; others, after varying terms of detention, were given minor posts and stripped of any political influence.

Czech experiments with the concept of "socialism with a human face" failed in part because of the blind enthusiasm of many participants in the reform movement. They did not take sufficiently into account the rising anxiety of the Soviet Union, East Germany, and Poland. The Soviet Union could not afford to chance Czechoslovakia's defection from the WTO. Its geographical location is such that it forms a salient into the Ukraine, an area of the Soviet Union highly important for both agricultural and industrial production. The Soviet Union joined East Germany and Poland in wondering what effect a rapidly liberalizing Czechoslovakia would have on their more orthodox regimes, already experiencing dissent and calls for greater liberation.

Politics in the Early 1970s:
East Europe after the Czech Invasion of 1968

Czechoslovakia experienced conditions in the early 1970s that were reminiscent of the early 1950s: subservience to Moscow, police repression, and censorship. After Husák replaced Dubček, a thorough purge of party leadership and membership took place. Carefully staged elections in November 1971 and the Fourteenth Party Congress in May 1971 were also part of the process of "normalization." Among the problems remaining, however, were the apathy of many members of the Czechoslovak Communist Party and the difference of opinion between the pro-Soviet hard-liners and the more moderate leaders such as Husák, over what to do with the thousands of able people who had supported the reform movement but had not been leaders.

A good deal of emphasis was placed on the fifth five-year plan, which began in 1971. The hope was that many would forget about 1968 if the standard of living was improved. Husák achieved considerable success in the early 1970s in establishing his pragmatic and moderate policies at the expense of the hard-liners. He was less successful, though, in causing Czechoslovakians to forget 1968.

Poland, one of the states most alarmed by events in Czechoslovakia in 1968, changed in several respects in the years following.

First, Wladyslaw Gomulka was replaced by Edward Gierek in 1970. Gomulka was criticized for incorrect implementation of policies, more specifically for the economic difficulties experienced by Poland. Most of the leaders who followed Gomulka and his colleagues lacked training in the Soviet Union or experience in the anti-German underground in World War II. The post-Gomulka leadership traveled more and allowed more publicity about its meetings and decisions than before, so that the government appeared to be less aloof than it once had.

Several changes were made in agriculture, including higher prices for producers and the end of compulsory deliveries. Agricultural production and consumer goods were emphasized in the five-year plan for 1971 to 1975. Problems continued in industry with absenteeism, excessive production costs, and poor quality of production. Gierek tried to meet these by allowing private enterprise to play a small role in the economy and by emphasizing improvements in living standards. The change in regime did not lead, however, to liberalization or democratization in society and politics. Poland under Gierek continued to follow the Soviet lead rather closely in foreign affairs and to increase cooperation with the Soviet Union in a variety of ways.

Rumania, which did not take part in the invasion of Czechoslovakia, followed a path quite different from that of Poland. Under the leadership of the President of the Council of State, Nicolae Ceausescu, Rumania emphasized national sovereignty, the right to order her own affairs both at home and abroad. At home, although the stress remained on political control by the Rumanian Communist Party, there were attempts to encourage political participation. These efforts had only limited success. More successful were the efforts to educate the population and to make some progress toward higher standards of living.

Yugoslavia, long accustomed to following its own path within the international communist movement, faced two challenges in the post-1968 period. While foreign policy remained firmly grounded in the idea of non-alignment, despite some improvements in relations with the Soviet Union, Yugoslavia took on two, interrelated domestic issues. One involved the heirship to Tito and the second, closely connected with the first, dealt with the revival of nationalism and ethnic rivalries among the six republics constituting Yugoslavia. In large part, the two problems were given their particular shape by the decentralization of political and economic power which, in turn, made the republics important and influential in political and economic life and reduced the power of the national League of Communists of Yugoslavia (LCY). A downturn in the economy in 1970-1971 and a student strike in Croatia in December 1971, which emphasized Croatian interests, led Tito to move toward a policy of recentralization of politics and greater power for the LCY. A purge of several organizations on the level of the republic followed in 1972, as Tito sought to create a party that could deal with the economic crisis and bank the fires of national and ethnic competition. Like his counterpart in China, Mao Zedong, and at somewhat the same time but on a much reduced scale, Tito found it necessary to attempt to re-establish the revolution in Yugoslavia. Yugoslavia was rather an exception to the general picture in eastern Europe where, after the excitement of events in Czechoslovakia, there was almost no experimentation in politics. A great deal of attention was paid to economic matters as governments struggled to meet desires for a better standard of living and to deal with the problems involved in sustaining economic development.

Brezhnev's Russia

In the several years following the events of 1968, Leonid Brezhnev emerged as the major figure in Soviet politics despite continued references to the premier, Alexei Kosygin, and occasional mention of the president, Nikolai Podgorny. Changes in the Politburo in the early seventies assured Brezhnev of a solid base of power in that organization, the chief policymaking body in the Communist Party. Brezhnev and his supporters were faced with several important domestic issues, issues that made détente with the United States seem even more attractive in that an easing of tension in international matters made concentration on internal affairs easier. In addition to the perennial issue of the economy, the Soviet Union also faced important difficulties in its policies toward nationalities and dissidents.

Soviet dissidents protested the invasion of Czechoslovakia in 1968 and several were arrested for protesting in Red Square in Moscow. *Samizdat* (literally, "self-publishing"; hand- or typewritten manuscripts circulated illegally) publications continued to appear in the Soviet Union. Aleksandr Solzhenitsyn emerged in the late sixties and early seventies not only as a major figure in world literature but also as one of the mainstays of the dissident movement. He was not allowed to accept the Nobel Prize for literature in 1970 because of his prominent role in the movement. Andrei Sakharov, an eminent

Russian physicist, was perhaps even more important because of his work with the Committee for Human Rights. The official Soviet line toward dissidents remained harsh. Similarly harsh were reactions to nationalist movements in Lithuania, the Ukraine, and elsewhere. Part of the general campaign to control intellectual and cultural life and to restrict the expression of nationalist or ethnic sentiments were the efforts to hamper the emigration of Soviet Jews through special taxes and other policies.

Ever-present and basic to the maintenance of power in the Soviet Union was, of course, the economic question. The year 1972 was particularly bad, with a harvest 15 percent below planned levels and a growth rate in the overall economy of only 4 percent, the lowest since 1963. Partially behind the move toward détente were plans to rejuvenate the Soviet economy by massive injections of Western technology and investment. Another hope was the exploitation of the vast quantity of natural resources in Siberia. Neither was likely, however, to eliminate the basic problems that emerged in the 1960s and led to lower growth rates in the 1970s. One problem had to do with the technological lag of the Soviet Union. The government found it difficult to move from the relatively simple technical requirements of basic heavy industry to the more sophisticated demands of high technology. Computer development lagged, for example. Another problem was directly connected with the rate of growth of the economy. In part, the economy had expanded in the past because of an annual enlargement of the labor force and an increase in the amount of capital available for investment. Increases in productivity are another way in which an economy grows, but this had not figured prominently in the Soviet economy's development between 1930 and 1970. In the 1970s Soviet economic planners found that the automatic increase in the size of the labor force could no longer be counted on because population growth was slowing. Nor could investment necessarily increase year after year. It had reached a point where any substantial increase would come at the expense of consumption or at the expense of "social investment," money put into facilities or services that would increase the public welfare. Given the strong press for improvements in the standard of living beyond what had already been reached, it was not wise to divert investment capital from "social investment" to industrial needs.

In 1973 the Soviet Union attempted another reorganization of the economy, involving mergers of similar enterprises into associations to gain the benefits of economy of scale without losing sight of the priorities and peculiarities of each component within the association. This has failed, like so many other past fluctuations between centralized and decentralized economic organizations. At the mid-point of the 1970s, the Soviet Union remained plagued by domestic problems that were only partially offset by foreign policy successes.

West European Politics: Brandt's *Ostpolitik*

Politics in western Europe after the failure of the radical movements at the end of the sixties produced little in the way of accomplishment. The great leaders of the postwar era no longer played a role in European politics after De Gaulle's retirement in 1969. The new leaders were, for the most part, rather cautious and moderate in their policies, managers rather than visionaries. The major exception to the prevailing political stagnation were the policies of Willy Brandt, in particular his *Ostpolitik*. The emergence of the German Social Democratic Party (SPD), first as a coalition partner of the Christian Democrats (CDU) and then as the government party in 1969 in coalition with the Free Democrats, was the key development. The SPD in power made few changes in the economic and social arrangements in West Germany, but it did initiate a series of highly significant developments in foreign policy. These developments, collectively labeled the *Ostpolitik* (east policy) and part of the general détente between east and west, had begun when Willy Brandt, the leader of the SPD, was foreign secretary in the great coalition with the CDU. When the SPD came into power on its own, *Ostpolitik* began in earnest. It involved the reopening of diplomatic relations with various east European states, the recognition of East Germany, and acceptance of the existing Polish-German boundaries. Brandt remained in power until 1974, despite an economic slowdown beginning in 1973. While disappointed in progress made toward social reform and European unification, he resigned primarily because of the scandal created by the discovery of an East German spy among his advisers. His successor, Helmut Schmidt, has been much more of a pragmatist and gradualist.

France Under De Gaulle and Pompidou

Although Georges Pompidou was able to steer France through the crisis of 1968 and although the nation responded one more time in the elections that year to the charisma of De Gaulle, the events were a fateful step in the direction of the decline of Gaullism. The next year

De Gaulle retired after losing a referendum on a relatively unimportant aspect of government reorganization. His successor, Pompidou, continued most of the Gaullist policies but, because he saw his role in less grand terms and because he soon became ill, Pompidou moderated most of these policies. In the 1974 elections, the Left Federation under François Mitterand, who had put the French Socialist Party back together again and had made it into a strong force on the left, gained 48 percent of the vote. Valery Giscard d'Estaing, the Liberal party candidate, was second, with the Gaullist candidate a poor third. In the runoff election, the right threw its weight behind Giscard d'Estaing and elected him. Politics shifted then in the several years after 1968 from the right to the center. Giscard was far less authoritarian and visionary than De Gaulle. He tended, as did Schmidt in West Germany, to respond to events rather than to shape them.

Britain and Italy: Two Nations in Trouble

In Italy, even more than in France, the expectation in the early seventies was that the left would gain power. To the disappointment of many, dissension on the left made it impossible for socialists and communists to take advantage of widespread discontent with the Christian Democratic government. Italy, unlike Germany and France, continued after 1968 to be plagued by social unrest. Student activity, wildcat strikes, the growth of extremist groups (especially on the left), political corruption, economic instability despite substantial growth, and a general failure to meet the expectations of the public contributed to a sense of decline and anarchy in public life. The problems associated with OPEC and the rise in oil prices in 1973 only brought into bold relief Italy's manifold problems.

In Britain the Conservatives returned to office in 1970 under the leadership of Edward Heath. Their efforts to deal with inflation and Britain's unsound economy led to several declarations of states of emergency and to confrontations with the coal miners. The economy remained troubled through the midpoint of the seventies, despite the return of the Labour Party and Harold Wilson. To a great extent Britain was no longer competitive, productive, and efficient in comparison with other advanced economies. Prospects for both Britain and Italy seemed rather dismal by 1974-1975, although for different reasons.

The Smaller States

In many of the smaller countries, changes in the government had little effect on politics or on social and economic policies. In Austria, for example, a Social Democratic government under Bruno Kreisky came to power in 1969. Its aim was to make Austria into a modern industrial state rather than to fulfill any doctrinaire programs from the past. No major shifts in policy took place. The same was true in Denmark and Norway, where the Socialists lost power, and in Sweden, where their majority was reduced. In the Netherlands, a coalition headed by a socialist, Joop Den Uyl, came into power in the early seventies, again without altering the life of the country to any large degree. In all the countries just mentioned, the mixture of social welfare statism and private enterprise, different from country to country, continued and, on the whole, were successful.

More dramatic activity took place in Greece, Spain, and Portugal. Highly important developments took place in Greece, where the military junta was forced to relinquish power in 1974 after seven years of military dictatorship. The junta's fall from power came after attempts to establish control over Cyprus led to a Turkish invasion of the island and to the threat of war between Greece and Turkey and civil war in Greece. The junta recalled George Karamanlis, a center politician, who restored the 1952 constitution and won a victory in the 1975 elections. King Constantine, who had been forced into exile several years previously, after an abortive coup against the junta, was not allowed to return.

In Spain arrangements had been made for a successor to General Francisco Franco in the person of Don Juan Carlos and for a loosening of political controls. Franco's death in November 1975 allowed the process to begin in earnest.

In the meantime, events in Portugal ended the regime of Antonio Salazar. Junior officers, aided by a few sympathetic generals and organized in the Armed Forces Movement (MFA), toppled the government of Premier Marcelo Caetano, successor to Salazar. The coup was directly connected with the long Portuguese struggle to maintain colonies in Angola, Guinea-Bissau, and Mozambique. The military, like the French military at the end of the fifties, had grown tired of fighting a difficult war with inferior equipment and with little recognition for their sacrifices. They had also been "infected" in part by the radical ideas of the captured guerrillas and Portuguese university students in the army. By 1974 the MFA had strong socialist-communist sympathies.

245

245

The MFA soon clashed with the government led by General Antonio de Spinola. Spinola had been popular in Portugal because before the coup he had called for political democratization in Portugal and an end to the colonial wars. The MFA had originally supported Spinola because it had anticipated that his presence in the government would lend respectability to the revolutionary government. Differences of opinion between Spinola and the MFA led the former to resign in September 1974, in the hope that he could return later on his own terms. Such was not to be. However, Communist party influence within the militarty was weakened by events in 1975 and parliamentary elections the next year resulted in a victory for the Socialist party under Mario Soares. The Portuguese revolution appeared at that point to have reached a moderate and relatively stable stage.

OPEC and the Crisis of the European Economy

On the whole, the issues affecting the eastern European states in the first part of the 1970s were political rather than economic. They involved problems of succession in the leadership—actual problems in Czechoslovakia, East Germany, and Poland, potential problems in the Soviet Union and Yugoslavia. After the "Prague Spring" of 1968, eastern European communist parties re-evaluated their positions within the state and their memberships. Economic issues were of great importance, of course. Perennial difficulties with agricultural production and failures to satisfy consumer demand now coexisted with a realization that the impressive growth rates of the past could not be maintained. Nonetheless, economic problems could be relegated to second place not only because of the urgency of some political problems, but also because of the prospects of relatively cheap energy from the Soviet Union and new prospects of credits and technology from a West eager to do business.

For western Europe, however, the situation was more or less reversed. Economic problems, especially after 1973, seemed to hold the key to future events. Politics were significant to the extent that they offered a possibility of dealing successfully with economic developments.

Although the Arab oil embargo and OPEC's quadrupling of oil prices certainly were the most dramatic aspects of Europe's economic difficulties, signs had already appeared before 1973 that the long period of growth and economic stability was coming to an end. Inflation had already hit some western European countries in the

1960s. By 1973 it was rampant. After the oil crunch, it became even worse. By 1976, however, inflation had tailed off somewhat, although in some countries, such as Great Britain and Italy, it remained a serious problem.

Most western European states recovered fairly quickly from the recession of 1974 and 1975, the "slumpflation," despite the oil crunch and a variety of other problems. Several things became apparent, however, in the course of the recession. One was that the economic problems were not confined to Europe. In fact, developments beyond Europe's control, such as the United States' economic problems and the increase in oil prices by OPEC, created many of the difficulties that Europeans contended with in the mid-seventies. The economic difficulties were worldwide, with Europe as one of the principal trouble spots. On the other hand, some countries within Europe experienced much greater difficulty than others. Differing inflation rates made it clear that western Europe still did not form an economic unit. In this period, each state managed its own monetary policy and tended to seek its own solution to the energy crisis.

Several western European countries had obviously strong economies and recovered well from the problems of the 1973-1975 period. Switzerland, for example, despite a large component of guest workers (roughly one-eighth the population), as of 1977 had an unemployment rate of 0.4 percent, an inflation rate of 1.3 percent, a healthy growth rate of 4.3 percent and a surplus of exports over imports of $3.25 billion. Figures for West Germany were not as spectacular, but followed the same pattern. West Germany and Switzerland escaped most of the economic difficulties experienced by other European countries by adhering to conservative economic policies. Government budgets were balanced, as were payments for imports and exports. The government emphasized tight credit and sound currency. Productivity in industry increased more rapidly than wages and benefits. Full employment was maintained, sometimes through manipulation of the pool of guest workers.

For countries such as Norway and Sweden, the economic picture was mixed: low unemployment but limited or no growth in the economy and a balance of payments deficit. France showed a different mix with relatively high unemployment and a balance of payments deficit, but an economy that was growing relatively rapidly. Countries such as Britain and Italy, with high unemployment, high inflation rates and, in the case of Britain, low growth rates, were clearly not doing well. North Sea oil helped to ease the economic pressure in Britain. In Italy political instability fed economic instability.

The results of the end of the long period of economic growth in Europe are difficult to predict. Indications are that the Western European economies have come through the transition period in good shape. Protectionism (the tendency to resort to tariff protection or to special arrangements with oil-producing countries) has increased, but, on the whole, trade and capital still flow smoothly from country to country. Technological development continues at a rapid pace. The energy situation is problematic, but at least now much thought and investment are being given over to the search for solutions. European economic integration through the European Community, despite its deficiencies, remains impressive and important. On the whole, western Europe has managed well in the extraordinarily rapid rearrangement of the world economic scene.

Not only in economics but in virtually every aspect the world changed greatly in the span of less than a decade. Between 1968 and 1975 Europe faced the first hard tests of the durability of postwar recovery and reconstruction. Although its performance in the adverse conditions of the early 1970s was often hesitant and confused, many Europeans were reassured by the soundness of most institutions and arrangements. To be sure, most of the visions entertained by radicals in the late 1960s did not take shape in reality. And on a more mundane level, complex political and economic tangles remained to be dealt with in eastern Europe and in the countries on the northern rim of the Mediterranean. Despite this, Europeans had reasons to be optimistic about the last quarter of the century and the role they might play in it. It would be a role different from those Europe had played before. No longer the leading role, it was nonetheless a supporting role of great potential significance. How the twentieth century ends will no doubt depend to a large extent on how well Europe plays its role in the 1980s and 1990s.

Suggested Readings

Alastair Buchan, *The End of the Postwar Era* (1974)

Walter Laqueur, *A Continent Astray, Europe, 1970-1978* (1979)

John Ardagh, *A Tale of Five Cities: Life in Provincial Europe Today* (1980)

Norman Luxenburg, *Europe since World War II: The Big Change* (rev. ed., 1979)

Jane Kramer, *Unsettling Europe* (1981)*

Michael Crozier, *The Stalled Society* (1973)

Gianni Statera, *Death of a Utopia: Development and Decline of Student Movements in Europe* (1975)

Richard Johnson, *The French Communist Party versus the Students* (1972)*

Bernard E. Brown, *Protest in Paris: Anatomy of a Revolt* (1974)

Alain Touraine, *The May Movement: Revolt and Reform* (1979)*

Neil McInnes, *The Communist Parties of Western Europe* (1975)

Galia Golan, *The Czechoslovakian Reform Movement: Communism in Crisis, 1962-1968* (1971)

_____, *Reform Rule in Czechoslovakia: The Dubček Era, 1968-1969* (1973)

H. Gordon Skilling, *Czechoslovakia's Interrupted Revolution* (1976)*

William Shawcross, *Dubček* (1971)

Rudolph L. Tokes, ed., *European Communism and Detente* (1978)*

Andrei Amalrik, *Will the Soviet Union Survive until 1984?* (1970)*

Nora Beloff, *Inside the Soviet Empire: The Myth and the Reality* (1980)

Joseph Korbel, *Detente in Europe: Real or Imaginary?* (1972)*

William Griffith, *The Ostpolitik of the Federal Republic of Germany* (1978)

Walter Hallstein, *Europe in the Making* (1973)

R. E. Tyrrell, ed., *The Future that Doesn't Work* [Britain] (1977)

G. N. Minshull, *The New Europe: An Economic Geography of the EEC* (1978)

*indicates paperback edition available

12

Contemporary Europe, 1975-1980

A case can be made for seeing the history of Europe in this century as essentially a tragic one, a fall from greatness to a position of relative insignificance in comparison to major powers such as the Soviet Union, the United States, or the People's Republic of China. In this view Europe's influence lies largely in the past, when it helped to shape the present contenders for world power and, in so doing, contributed to what some have called a world civilization based on urban life-styles and industrial products.

While one should not underestimate the significance of Europe's decline from its preeminent position in 1900, with all the consequences that it entailed, one can construct a more optimistic interpretation of developments in the twentieth century by viewing Europe from the perspective of 1945. Since that date, Europeans have made enormous progress in terms of political stability and economic well-being. Europeans have led the way in many areas of social policy, in economic cooperation and integration, and in concern for the problems of the so-called Third World. The decade of the seventies was a time of testing for the political, social, and economic systems that evolved in Europe in the two decades after World War II. It is too early to say how well these systems have stood the tests, mostly economic, to which they have been subjected. Some observers, such as Walter Laqueur in *A Continent Adrift*, are deeply pessimistic and emphasize political drift, ineffective government, sluggish economies, and vague but nonetheless troubling feelings of cultural malaise.

Others take a more optimistic approach and stress that the important fact is that even after a decade of inflation, unprecedented energy problems, and political terrorism, most European polities and economies are in reasonably good shape. Perhaps even more important here is the fact that Europe can still serve as an alternative model for advanced industrial societies. There are many issues which the great powers, preoccupied by strategic and military considerations, have tended to neglect. European states have taken the lead in dealing with some of these issues. For example, West Germany has consistently devoted a larger share of its national economic product to aiding developing nations than have other industrial powers. It has shown a great deal more concern about the tensions between developed and developing nations than most other industrialized nations. In another area, the Netherlands has worked in various ways to keep the older members of society involved in the mainstream of that society's affairs. An example of this can be found in the construction of housing which permits the aged to live in quarters specially designed for their needs but yet not segregated in any way from housing occupied by younger people and people with families.

In most important ways Europeans are quite similar to people living in other urbanized, industrialized, and affluent areas of the world. They are different, however, in that they inhabit a relatively large area with a long common history and a heritage of leadership. Europe can have more influence in some ways than the United States in that it is not so overwhelmingly powerful. At the same time, it will ordinarily be more influential than Japan or Australia because of its size and weight in world affairs. Europe, then, should continue to offer the rest of the world examples and guidance in the last two decades of the century. While it will not likely ever dominate world affairs as it once did, it will be influential in the resolution of the various problems now confronting people around the world.

Economic Questions: An Overview

Several factors have affected the performance of the economy in Europe. One that has long been a source of controversy both in western and eastern Europe is the welfare system, its costs and benefits. At least two other factors are crucial. One is the rapid increase in the price of petroleum products since 1973. This is particularly important since most European countries are heavily dependent on oil imports for energy supplies. Another factor, affecting western Europe primarily, has been the influence of American economic difficulties over

MEMBERS OF

- NATO (plus U.S.A. and Canada)
- WARSAW PACT
- COMMON MARKET *
- COMECON (plus Mongolia and Cuba)

* Negotiations with Greece completed and entry expected in 1981.

ICELAND

ATLANTIC

NORTHERN IRELAND

EIRE

UNITED KINGDOM

NORWAY

SWEDEN

FINLAND

DENMARK

BALTIC SEA

SOVIET

UNION

OCEAN

NETH.

BELG.

LUX.

EAST GERMANY

WEST GERMANY

POLAND

CZECHOSLOVAKIA

FRANCE

SWITZ.

AUSTRIA

HUNGARY

YUGOSLAVIA

RUMANIA

BLACK

SEA

PORTUGAL

SPAIN

ITALY

BULGARIA

ALBANIA

GREECE

TURKEY

MEDITERRANEAN

0   400
SCALE IN MILES

SEA

Economic and military alignments. The Warsaw Treaty Organization and Comecon are virtually identical in composition, the difference being that Comecon includes two non-European members. NATO and the Common Market differ considerably in memberships although, of course, a number of nations belong to both.

the past decade. A related problem, and one of great significance for eastern Europe, has been the performance of the Soviet economy in recent years.

Efforts to deal with economic problems have largely been national in scope. Few efforts have involved the entire continent. Even the response to Poland's severe economic difficulties, while involving a large number of European states, has been carried out on a national basis. Both the European Community (EC) and the Council for Mutual Economic Assistance (Comecon) continue to bring a number of states together in close cooperation. Within Comecon there are several joint ventures at work on the production and distribution of energy resources. The EC, which has grown over the past few years to ten members, still faces difficulties in integrating. The British, in particular, have complained that they contribute more than their share, to the benefit of France and Germany. Questions have been raised about the inclusion in the EC of much poorer countries, such as Greece. The direct election of members to the European Parliament (the legislative body of the EC), while an important political initiative, is unlikely to affect the economic policy of the EC greatly. Work to stabilize currency fluctuations through the European Monetary System has been successful. However, attempts to design energy-sharing plans have not worked out.

The era of rapid economic growth now seems over for both western and eastern Europe. Multinational efforts to deal with economic problems have made some progress, but not as much as critics would hope. Problems remain in inflation, the cost of social services, and the price of energy. There have been some extraordinary successes and some resounding failures among the European economic systems. The next several years will be difficult years in many states. No easy answers exist in either part of Europe, but Europeans have accumulated a vast amount of experience and demonstrated a general willingness to be innovative and flexible in their approaches to economic problems. What they do in the next several years will be not only important to Europeans but may also provide some answers to pressing economic questions outside Europe.

Welfare Societies

Since the war European states have fashioned one or another variant of the welfare state system as a means for meeting social and economic needs. A comprehensive system of education, health care, employment benefits, and the like have now come to be viewed as standard in many areas of the world. There are, however, many doubts about this kind of approach. Europe's recent experience with the welfare state is crucially important to the debate about whether the welfare state might be modified and retained or, as many have insisted, must be severely restricted.

The debate on the welfare state stems in large part from the fact that it is growing increasingly difficult to pay for the many programs put into place over the years. European economies are no longer growing as rapidly as they did in the fifties and sixties so that even maintaining presently available benefits is sometimes difficult. There is, however, continued pressure to expand the system as generations grow up within it and come to expect improvements almost as a matter of course. Some believe that the main purposes of the welfare state have been lost and that all too often desirable services are provided to the neglect of the most essential. Others are concerned with incentives and the will to work. In Sweden, one can work half time and make almost as much as a person working full time because of child benefits and rent subsidies. In Sweden, too, the specter of a relatively small group of workers supporting a large number of those receiving benefits is in sight. Already a work force of about four million helps to support around one million pensioners.

It is worth examining the Swedish case in some detail since it has long been seen as the foremost example of a welfare state. Problems exist now that may spell an end to what Marquis Childs first described in 1936 as "the Middle Way." While much about "the Middle Way" is unique, its past successes and present difficulties offer many insights into the possibilities and problems of the welfare state.

First, it is important to note that the Swedish economy is a capitalist economy. More than 90 percent of industry is privately owned with a rather small number of firms, many family-owned, dominating. Serving as a context for private enterprise has been a rather comprehensive welfare system that provides a generous assortment of benefits from birth through retirement. The system is now under considerable strain because of Sweden's declining share in the world export market, down from 7.5 percent in 1961 to 3 percent in 1976. This decline resulted from the availability elsewhere of cheaper raw materials such as iron ore and forest products, once mainstays of Swedish exports, and the expensiveness of Swedish labor in comparison to that of other countries. There does not seem to be an easy way out. Suggestions have been made that would lead to what the economist Robert Heilbroner has called "bourgeois socialism." This would involve ownership or at least working control of an enterprise by those working in it. This, however, would not necessarily increase efficiency. Here, Heilbroner suggests that a Nordic union of Sweden with Denmark and Norway might create an economic unit strong enough to permit the rather drastic rearrangement of economic ownership and control envisioned by some to take place.

Other countries will not be able, of course, to follow very closely the particular policies that Sweden undertakes in dealing with the crisis of the "Middle Way," but its experience should be instructive. Few would now suggest dismantling the welfare state. Attempts in various corners of Europe to reform it or to refocus its efforts will take various forms. Each will offer those outside Europe some guidance in dealing with their own particular problems.

Problem Areas: Britain

One of the most interesting countries in terms of its struggles with economic and political difficulties is Britain. While the British situation has been relieved somewhat by the discovery of oil in the North Sea, the relief will be only temporary. The economy as a whole remains as it was before the North Sea oil discoveries: less productive and less competitive in comparison with most other industrial powers.

The debate over Britain's future concerns whether the country will be better served by a return to an economy in which the private sector has greater room for maneuver and fewer governmental restrictions, the Conservative position, or by an extension of the welfare state and a new wave of nationalization of industry, the position taken by the left wing of the Labour Party. In the debate, Prime Minister Margaret Thatcher has stated unequivocally that Britain will be better served by the revitalization of industry and the creation of a more favorable climate for business. Policies designed to accomplish these goals include tight credit, a reduction in government spending, reduction in income taxes, the end of subsidies for unprofitable industries, and the return of some nationalized industries to the private sector. Through the first half of 1981, the government met with little success. Unemployment rose to more than 10 percent with nearly 2.5 million people out of work. The growth of the Gross National Product dipped from 1.5 percent in 1978-1979 to a minus 3 percent in 1979-1980. The inflation rate fell from the 22 percent of the summer of 1980 but remained in double digits, at 15 percent, later in 1981.

In British politics, the Labour Party has split into a somewhat weakened Labour Party, heavily influenced by its left wing, and a Social Democratic Party representing many of the moderate forces from the old Labour Party. The split may cause British politics to change dramatically in the next few years, provided the new Social Democratic Party in coalition with the Liberal Party can capture a substantial percentage of votes. It is unlikely, however, that a realignment of British politics, even an extensive one, would contribute greatly to the solution of economic difficulties or to a resolution of the tragic situation in Ulster, which constantly threatens to deteriorate further. There is, in addition, growing racial tension resulting from the resentment of many Britons toward the influx of hundreds of thousands of immigrants from former British colonies. Finally, discontent among the young, a large percentage of whom are unemployed, seems on the rise. These problems each contribute to the central problem of an economy that is outmoded and inefficient, an ironic dilemma for the nation which a century ago was the paramount industrial power in the world.

Problem Areas: West Germany

Britain has been for some years one of the weakest of the west European economies. The strongest in the same period has been that of the Federal Republic of Germany. In 1980 and 1981 it began to falter. Most other countries would be pleased if their economies performed as well as that of West Germany even with the new problems, but Germans have become alarmed by some indications of difficulties ahead. More than Britain, West Germany reflects the difficulties

An example of modern residential architecture in West Germany. "Blumenhügelhaus" (Flower Hillhouse) is an attempt to blend environment and structure harmoniously. The design is not only beautiful but also practical. Among other features, a highly efficient solar heating system is built into the roof. (Sven Simon/Katherine Young)

caused by the round of oil price increases in 1979 and by the world-wide recession. Germany's rate of inflation is still among the lowest in Europe as is its rate of unemployment, but the balance of payments deficit (which formerly did not exist at all) stood in 1981 at some twenty-eight billion marks (slightly less than fourteen billion dollars). When Germany's present record is compared to its past accomplishments, the reasons for viewing the future somewhat pessimistically became apparent.

The elections of October 1980 left the Social Democrats, in coalition with the Free Democrats, in control of the Bundestag and once again Helmut Schmidt became Chancellor. His position in Germany and in Europe, especially after the defeat of Giscard d'Estaing in the French presidential elections in April and May 1981, is a strong one. Schmidt faces some political problems at home, but the major issue in the period to come will be the German economic performance.

Elsewhere in Western Europe it appears likely that economic developments will only lead to more of the same, as in Italy, or will follow rather closely the trend of political development, as in Spain after the attempted coup by a right-wing segment of the military in 1981, or in France following the election of François Mitterand, a Socialist, as President. For some countries a dramatic new development might make a substantial difference. An example here would be the 1981 victory of the left-wing Panhellenic Socialist Movement in elections in Greece, a victory which could affect Greece's membership in NATO and the EC.

Problem Areas: Poland

In Eastern Europe, the most dramatic development has been one that has affected both economic and political considerations: the formation of an independent union in Poland. Events in 1980 and 1981 that led to the formation of Solidarity for the workers and Rural Solidarity for the farmers were based on previous clashes with the government in 1970 and 1976. A great deal of experience was gained in the 1976 protests, particularly by those workers who took part. Also, a movement of dissident intellectuals organized after the 1976 riots as the Committee for Social Self-Defense (KOR). This group established connections with the workers involved in the 1980 strike movement and provided help in seeing the larger issues. A factor that sets Poland apart from other Eastern European countries is the strong position of the Roman Catholic Church. The church aided the strikers in various ways and used its influence with the great majority of the population to help keep government responses to events fairly moderate.

The events of 1980 began in mid-August with a strike of 16,000 workers at the Lenin Shipyard in Gdansk in protest against projected price increases for meat. By the end of the month the strike had spread to factories and enterprises in other cities. An Interfactory Strike Committee was established to negotiate with the government. More was at stake than just wages and working conditions. Early in September the right to organize free trade unions was granted. The right to strike was recognized. In return the unions agreed to recognize the supremacy of the Polish Communist Party in national affairs and to forego any political role.

In mid-September Edward Gierek was replaced as head of the Polish Communist Party by Stanislaw Kania, a Politburo member since 1975. Kania and Wojciech Jaruzelski, who succeeded him in October 1981 as first secretary of the Polish United Workers Party, have worked in the time since then with three different but related problems. Perhaps the most important concerns the state of the Polish economy. Gierek had gambled in the 1970s on rapid modernization of industry and the establishment of a significant volume of trade with Western nations. His plan did not work because of mismanagement, the reduction of the size of Western markets through recession, and the spiraling cost of oil. Poland was left with a $20 billion international debt.

The second problem involves Solidarity's role in national life. A great deal of friction has resulted from government obstruction of Solidarity's efforts to organize and function as a trade union. It has created some problems for itself in speaking out for free discussion, in opposing government persecution of dissidents, and in supporting the right of farmers to organize. The third problem has been the response of the Soviet Union to turmoil in Poland. Although there was considerable apprehension in the latter part of 1980 and the first part of 1981, the Soviet Union did not choose to use force to deal with the Polish crisis. It seems to have, first, more confidence in the present Polish leadership than it had in the Czech leadership in 1968, and also it is aware of the strong feelings of Polish patriotism and of the anti-Russian sentiments which made it likely that an invasion would be strongly resisted.

Poland, for all its unique qualities, symbolizes the difficulties most East European states find themselves in presently. Highly dependent

A panoramic view of "Gropius City," a part of Berlin. The city is named for Walter Gropius, the famous German architect who headed the Bauhaus movement in the 1920s. Many Europeans now live in high-rise apartment buildings, each apartment with its own balcony. Single-family dwellings are increasingly the exception. (Sven Simon/Katherine Young)

on the Soviet Union for energy, deeply in debt, unable to compete effectively on the open market, Poland faces some difficult choices. Potentially, however, the formation of Solidarity could serve to pull the nation together behind the government in a common endeavor to put the economy back on its feet.

Problem Areas: East Germany

Even more than West Germany, East Germany's economic performance in the sixties and seventies was a *Wirtschaftswunder* (economic miracle). On the basis of rather limited resources East Germany constructed an economy unrivaled in Eastern Europe with the exception perhaps of Hungary. It is now ranked among the ten major industrial powers in the world. Basically, it has concentrated on the production of high-quality finished products for export. So far it has managed to avoid both unemployment and inflation.

Some problems exist, however, which may become more severe in the future. Existing plants and equipment are sometimes under-utilized because of inefficient planning or inadequate transportation.

Even more important, equipment and facilities are becoming obsolescent. East Germany's relatively limited financial resources make it difficult to re-equip or carry on trade with the West. Political stability has been achieved on the basis of a relatively high standard of living. Should that standard of living cease to improve or begin to decline, East Germany could face real problems. It might be able to deal more successfully with some of its economic challenges were it not for its special relationship with the Soviet Union and its close ties with other East European states. It could not change these relationships even if it wanted to. East Germany is too important to the Soviet Union. In turn, East Germany depends heavily on the Soviet Union for a variety of resources.

Problem Areas: The Soviet Union

The major problem that the Soviet Union now faces is political and concerns who or what group will replace the present secretary of the Communist Party, Leonid Brezhnev. Brezhnev is clearly ailing and unable to sustain a full schedule. Most of the present leaders are from his generation. They are also people who have largely distinguished themselves by their loyalty to Brezhnev rather than by the quality of their work. It is unlikely that they would be able to provide the vigorous leadership needed in the period after Brezhnev's death.

Strong leadership is needed in the Soviet Union to deal with a number of problems that continue to plague the Soviet government. The most persistent and intractable problem is that of agriculture. Production fluctuates widely, as figures of 140 million metric tons of grain for 1975-1976 and 224 million metric tons for 1976-1977 demonstrate. The regime committed considerable resources to the modernization of agriculture in the seventies with, however, disappointing results. The Soviet Union does not always produce enough foodstuffs to feed its citizens in any given year and even in those years when it does, shortages of fruits, vegetables, and meat are the rule rather than the exception.

The Soviet consumer fared better in the 1960s than in previous decades although his or her options were far fewer than those open to west Europeans and even to some east Europeans. Between 1965 and 1975 the production of television sets tripled, as did that of washing machines and vacuum cleaners in the same period. The number of refrigerators produced increased eight times. There are still problems with quality, attractiveness, availability and range of styles and types. Russians are no longer eager buyers regardless of the quality of goods available. Badly made or unattractive products often will not sell, even in the country where there are special difficulties with availability of consumer goods and with service after purchase. What most Soviet citizens seem to want is a car of their own, despite the headaches of owning one. However, even with the obligatory bribe, waiting time may run from three to five years.

Beyond the perennial problems of agriculture and the difficulties the Soviet Union has in fulfilling demands for consumer products, there is some evidence at hand that points to a serious social and economic crisis ahead. Data suggests, for example, that both the Soviet population as a whole and particular groups within it have become less healthy over the past two decades. Infant mortality rates increased by more than one third between 1970 and 1975. Official statistics have not been presented for the period after 1975, was Western observers think that the mortality rate could be as high as forty per thousand (in Western Europe and the United States the figures are under thirteen per thousand). Life expectancy appears to have declined in the last decade and may now be lower than it was in the late fifties.

Rising infant mortality rates and declining life expectancy are two indications of a serious social crisis. There are other indications, among them alcoholism (the per capita consumption of hard liquor in the Soviet Union is twice that in the United States), pollution, and extraordinarily high numbers of industrial and traffic accidents (with only a tenth as many cars as in the United States, the Soviet Union has just as many accidents). The indications are that the Soviet Union, its massive military power and great economic potential notwithstanding, faces over the next several years a very serious and difficult set of problems. The title of the famous book by the Soviet historian Andrei Amalrik, *Will the Soviet Union Survive Until 1984?*, may be overly dramatic, but the Soviet Union does face a more troubled future than any other state in Europe.

Terrorism

While developments in the economic sphere—the rapidly rising cost of energy, a general slowing of investment and growth in the economy, inflation, and unemployment—seem to have dominated events over the past several years, political happenings have had a significant influence as well. One of the most important and, in some ways, unexpected political phenomena has been terrorism. At first, terrorism seemed largely an external affair that occasionally spilled over into Europe. Such were the triple skyjackings of airliners during the summer of 1970 and the Olympic Games massacre in 1972 in Munich, both engineered by the Popular Front for the Liberation of Palestine. For a time, the situation in Northern Ireland, where militant Protestants and Catholics used terror against one another and on their own groups, seemed to be the only European example of the extensive use of terror in politics. By the end of the 1970s, however, there were terrorist groups in operation in nearly every country in western Europe; most were linked informally to one another, to Palestinian and Latin American radical movements, and to some eastern European countries as well.

The two most important groups were the Red Army Faction (the Baader-Meinhof gang) in West Germany and the Red Brigade in Italy. The Red Army Faction, a product of the radicalism of the late sixties like the Weathermen in the United States, originally formed around Ulrike Meinhof, a radical journalist from Hamburg, and Andreas Baader, a former student activist. It attracted probably more attention than warranted because of the anxiety that many Germans felt when confronted by extremists. Then, too, its brutal, vicious, often senseless methods seemed out of keeping with a Germany characterized by a strong economy, a stable polity, and an earnest concern for social welfare. While Germany might be criticized for being somewhat sterile and soulless, the Red Army Faction offered nothing to take its place but blind fanaticism.

In contrast to the Baader-Meinhof gang, which often appeared to be simply criminal rather than politically committed, the Italian Red Brigade has been distinguished by a dedicated professionalism and by carefully planned, highly sophisticated political action. Originally drawn from those involved in the 1968 movement, members of the Red Brigade now are highly trained and equipped with precision weapons from eastern Europe and specially-built cars. Their major operation was the kidnapping and eventual murder of Italy's most prominent political figure, Aldo Moro of the Christian Democratic Party, in 1978. In the years since the murder, however, the Italian police have made substantial progress in arresting some activists in the Red Brigade. The organization appears to have been badly damaged.

In 1980 and 1981 observers also began to speak of a right-wing terrorism. Three incidents in 1980—the explosion in August of 1980 in the Bologna central railroad station, the one in September at the entrance to Munich's Oktoberfest, and, finally, the explosion in front of the synagogue in Paris a week after the one in Munich—appeared to signal the start of a right-wing campaign of terror. Right-wing extremist organizations exist in Britain, France, Spain, Belgium, Germany, and Italy. At least in France and in Italy there is evidence pointing to a linkage between terrorist organizations and institutions such as the police, the judiciary, the secret service, and the army. What makes right-wing terrorism potentially extremely dangerous are the ties that it may have to those institutions of the state most dedicated to the destruction of left-wing terrorism, in particular the police and the judiciary.

It seems likely that terrorism as a factor in politics peaked with the kidnapping and murder of Aldo Moro in 1978. It is, of course, still a factor in political life in Northern Ireland, Italy, and Spain. And in Spain at least, where the attempted coup in 1981 indicated a large degree of dissatisfaction with the existing parliamentary structure of government among the military and the police, a continuation of terrorism by the *Euzkadi ta Azkatasuna* (ETA—Basque-Land and Liberty) could lead to a situation in which the military would sponsor a successful coup. The possibility of atomic terrorism—not, of course, simply a problem for Europe, increases yearly. Nonetheless, the wave of terrorism that Europe has experienced in recent years appears to be ending along with many of the Latin American and Middle Eastern movements that provided a context for it.

Eurocommunism

Another important political phenomenon of the seventies was Eurocommunism. The term first came into use in the mid-seventies and was employed to describe various national communist parties that appeared to be willing to play by the prevailing democratic political rules of their respective countries. If they were to gain power, it would be through legal means: elections, parliamentary majorities and the like. In power, they would abide by and protect the constitution. If they were to lose power, they would surrender their position in government and return to the legal struggle to regain power. The major Eurocommunist parties were the Italian, Spanish, and French Communist Parties.

The Italian Communist Party (PCI), under the leadership of Enrico Berlinguer, has been the most consistent supporter of the Eurocommunist position. Italian Communists have long participated in government on the municipal and regional levels. In fact, their accomplishments in the administration of the city and region of Bologna have given them a reputation for honest, efficient, and effective government. On the national level, the PCI has taken an active part in parliamentary committee work, an important part of the legislative process under the Italian system. Since about 1973, tacit collaboration between the PCI and the various coalitions ruling Italy has been a political fact of life.

Despite the PCI's reputation as the most liberal of European communist parties and its many Italian characteristics, there is a tendency not to trust it fully. While it clearly is not a revolutionary party, there is some feeling that it is not entirely committed to democracy. For one thing, some observers are concerned about the lack of democratic procedures in the workings of the PCI itself.

Beyond Italy, where the question of the participation of the PCI in a national coalition government remains unresolved, Eurocommunism seems to be a passing phenomenon. The Spanish Communist Party is outspoken in declaring its independence of Soviet communism, but it plays a relatively minor role in Spanish politics. The French Communist Party can no longer be classified as Eurocommunist. Whatever the extent of its participation in the French Socialist government, it will have to be recognized as a political party that has yet to accept in all respects the rules governing the operation of a constitutional and democratic form of government.

Unanswered Questions

For each European nation there are important and vital questions that will be discussed and perhaps also resolved in the near future. For example, how will France fare under the Socialist government of Mitterand? Will the successors of Tito in Yugoslavia be able to deal with the economic problems and ethnic rivalries of that country? What is the likelihood that democratic institutions will continue to exist and function in Portugal and Spain? Various specific questions might be asked of regional or multi-national organizations as well.

Beyond questions that refer to particular situations, there are a number of questions that deal with more general concerns. In Europe a growing dislike of highly centralized and impersonal bureaucracies has led to the growth of movements for political devolution, the delegation of political authority to regional or local institutions by the central government, and also to movements for independence. Such movements exist not only among the Basques in Spain and the Catholics in Northern Ireland but also among the Welsh and Scottish in Britain, the Flemings and Walloons in Belgium, the Bretons in

France, and the Croatians in Yugoslavia. In addition to movements for political devolution and political independence, there are other and smaller ways in which people have tried to protest against centralized and impersonal institutions.

Feminism in Europe has developed less rapidly than in the United States despite the fact that many important sources of feminist thought are European (for example, the books *The Second Sex* by Simone de Beauvoir and *The Female Eunuch* by Germaine Greer). A long struggle was necessary in the 1970s to secure a divorce law in Italy and legalized abortion in France. Feminism has made the most progress in the Scandinavian countries, the Netherlands, and Britain. Attitudes are still quite conservative in the countries bordering on the Mediterranean. In eastern Europe and the Soviet Union a theoretical equality exists, but the reality is often quite different. For example, in the Soviet Union many doctors are women, but doctors there are not as well paid nor do they have the same status as doctors in western Europe and the United States. Also, a large number of women in the Soviet Union and some east European countries work. They are nevertheless expected to take care of most tasks associated with child care and housekeeping. Husbands rarely volunteer to help, although this attitude is beginning to change. Without question, feminism or, at the least, a different attitude toward the rights and capabilities of women will continue to develop throughout Europe.

Basic questions continue to exist about human rights and Europeans have often taken the lead in discussing these. The promising steps taken in the "Final Act" of the Helsinki Conference in 1975 with regard to human rights have, however, not produced much progress toward greater human rights. The reviews of the Helsinki Agreements at Belgrade in 1977-1978 and at Madrid in 1980-1981 accomplished little beyond providing a forum in which Americans and Russians could criticize one another.

Another promising development, the Lomé Convention, also reached in 1975, this time between the members of the European Community and forty-six developing countries, allowed the developing nations to send their products without hindrance to the markets of the European Community. Aid and investments were also granted. This agreement, while a step in the right direction, will not be sufficient in itself to meet the needs of developing nations. However, Europeans will no doubt continue playing an important role in North-South dialogues and will contribute to the resolution of Third World problems.

Perhaps the most important questions are those that concern the ways in which daily life is lived. In this respect, Europe has much to offer. Contrary to fears expressed in the sixties, it has not been overwhelmed by either American or multinational corporations. It retains its own vigorous culture and distinct approaches to political, economic, and social questions. It is, at least in western Europe, largely not interested in military matters. Understandably, having been through two ruinous wars and having lived after the second of those wars under the threat of a nuclear holocaust should another major war break out, Europeans prefer not to contribute to large armies and massive weaponry. In eastern Europe and the Soviet Union, the same fears exist, but the response there has been to create large military establishments, ostensibly for defensive purposes.

Unlikely to dominate the world again militarily or politically, Europe has a certain leeway now to commit resources and attention to social questions. And much is being done to deal with the problems of mass transit in urban environments and policy toward those entering the work force and those about to leave it, just to cite two examples, that will be of interest to people outside Europe. Without a doubt Europe will continue contributing in the last decades of the century in significant ways to political, economic, social, and cultural developments. It is no longer the only part of the world in which innovative developments take place and it no longer dominates the rest of the world as it once did. It has instead become something of a reference point. The achievements of European civilization to date will not accord with everyone's definition of progress, but they do furnish a means of determining one's location in the flow of history— and serve as a source of ideas and models for the future as well.

Additional Readings

The historian, faced with the task of suggesting readings that would help in understanding and evaluating events of the last few years and present-day situations as well, would prefer most often to avoid that task by insisting that "it isn't history yet." History or not, it is important to deal with the recent past and the ongoing present as best one can. The following are some items among the wealth of material that might be consulted.

Several books might be mentioned in addition to those cited in the Suggested Readings for Chapter 11. Each helps to put the present in a wider perspective.

> Alan Bullock and Oliver Stallybrass, eds., *The Harper Dictionary of Modern Thought* (1977)
> J. P. Cole, *Geography of World Affairs** (fifth edition, 1979)
> Michael Kidron and Ronald Segal, *The State of the World Atlas** (1981)
> Alan Palmer, *The Penguin Dictionary of Twentieth Century History, 1900-1978** (1979)

Also in the same category is the special issue of *Scientific American* on "Economic Development" (September, 1980).

A number of yearbooks and annuals are available. Among these are:

> *The Europa Year Book*
> *The Statesman's Yearbook*
> *The Annual Register: A Record of World Events*

Facts on File
Yearbook on International Communist Affairs
USSR: Facts and Figures Annual

Mention should also be made of *Current History*, which publishes a special issue on the Soviet Union each October. Special issues appear from time to time on west Europe and east Europe. The most recent of these are April 1981 for east Europe and May 1981 for west Europe.

There is an abundance of material in periodicals and newspapers; most of it, however, is repetitious and superficial. The following can be especially recommended as better than most:

Daedalus, special issues on "Old Faiths and New Doubts: The European Predicament" (Spring, 1979) and "Looking for Europe" (Winter, 1979)
The Economist (Britain)
Foreign Affairs
Manchester Guardian Weekly (Britain)
Le Monde (daily or weekly, France)
The New Republic
Problems of Communism
Survey (Britain)
The Christian Science Monitor (daily, Boston)
The New York Times (daily)
The Washington Post (daily)

Appendix of Abbreviations and Acronyms

Two lists, each arranged alphabetically, follow. The first is composed of titles of institutions, parties, and the like together with the abbreviations or acronyms used as short forms of reference. The second is made up of the abbreviations and acronyms together with the corresponding titles.

Royal Air Force .... RAF
Russian Social Democratic Labor Party (Bolsheviks; Mensheviks) .... RSDLP
Schutzstaffel (Elite Guard) .... SS
Socialist German Student Federation .... SDS
Socialist Party, France .... SFIO
Socialist Party, Germany .... SPD
Socialist Party, Russia .... RSDLP
Socialist Revolutionaries .... SR
Sturmabteilung (Stormtroopers) .... SA
Trades Union Council .... TUC
Warsaw Treaty Organization .... WTO
West Germany (Federal Republic of Germany) .... BRD

BRD .... Federal Republic of Germany (West Germany)
BUF .... British Union of Fascists
CLNAI .... Committee of National Liberation for Northern Italy
COMECON .... Council for Mutual Economic Assistance
COMINFORM .... Communist Information Bureau
COMINTERN .... Communist International (Third International)
CPSU .... Communist Party of the Soviet Union
DC .... Christian Democratic Party of Italy
DDR .... German Democratic Republic (East Germany)
EC .... European Community
ECSC .... European Coal and Steel Community
EDC .... European Defense Community
EEC .... European Economic Community
EFTA .... European Free Trade Association
ETA .... *Euzkadi ta Azkatasuna* (Basque-Land and Liberty)
KOR .... Committee for Self-Defense
KPD .... Communist Party of Germany
KRA .... *Kriegsrohstoffabteilung* (War Raw Materials Administration)
LCY .... League of Communists of Yugoslavia
MFA .... Armed Forces Movement
MRP .... Popular Republican Movement
NATO .... North Atlantic Treaty Organization
NEP .... New Economic Policy
NSDAP .... National Socialist German Workers' Party
OEEC .... Office of European Economic Development
PCI .... Communist Party of Italy
RAF .... Royal Air Force
RSDLP .... Russian Social Democratic Labor Party (Bolsheviks; Mensheviks)
SA .... *Sturmabteilung* (Stormtroopers)
SDS .... Socialist German Student Federation
SFIO .... Socialist Party of France
SPD .... Social Democratic Party of Germany
SR .... Socialist Revolutionaries
SS .... *Schutzstaffel* (Elite Guard)
USPD .... Independent Social Democratic Party of Germany
TUC .... Trades Union Council
WTO .... Warsaw Treaty Organization

Index

Christian Socialists (Austria), 149, 197
Churchill, Winston, 161, 166, 172-173, 175, 191, 203
Circle of industrialization and urbanization, 2
Civilization and Its Discontents (Sigmund Freud), 72
Clemenceau, Georges, 36, 61-62
Cold War, 175-177, 178-180, 188-189, 209-210
    American policy and, 179
    Berlin Blockade and, 178
    formation of NATO and, 179
    Marshall Plan and, 176, 180, 188-190, 204,
    origins of, 175-176
    Soviet policy and, 179
    Truman Doctrine and, 176
Collaboration, *see* World War II
Collectivization (Soviet Union), 109, 128-130
Colonialism, *see* imperialism
Committee for National Liberation, 194
Committee for Self-Defense, 256
Committee of National Liberation for Northern Italy, 194
Communism, 79-80, 95, 131-133, 223, 236, 245
Communist Information Bureau, 176, 179, 203
Communist International, 79-80, 82, 88, 95
Communist Party
    France, 82, 122, 144, 192-193, 262
    Germany, 95, 123-124, 126-127, 195
    Italy, 85, 194-195, 243, 262
    Poland, 199-200, 256-258
    Portugal, 245
    Soviet Union, 86-88, 108-109, 127-128, 130-131, 162-163, 198-199, 240, 259
    Spain, 263
Congress of Europe (1948), 203
Conservative Party (Great Britain), 83, 191, 243, 254
Constantine (king of Greece), 244
Council for Mutual Economic Assistance, 204, 252
Council of Europe, 203
Croatia, 240
Croix de feu, 122
Cuban Missile Crisis, 209-210
Czechoslovakia, 66, 107, 149-150, 178-179, 201-203, 220, 236-238

Dadaism, 73-74

Dawes Plan (1924), 80, 91-92
Decline of the West, The (Oswald Spengler), 72
De Gasperi, Alcide, 194-195, 203
De Gaulle, Charles, *see* Gaulle, Charles de
Democratic Party (Germany), 80, 124
    See also Progressive Party
Den Uyl, Joop, 244
Denmark, 196, 214, 244
Depression, *see* the Great Depression
De-Stalinization, 198-199
    See also Soviet Union, politics
Dien Bien Phu, fall of, 211
Disarmament, 93, 115
Disarmament Conference (1933) 93, 133, 146
Doctors' Plot, 198
    See also Soviet Union, politics
Doriot, Jacques, 122
Dovzhenko, Aleksandr, 102, 129
Dubček, Alexander, 237-238
Duce, Il, see Mussolini, Benito
Dutschke, Rudi, 233

East Germany, *see* German Democratic Republic
Ebert, Friedrich, 56, 57
Eden, Anthony, 191
Eisenstein, Sergei, 102
Elites, 217-219, 220
Enabling Act (Germany), 127
Erhard, Ludwig, 196, 223
Eurocommunism, 262-263
European Coal and Steel Community, 204
European Community, *see* European Economic Community
European Defense Community, 204
European Economic Community, 204-205, 222, 247, 252, 264
European Free Trade Association, 204
European Monetary System, 252
European Recovery Preogram, *see* Marshall Plan
Euzkadi ta Azkatasuna, 262
Expressionism, 73-75

Falange, 147
Farmers, 216, 218-219
    See also peasants
Fascism, 133, 135-138, 148
    See also Italian Fascist Party and National Socialist German Workers' Party
Federal Republic of Germany
    origins of, 178